D1566362

Republic of Readers?

Republic of Readers?

The Literary Turn in
Political Thought and Analysis

Simon Stow

State University of New York Press

Published by
State University of New York Press, Albany

© 2007 State University of New York

Printed in the United States of America

For information, address State University of New York Press,
194 Washington Avenue, Suite 305, Albany, NY 12110–2384

Production by Michael Haggett
Marketing by Anne M. Valentine

Library of Congress Cataloguing-in-Publication Data

Stow, Simon, 1970–
    Republic of readers? : the literary turn in political thought and analysis /
Simon Stow.
        p. cm.
    Includes bibliographical references and index.
    ISBN-13: 978-0-7914-7089-3 (hardcover : alk. paper)
    1. Political science—Philosophy. 2. Politics in literature. I. Title.

JA71.S792   2007
320.01—dc22   2006020830

10 9 8 7 6 5 4 3 2 1

For my parents, Graham and Christine Stow,
and in memory of Alexander Keith Wood (2002–2003)

Dear Homer, if you are not a third from the truth about virtue, a craftsman of a phantom, just the one we defined as an imitator, but are also second and able to recognize what sorts of practices make human beings better or worse in private and public, tell us which of the cities was better governed thanks to you.

—Plato, The Republic

Contents

Acknowledgments

A first book necessarily incurs a great many debts, and I am delighted to acknowledge them here. This project began life as a doctoral dissertation at the University of California, Berkeley, where I am immensely grateful to Mark Bevir, Eric Naiman, Hanna Pitkin, the late Michael Rogin, and Shannon Stimson for their help, advice, and criticism. The manuscript was completed with the assistance of a Faculty Summer Research Grant from the College of William and Mary. At William and Mary I am fortunate enough to have a number of colleagues I also consider friends. In particular I would like to thank Larry Evans, Christine Nemacheck, Ron Rapoport, Joel Schwartz, and Mike Tierney for their feedback and support. At State University of New York Press I am grateful to Michael Rinella, Michael Haggett, Michele Lansing, and also to the two anonymous reviewers for their insightful comments on an earlier draft of the manuscript.

Equally important to the completion of the book are a number of friends without whom both it and my life would be considerably less rich. Ben Bowyer, Kip Kantelo, Naomi Levy, Robyn Marasco, Gemma and Jessica Newton, Ara Osterweil, Jack Porter, Rosalind Porter, Matthew Rudolph, Clare, Daniel, and Sam Schoenheimer, and Jonathan and Karen Wood all deserve far more thanks than this simple acknowledgment suggests.

A central claim of the book is that, by itself, reading cannot make us better people, but that the process of moral improvement depends crucially upon interacting with others. For me there could be no greater evidence of this than the company of Caroline Hanley, to whom I am fortunate enough to be married. She makes me and my life better and happier than I could ever have possibly imagined, and I thank her.

Finally, I wish to thank my parents, Graham and Christine Stow, without whom none of this would have been possible. It is to them that this book is dedicated with gratitude and love.

Introduction

When politicians and politically minded people pay too much attention to literature, it is a bad sign—a bad sign mostly for literature, because it is then that literature is in most danger. But it is also a bad sign when they don't want to hear the word mentioned, and this happens as much to the most traditionally obtuse bourgeois politicians as to the most ideological revolutionaries.

—Italo Calvino, *The Uses of Literature*[1]

A brief stroll through the humanities and social science sections of any North American university bookstore reveals that the study of literature and the study of politics have become somewhat indistinguishable enterprises. In the sections set aside for literature courses, novels—canonical and otherwise—now rub spines with books by thinkers such as Marx, Habermas, and Adorno, while in the section set aside for government or political science classes, in addition to impenetrable—for this reader at least—volumes on statistics and formal modeling, novels have begun to appear, and alongside them, books by thinkers and critics such as Judith Butler, Terry Eagleton, and Richard Rorty: works that do not appear to fit neatly into either category, politics nor literature. Much the same can be seen in both the law and philosophy sections. Novels now pop up on course reading lists, and with them books by figures such as Martha Nussbaum and Richard Posner debating the relative merits of a "literary" approach to legal and philosophical study. In literature departments and in the popular press, this apparent merging of disciplines produced (occasionally) headline-grabbing battles over "political correctness," tenure disputes, and a largely circular debate in which "conservatives" asserted that the "radical" obsession with issues of class, gender, ethnicity, and sexuality is simply a way of doing violence to the text; and the "radicals" countered that the "conservative" obsession with the text is simply a way of doing violence to issues of legitimate political concern.[2] Indeed, so pervasively did this conflict—sometimes known as the "Culture" or "Canon Wars"—embed itself in the study of literature that it became the stuff of literature, with writers as diverse as Philip Roth, A. S. Byatt, and David Lodge alternately lamenting and lampooning these academic debates in novels such as *The Human Stain*, *Possession*, and *Small World*.

1

In political science departments there has, however, been much less publicity for, and much less critical reflection on, a similar merging of the political and the literary in our approaches to thought and analysis. While many theorists working in political science departments now study narratives, rhetoric, and language—areas traditionally associated with the study of literature—much of the ground on issues such as class, gender, and colonialism—areas more traditionally associated with political science—appears to have been usurped by literary critics such as Terry Eagleton, Gayatri Chakravorty Spivak, and the late Edward Said. Furthermore, some political scientists appear to have been tempted to adopt the latter's methods in an effort to reclaim lost territory. There has, that is to say, been something of a "literary turn" in contemporary political thought and analysis. It is one that, while deeply influenced by a "political turn" in literary and cultural analysis that preceded it, has nevertheless failed to generate the sort of self-reflexive, potentially self-correcting debate that has marked the political turn in the study of literature.[3] This book is an attempt to start and to contribute to such a debate. As such, its claims are, by necessity, likely to be somewhat controversial, and occasionally, perhaps, undertheorized, not least in its suggestions about how we might more coherently utilize literature in political thought and analysis in the future. Such potential weaknesses might, however, be forgiven, for the book is—to utilize that most overworked and oftentimes disingenuous of methodological disclaimers—the work of a philosophical underlaborer, intent on clearing some paths toward future discussion. Its aim is not to *dismiss* the suggestion that literature can be a valuable source of information about the political but rather to try to *place* it. Recognizing that the literary has much to offer us as social scientists and political thinkers, this study seeks to identify what is of value in the current work in this area. It also seeks to identify what is problematic about the ways we currently use literature in political thought and analysis. It does so in order that we might add literature and literary analysis to our methodological tool kits without sacrificing either conceptual clarity or analytical rigor. In this, the concern of the book is that of the good lover in Plato's *Phaedrus*: one who highlights the object of his affection's defects in the hope that the object—in this case the use of literature in political thought and analysis—might become more perfect.

The focus here is not, however, entirely academic. Underpinning much of this discussion is a concern with the way in which politics—and political *debate* in particular—is currently practiced in liberal-democratic societies. Both the "political turn" in literary studies and the "literary turn" in political studies have, it will be argued, combined to produce a generation of students for whom *readings* are more important than *arguments*. The problem with this mode of debate is—as the claim will be developed in greater detail later—that *readings*, unlike *arguments*, have no more or less agreed-upon standards for validity, nor do they have any underlying principles to which to retreat in order to adjudicate between competing claims, especially now that texts are widely regarded as being open to a multiplicity of possible interpretations. For this reason, it will be suggested, the literary mode of political debate is marked by what Alasdair MacIntyre called—in another context—a certain "shrill tone" among the participants.

SHRILLNESS AND LITERARY DISCOURSE

In *After Virtue*, Alasdair MacIntyre argues that the contemporary polity is marked by an absence of agreed-upon principles about how to adjudicate moral debate: arguments about rights and individuality are, he says, met with arguments about universalizability; arguments about liberty met with arguments about equality. The result is, he suggests, incommensurability and stalemate. "From our rival conclusions" he notes, "we can argue back to our rival premises; but when we do arrive at our premises argument ceases and the invocation of one premise against another becomes a matter of pure assertion and counter-assertion."[4] It is a condition, he suggests, with both public and private consequences:

> . . . if we possess no unassailable criteria, no set of compelling reasons
> by which we may convince our opponents, it follows that in the process
> of making up our own minds we can have made no appeal to such cri-
> teria or such reasons. If I lack any good reasons to invoke against you,
> it must seem that I lack any good reasons. . . . Corresponding to the
> interminability of public argument there is at least the appearance of
> a disquieting private arbitrariness. It is small wonder if we become
> defensive and therefore shrill.[5]

In these circumstances, moral debate has something of a double shrillness. The impact of this unfortunate development upon the broader political culture is perhaps evidenced in the similarly shrill tone of much contemporary political debate. We see this most clearly in popular political books, where precisely due to a lack of shared principles in interpretation, disagreements over how to re-gard political facts and figures are presented as the difference between the writer's own Truth and the "lies" of his or her political opponent, an approach that is, alas, prevalent across the entire political spectrum.[6] Somewhat unfor-tunately, there also appear to be strong parallels between MacIntyre's descrip-tion of our contemporary moral discussions and our literary-political debate.

In the absence of agreed-upon principles to adjudicate between literary interpretations, the literary mode of debate generates a similar tendency toward assertion and counter-assertion. This is especially true when political claims are thought to turn cn such debates. As a result, philosophically and politically important distinctions are often ignored in the ensuing melee of personal insults and attacks. It is, perhaps, for this reason that the debate over the canon has been so circular. In training a generation of students to engage in political *readings* as opposed to political *arguments*, the political turn in literary studies and the literary turn in political analysis are undoubtedly contributing to and perpetuating this problematic aspect of our contemporary political discourse. The process by which academic debates impact upon the broader political culture is, nevertheless, too random and imprecise to draw a direct causal arrow between any single instance of one affecting the other. So although this study evinces a concern with broader political questions—placing itself somewhere between Stanley Fish's assertion that academic debates are merely fun[7] and the poststructuralist assumption that these debates are a form of political work in and of themselves—it will largely be focused on the more tightly argued debates about the proper role of literature in political thought and analysis. The claims about the significance of this work for the world outside of academia will, by necessity, be somewhat more speculative.

LITERATURE AND POLITICAL ANALYSIS

Literature has, of course, been part of political thought and analysis since the beginning. The quarrel between philosophy and poetry was already "old" when Socrates identified it in the *Republic*, and many early classics of the discipline have a distinctly literary bent. The emergence of behavioralism and statistical modeling in post-World War II political science, along with the apparent dominance of analytical philosophy in certain key areas of political thought—most notably in the discussion of justice—seemed, however, to diminish the significance of literary approaches in political science departments, even as political approaches to literature were gaining ground in the literature departments housed in the older, and usually nicer, buildings across campus. In recent years, however, there has been something of a revival of the literary approach to political study with the establishment of a "Politics and Literature" (now expanded to include film) organized section of the American Political Science Association and the publication in leading journals of—albeit a few—reflections on the role of literature in political analysis and indeed a number of politically inspired readings of literary texts.[8] In the American context, such work has been largely dominated by one method: the "classical perspective." Drawing on the work of the political theorist Leo Strauss, the classical perspective argues that some literature is a worthwhile object of political analysis because of the special genius of its authors: figures capable of raising themselves above the perspective "of the era, the community, or the regime" to offer us unique insight into the political.[9] The apparently widespread acceptance of this method in American political science journals has, however, not only precluded self-reflexive rumination on the *value* of the approach—that which has begun to act as a corrective to some of the more extreme claims made by proponents of the political turn in literary criticism—it has also obscured the *pervasiveness* of the turn to the literary in contemporary political thought and analysis. There is more to the literary turn than a mere revival of interest in reading novels and plays among certain groups of political scientists.

This study identifies three key aspects of the literary turn. It concerns itself with the questions they raise for the use of literature and literary-critical methods in political thought and analysis. Each expands the definition of the literary in the political far beyond the classical perspective discussion of the "political lessons" offered to us by particular authors and their works. The first of these three aspects is the *epistemological and ontological* question concerning the nature and role of *argument* in philosophical and political justification. The second is the *moral and political* question concerning the plausibility of the attempt to use literature as an emotional foundation for liberal democracy. The third is the *methodological* question concerning the validity of the turn to literature as a source of insight into the political that is allegedly unavailable through behavioral social science or philosophy, at least as each is traditionally conceived.

The Epistemological and Ontological Question

For postmodernists and poststructuralists, analytic philosophy is, at best, a set of pseudo-problems and, at worst, dead. For such thinkers, arguments of the form "All men are mortal, Socrates is a man, Socrates is mortal" are simply another form of *narrative*, one whose validity rests not upon some logical structure or state of the world but rather upon the widespread acceptance of the argument by similarly situated beings. Having embraced this claim, a number of thinkers such as Richard Rorty and Judith Butler have turned to *redescription* as a source of political critique and construction. For them, political critique often seems to be simply a matter of redescribing, both one's own position and that of one's opponents, until the former appears more attractive than the latter. Persuasion, not careful and deductive argument, rules the day. Political construction in these circumstances is similarly a matter of marshalling *support* but not necessarily *evidence* for one's position. This approach to political critique and construction relies for its critical purchase on the rhetorical power of its *language* and not the force of its *argument*. It is this concern with *language* and *narrative* that leads thinkers such as Butler and Rorty to prioritize—both consciously and unconsciously—the methods of literature and literary criticism over those of philosophy.

It is an approach that calls into question many of the traditional philo-sophical assumptions about *what* and *how* we know and, of course, the onto-logical status of arguments. It is, furthermore, an approach that has become so pervasive that even political theorists and moral philosophers with little time for the claims of postmodernity and/or poststructuralism have made a *partial* literary turn, at least as far as the *ontological and epistemological* question is con-cerned. Martha Nussbaum, a thinker who has openly scorned many of post-structuralism's central claims, has, for example, offered a number of seemingly powerful arguments for incorporating literature into philosophical reasoning and social science.[10] She seeks, however, not simply to replace philosophy with the methods of literature and literary criticism, in the manner of a Butler or a Rorty, but rather to augment it. Nussbaum wishes to embrace certain key ele-ments of the turn toward literature while maintaining a fairly fixed view of the world and the role of Reason in it. She argues for a more modest philosophical position than either Butler or Rorty. Simply, that when combined with tradi-tional analytical philosophy and formal modeling, the insights generated by lit-erary analysis will offer a more complete picture of that world than that offered by Reason alone.[11]

This first aspect of the literary turn in contemporary political thought and analysis obviously goes much deeper than the classical perspective claim that literature can offer us critical insights unavailable elsewhere: it concerns the very foundations (or potential lack thereof) of philosophical inquiry and polit-ical argument. As such, it is intimately connected to the second aspect of the literary turn, the attempt to use literature as moral and/or emotional founda-tion for liberal democracy. The nature of this alleged connection, however, dif-fers according to the philosophical perspective of those proposing it. For those who accept the value of philosophical argument, literature is merely a way to augment the existing practices; for those who reject philosophical argument, literature is both a way to justify and to maintain liberal-democratic societies.

THE MORAL AND POLITICAL QUESTION

In his 1971 work *A Theory of Justice,* John Rawls presented a defense of liberalism that attempted to separate the Right from the Good, offering a theory of "Justice as Fairness."[12] In an America whose social fabric was being torn apart by con-flict over civil rights, the role of women, and the ongoing strife over the war in Vietnam, Rawls sought a way to regulate rather than overcome what appeared to be fundamental differences of opinion and political perspective: to offer a the-ory of *pure procedural justice* to which any citizen could subscribe regardless of whatever else he or she believed. The philosophical underpinnings of Rawls's

approach were largely Kantian, and his theory appeared to rely on the metaph
cal claim that the self was ontologically prior to its ends. As such, it drew howls of
protest from a group of thinkers who came to be known as "communitarians."[13]
Not only was Rawls's account of the self inherently implausible, they suggested,
but his theory was parasitic upon a conception of community that it not only did
not acknowledge but that it actually undermined. In response to their criticism,
Rawls revised his original theory, moving from the claim that "Justice as Fairness"
was a mere *modus vivendi* for competing conceptions of the good, to the suggestion that it was itself a rather more substantive—albeit very thin—conception of
the good that could be defended on minimalist terms.[14] There was, he suggested,
a definite context for his theory: that of American-style liberal democracy.

Rawls's acceptance of the communitarian claim that liberalism requires
some recognition of its own social context—that rights are not by themselves
enough, but that they must also be situated amid a culture of respect for those
rights—paved the way for a debate about the best way to cultivate and support
this democratic culture. The work of Robert Putnam was illustrative of this
revived interest in the cultural foundations of liberal-democratic societies.
Reaching back to Tocqueville's discussion of the importance of "secondary institutions," Putnam argued for the importance of choirs, bird-watching groups,
and, most famously of course, bowling leagues in generating what he calls the
"social capital" necessary to the proper functioning of liberal democracy.[15]
Martha Nussbaum and Richard Rorty similarly turned to literature as a source
of stability and cohesion for liberal-democratic societies.[16] Both thinkers
argue—albeit from very different perspectives and in very different ways—that
a well-read citizenry will enhance the practice of liberal democracy by generating an empathy and/or a solidarity that will promote respect for other viewpoints, an understanding of other ways of living, and a recognition of the
contingency of one's own perspective; in short, the values of civil society. This
enhanced civil society, they suggest, will serve to support the values and institutions of liberal democracy, the very values that Rawls identifies as a prereq-
uisite for a stable political system but that his theory fails to generate.

This question of the moral and political value of literature in liberal
democracies is not only significant for the actual practice of liberalism, it also
raises a number of questions about disciplinarity and method in the humanities
and social sciences. Such questions have become all the more pertinent, given
the recent revival of interest in the ethical value of literature,[17] for central to the
consideration of literature's power to generate moral and political insight are
the questions of what we can legitimately derive from the texts under study,
whether this differs according to the *way* that we read texts in and across different disciplines, and whether this *should* differ by discipline and the information and insights we are seeking from what we read.

The Methodological Question

The apparently circular debate of the 1980s and 1990s between "conservatives" and "radicals" in literature departments over the value of the traditional "dead-white-male" canon in a multiethnic, multigendered world was, it has been suggested, the product of a distinct "political turn" in literary studies. For certain critics the study of literature as a quest for textual meaning, authorial intent, poetic allusion, or metaphor gave way to a study of the ways in which literature reflected and contributed to underlying social tensions such as class struggles, colonial repression, or the construction of gender. In his reading of *Mansfield Park*, for example, Edward Said famously argued that Mr. Bertram's failure to respond to Fanny Price's question about the slave trade was indicative of the reluctance of characters, the author—and, by extension, nineteenth-century England—to question the colonial equation of material comfort with moral superiority.[18] Indeed, for thinkers such as Terry Eagleton, the study of literature became a matter of identifying the social tensions inherent in texts: highlighting the repressed, the forgotten, or the hidden as a way of placing literature in its social context. No longer divorced from its social surroundings as an object of aesthetic appreciation, such politically motivated literary critics suggested, the book, the novel, the play, or the poem became a material object of cultural analysis. In effect, literature *became*—or, depending on the claims of the theorist, *was revealed as*—another arena in which politics was practiced. Implicit in this political turn in the study of literature were two key methodological assumptions that we might label the *privileged observer* claim and the *portability* claim.

The *privileged observer* claim suggests that literature can tell us something about society—its politics in particular—that is simply unavailable through the more traditional methods of social science. Whereas the latter is focused on the observable, the countable, and the empirical, the former gives us insight into the way that social forces shape what people think, write, and create. Gayatri Chakravorty Spivak, for example, argues that social scientists have "long feared the radical impulse in literary studies," and that this has mistakenly led them "to measure success by statistics or photo-ops."[19] Literature, it is suggested, in its complexity, nuance, and context, can highlight that which is obscured by the abstraction and consequent distortion of the social scientific method.

The *portability* claim suggests that the skills and methods of the literary critic are equally applicable in other fields and that furthermore the insights into the nontextual world generated by reading literature are as valid as those generated by the social sciences. Emboldened by arguments from thinkers such as Rorty about academic disciplines being less about specialized areas of study and more about the kind of books we read, literary critics have expanded their concerns well beyond the traditional domains of literary analysis. The work of literary critic Elaine Scarry on the crash of TWA Flight 800 on July 17, 1996, is a case in point, with Scarry expanding the claim for the validity of literary methods into even the *natural* sciences. Despite a distinct lack of training in aviation or electromagnetics, Scarry presumed to explain the cause of the crash as electromagnetic interference, later extending her claims to encompass the fall of Swissair Flight 111.[20] She explained her qualifications thusly: "There is nothing about being an English professor that exempts you from the normal obligations of citizenship. In fact, you have an increased obligation, because you know how to research."[21]

It is, perhaps, indicative of the influence of the political turn in literary studies on political thought and analysis that both of these claims have been championed, consciously and unconsciously, by proponents of the literary turn. Martha Nussbaum and proponents of the classical perspective both argue—from quite different perspectives—for the *privileged observer* claim. Likewise, all of the thinkers who have turned to literature as a source of insight into the political—Butler, Eagleton, Nussbaum, and Rorty among them—seem to believe in some version of the *portability* claim.

SOME NOTES ON AIMS AND METHOD

Deeply influenced by the political turn in literary analysis then, the literary turn in political thought and analysis takes many forms: it incorporates claims about the status of philosophy as a discipline, practical claims about literature's power to generate moral capacities in its readers useful to the practice of liberal democracy, and claims about the role and value of literature as a source of critical insight into the political. All three of these aspects of the literary turn—which themselves subdivide into many smaller claims and debates—are, however, connected by the unifying suggestion that there is something about literature and literary criticism that gives us insights that are analytically or practically useful to the world of politics. It is this claim that is the focus of this study.

Previous work in this area, such as Valentine Cunningham's excellent *Reading After Theory* and the much earlier debate between Allan Bloom and Sigurd Burckhardt in the pages of the *American Political Science Review*, has focused on defending the study of literature from colonization by the theory and study of politics.[22] Here the aim is somewhat the reverse: to defend certain aspects of political science and political philosophy against the rival claims of the study of literature and literary criticism as a source of insight into the political. Briefly, these are the commitment to *reasons* over *persuasion*, *argument* over *redescription*, and the application of the correct *standards of justification* appropriate to the study of the literary and nonliterary worlds. Simultaneously, however, the book also aims to capture the ways in which the methods of literature and literary criticism might nevertheless enhance methods of political critique and construction, primarily perhaps by offering us new ways to think about old problems. Succinctly, the aim here is to establish a position that captures the creative freedom of the literary while simultaneously maintaining the methodological rigor of political science and political philosophy. In this there is a synchronicity between the aims of the book and its underpinning, postfoundational, philosophical position: one that rejects the epistemological and ontological claims of Enlightenment Reason about objectivity, universality, and Truth but which nevertheless accepts the value of philosophical reasoning and argument. This position will be developed in more detail in part 1. For those readers for whom postfoundationalism is of little interest, the arguments in part 2 about reading, literature, and political insight should still hold good. For those for whom the subject *is* of interest, an additional concern of the book will be to seek to demonstrate the plausibility and value of the postfoundational approach to political thought and analysis.

The method here will be to break down, into their constituent parts, the separate claims about the role of literature and the literary in political thought and analysis in the work of four thinkers: Judith Butler, Terry Eagleton, Martha Nussbaum, and Richard Rorty. Utilizing the postfoundational philosophical perspective set out in chapter 1, the study will seek to evaluate the plausibility of the claims made on behalf of literature and the literary in political life—theoretical, practical, and empirical—in order that we might assess what can safely be taken from this work and what we need to abandon. This process is, however, complicated by the myriad of ways in which the three questions of the literary turn overlap and intersect. Claims about the alleged moral and political benefits of reading (the *moral and political* question) are, for example, often predicated upon claims about the insights generated by reading (the *methodological* question). For this reason, the claims will be examined on a case-by-case basis in the work of specific theorists rather than by category across these thinkers' work. Such an approach will nevertheless allow us to develop a broader set of theses about the way in which literature is currently used and might be used in the future in political analysis. The book will proceed as follows:

In part 1, chapter 1, "*Arguments* and *Readings*: Philosophy in a Postfoundational World," sets out the philosophical underpinnings of this study. It examines the claim that the methods of philosophy are essentially those of literary criticism, and that *argument* can be safely abandoned in favor of *redescription*. It seeks, by contrast, to establish a postfoundational position between analytic philosophy and postmodernist skepticism: one that rejects capital "T" Truth, metaphysics, and representational epistemologies but that nevertheless embraces the notion of philosophical argument and reasoning underpinned by intersubjectively applicable standards of justification. Establishing this position serves two purposes. First, it provides a philosophical basis for the critical analysis in subsequent chapters. Second, it offers a basis for engaging in political philosophy in a postfoundational world; political philosophy that is separate from what Richard Rorty calls "literary criticism" but that is nevertheless informed by some of the latter's methods and concerns. This chapter addresses the *epistemological and ontological* aspect of the literary turn. Those for whom this issue is of little concern will hopefully find more of interest in part 2.

Part 2 examines the work of thinkers whose approach either exemplifies or provides impetus for the literary turn in political thought and analysis. Chapter 2, "Martha Nussbaum: Literary Imagination and the Public Life," examines the *methodological* and the *moral and political* aspects of the literary turn in the work of one of the most systematic and rigorous literary turn thinkers. Nussbaum's first claim is that literature gives us a particular type of insight into political life that is absent from the more traditional methods of social science. Illustrating the various ways in which the claims that make up the literary turn overlap and intersect, in Nussbaum's work the *methodological* claim is intimately connected to the *moral and political* claim. The insights generated by reading literature, she suggests, will themselves cultivate a certain moral capacity that she believes is essential to successful liberal-democratic practice. Given that Nussbaum's literary turn is only partial, the study will be concerned to show why Nussbaum's arguments—with which it might be thought to have broad sympathy—nevertheless fail to achieve the coherent and convincing synthesis that is here being sought between philosophy and the methods of literary-critical analysis.

Having addressed the *epistemological and ontological* aspects of Richard Rorty's work in chapter 1, chapter 3, "Richard Rorty: Non-Philosopher Kings and the Literary Republic," addresses both the *methodological* and *moral and political* aspects of the literary turn in the work of one of the most controversial figures in contemporary thought. The diversity of the work subsumed under the label "literary turn" is, however, illustrated by the different ways in which these questions manifest themselves in Rorty's writing. In Rorty's case, the evaluation of the *methodological* question concerns itself with the extent to which it might plausibly be claimed that literature is the source of specific moral insights useful to the political and the *moral and political* question with whether such insights are a source of potential solidarity that could act as a basis for liberal democracy. In addition, however, the *moral and political* questions raised by Rorty's work also concern the *type* of politics that might be thought to emerge from the postmodernist concern with redescription as a tool of political critique and construction. The chapter argues that the abandonment of Reason leads thinkers such as Rorty to believe that they can simply jettison the need to justify political positions with arguments, thereby contributing to the somewhat shrill politics described earlier. Such an approach also generates a potentially self-defeating liberalism: one whose elitism and manipulation of the population treat people as *means* and not as *ends*. It is a form of politics that emerges from a failure to distinguish between the world of the text and the world in which that text is written and from the subsequent failure to recognize the important moral differences between fictional and nonfictional persons.

Chapter 4, "Terry Eagleton: Is There a Class in This Text? Literary Criticism and Social Theory," focuses on the *methodological* aspects of the literary turn. It seeks to develop that which has been merely touched on in the preceding chapters, where the *methodological* claim is directly connected to the *moral and political* one. Eagleton, it will be noted, is a figure whose work precedes the literary turn; indeed, his work is rather more of an example—possibly the paradigmatic example—of the approach adopted by practitioners of the political turn in literary and cultural analysis. Examining the claims of a pioneer in the field of political-literary criticism nevertheless provides a number of insights into the promise and problems of utilizing literary criticism as a model for political thought and analysis. Foremost among these problems is that of confusing and conflating the different *standards of justification* that are appropriate to analysis of the literary and the political. Borrowing a concept from Paul Goodman, this chapter identifies and develops an important distinction between the *written* and *unwritten* worlds, between the world of the text and the world in which that text is written.[23] The distinction will serve not only to clarify some of the methodological confusion generated by the apparent merging of disciplines in the modern academy but also to act as the basis for a discussion of the ways in which political thinkers and analysts might incorporate literature into their methodological tool kits without sacrificing analytical clarity and rigor. It will also be useful for untangling the often complex and sometimes confusing work of Judith Butler in chapter 5, "Judith Butler: Politics, Literature, and Radical Democracy."

Judith Butler is possibly the leading proponent of the literary turn. "Proponent" may, however, be a somewhat misleading term. So completely has Butler collapsed whatever boundaries may have still existed between philosophy, politics, literary criticism, and rhetoric that she—unlike Terry Eagleton, Martha Nussbaum, and Richard Rorty—does not feel the need to justify her syncretism. Rather, she simply takes it as a given that literary readings of philosophical texts, novels, films, cartoons, legal documents, and even current events can provide not only hitherto unavailable insight into the political but also a perspective for the construction of alternative political formations.[24] Although Butler makes no overt *moral* claims for the act of reading—in the manner of a Nussbaum or a Rorty—she nevertheless combines all three aspects of the literary turn in her work on gender, sexuality, rhetoric, and radical democracy. Set in the context of the insights generated by the discussion of the work of Nussbaum, Rorty, and

Eagleton in previous chapters, the examination of Butler's work in chapter 5 illustrates most clearly the problems and promise of the literary turn in political thought and analysis.

In his *Dictionnaire des Idées Reçues*, Flaubert says of the Academy, "Always knock it, but try to belong if you can." Having established what is problematic about the philosophical underpinnings and the practical applications of the literary turn in parts 1 and 2, part 3 offers suggestions as to how some of these problems might be rectified. Chapter 6, "How to Read a Novel in a Democracy: Literature and Public Ethics," identifies what is useful about Martha Nussbaum's and Richard Rorty's attempts to utilize literature as a basis for, and an enhancement of, a liberal-democratic society. It argues that implicit in both thinkers' approach is a dialogic theory of literature and democracy, one that suggests that any moral and political improvements that might emerge from reading have more to do with the *discussions about* the texts than with the texts themselves. Crucially, however, the theory suggests that *how* we read is potentially more important than *what* we read, and the chapter closes with a discussion of how a certain kind of reading and discussion might make literature a potential source of political improvement for liberal-democratic societies. Chapter 7, "Beyond the Dolorous Haze: Literature in Political Thought and Analysis," offers an account of the ways in which the confusion over the *written* world of literature and the *unwritten* world in which that literature is produced might be untangled. It sketches a method by which we might use literature in political thought and analysis in a way that incorporates the rigor of social science and philosophy and the creativity of the literary.

The book concludes by suggesting the ways in which this study is itself an act of political theory. Having gone on a theoretical journey, the conclusion seeks to return these abstract questions to the consideration of problems in our contemporary political discourse. In this it seeks to become an example of the very thing it advocates: a work of postfoundational political theory inspired and influenced by the literary but underpinned by the rigor of philosophy and social science. This last claim is, however, contingent upon establishing that postfoundational political thought is a suitable basis for critical analysis and political argument. It is to this task that we now turn.

Part 1

Theoretical Foundations

Chapter 1

Arguments and *Readings*
Philosophy in a Postfoundational World

> To fit in with the change of events, words, too, had to change their usual meanings. What used to be described as a thoughtless act of aggression was now regarded as the courage one would expect to find in a party member; to think of the future and wait was merely another way of saying one was a coward; any idea of moderation was just an attempt to disguise one's unmanly character; ability to understand a question from all sides meant that one was totally unfitted for action.
> —Thucydides, *History of the Peloponnesian War*[1]

In the fifth century B.C. Greek historian Thucydides famously lamented the increasingly disparate relationship between Athens' words and deeds during her conflict with Sparta. With Pericles having declared in his Funeral Oration that "We Athenians . . . do not think that there is an incompatibility between words and deeds,"[2] the *History of the Peloponnesian War* shows what happens when Athens fails to live up to his boast.[3] Distilled from their connection to action, words became a heady brew, one that clouded good judgment and induced political chaos. "Any novelty in an argument," says Cleon to Athens during the debate over Mytilene, "deceives you at once, but when the argument is tried and proved you become unwilling to follow it; you look with suspicion on what is normal and are slaves of every paradox that comes your way."[4] Swayed by the cheap rhetoric of Diodotus—"(and only the most simple minded will deny this)"[5]—Athens chose a course of action that led to the physical carnage and linguistic chaos of the civil war in Corcyra. It was a time where in "order to fit in with the change of events words, too, had to change their usual meanings." Even Thucydides is led by the declining authority of the *logos* to abandon his

17

usual narrative mode: rather than describing what happened and leaving us to draw our own—albeit somewhat directed—conclusions, he is forced to tell us directly what we should think about these events. In the absence of a grounding connection to life as it was lived, words, the currency of democracy, became devalued: "a great mass of words that nobody would believe."[6]

The situation of Athens is not yet—despite some claims to the contrary—the situation in which moderns and postmoderns find ourselves.[7] The linguistic turn in philosophy, and the influence of figures such as Derrida and Lyotard on a generation of thinkers, has, however, created the possibility of a similar separation of words and deeds in the contemporary polity. As with the Ancients depicted by Thucydides, arguments, underpinned by mutually acknowledged premises and shared understandings about the world and the way that we live, seem to have become less important than the rhetorical and poetic power of language to sway us one way or the other in our deliberations over politics. Avoiding the potential linguistic and political chaos of a world in which words become separated from deeds is a key concern of this study. Doing so requires that we establish a connection between the language that we use and the lives that we live, one that will serve as the basis for meaningful debate and discussion.

In order that this study's words might match its own deeds, this chapter sets out the philosophical underpinnings of the broader project. They are predicated upon on a crucial distinction between *arguments* and *readings*. It is a position that while accepting the central tenets of postfoundationalism nevertheless embraces the value of philosophical argument and rejects the postmodernist and poststructuralist claim that the death of metaphysics means the death of philosophy. It is this philosophical position—one between the extremes of Enlightenment Reason and postmodernist skepticism—that can serve as the basis for a postfoundational political thought and analysis separate from, but nevertheless informed by, the methods of literature and literary criticism. In order to establish this position, it is first necessary to say something about how we arrived at this potentially critical juncture in the recent history of political thought.

POLITICAL PHILOSOPHY AND THE DECLINE OF REASON

In the latter half of the twentieth century, Anglo-American political philosophy was dominated by one man: John Rawls. His 1971 book, *A Theory of Justice*, set the terms of debate for political philosophy in Europe and America for the next twenty-five years.[8] In it, Rawls attempted to justify liberal political institutions—a system of justice as fairness—with two devices: the "Veil of Ignorance" and the "Original Position." Situated behind the Veil, agents would be denied knowledge of their skills, resources, preferences, and social status. From this Original Position, he said, they would choose the principles of justice for a democratic society. The outcome of this process was, Rawls argued, two principles: first, that each person was to have an equal right to the most basic liberty compatible with similar liberty for others; and second, that any social and economic inequalities were to be arranged so that they were reasonably expected to be to everyone's advantage and attached to positions and offices open to all.[9] It appeared to be an audacious attempt to found and justify liberal political institutions on the principle of Reason: the product of a correctly ordered mind.

The Kantian overtones of Rawls's project were clear and readily acknowledged by the author in *A Theory of Justice* and elsewhere.[10] Critics suggested that Rawls's theory was, however, too abstract, not least because it appeared to be predicated upon an empty conception of the self. So vacuous were the persons in the Original Position, it was claimed, that they could not be said to be either persons or choosers in any plausible sense of these terms.[11] As such, Rawls appeared to fall prey to a backlash against "metaphysics." Metaphysics, the claim that there are absolute values to which a certain cognitive capacity called "Reason" gives us access, had been dominant in Western philosophy since Plato enumerated his theory of the Forms. For many, however, Friedrich Nietzsche, Martin Heidegger, and their postmodernist and poststructuralist offspring had gradually undermined this notion over the last 150 years. Indeed, the claim that a faculty called "Reason" could no longer be relied upon to give us access to absolute values had become a philosophical commonplace by the time J. L. Mackie began his popular book on ethics by declaring: "There are no objective values."[12]

Mackie presented two arguments against the existence of objective values: the argument from *queerness* and the argument from *epistemology*. The first asserted that if there were indeed objective values "they would be entities or qualities or relations of a very strange sort, utterly different from anything in the universe."[13] The second said that "if we were aware of them it would have to be by some faculty of moral perception or intuition, utterly different from our ordinary ways of knowing anything else."[14] Even if one rejects Mackie's arguments for the nonexistence of objective values, there are many others. Most obviously, there is the high level of disagreement about the nature of these values among those who claim to have found them. Indeed, the values that people regard as being objective often seem to be directly correlated to their own prejudices and concerns. As Alasdair MacIntyre wryly noted, Immanuel Kant never questioned that the values he inherited from his virtuous parents where the ones that were objective and accessible by Reason.[15] It is little wonder that communitarian, Marxist, and feminist critics of Rawls's project concluded that "Reason" was simply a cover for the prioritization of certain individualist, elitist, and overly gendered values. The Enlightenment dream of founding a just and rational society on metaphysical values appeared to have had its last hurrah in Rawls's work: few would, perhaps, attempt such an ambitious project again. The response to this failure can be split into two schools: first, those who attempted to rehabilitate Reason by addressing the concerns of Rawls's critics; second, those who appeared to abandon philosophy, Reason, and argument altogether.

REASON REVISITED

Foremost among the political thinkers who tried to rehabilitate a conception of political philosophy based upon an amended notion of Enlightenment Reason was Rawls himself. In a series of books and articles that followed the publication of *A Theory of Justice*, Rawls responded to his critics by attempting to minimize the role of Reason and metaphysics in his theory. In a 1985 article, tellingly entitled "Justice as Fairness: Political not Metaphysical," Rawls asserted that "the aim of justice as fairness as a political conception is practical, and not metaphysical or epistemological. That is, it presents itself not as a conception of justice that is true, but one that can serve as the basis of informed and willing political agreement between citizens viewed as free and equal."[16] On this formulation, the Original Position was no longer a metaphysical thought experiment but rather a "device of representation" aimed at identifying "ideas implicit in the public culture" about justice in liberal democracies.[17] The device, wrote Rawls memorably, "no more commits us to a metaphysical doctrine about the nature of the self than our playing a game like Monopoly commits us to thinking that we are landlords engaged in a desperate rivalry, winner take all."[18] That even Rawls—a thinker with acknowledged Kantian sympathies—should be so keen to repudiate the apparently metaphysical aspects of his thought was, of course, indicative of the extent to which metaphysics and the belief in objective values had been discredited.

Nevertheless, Rawls's apparent apostasy did not solve the difficulties in his theory. There were still many problems in his later formulations, which suggested that Rawls's conception of justice was either, from a practical perspective, unworkable or, from a philosophical perspective, still overly metaphysical. In the first instance, Rawls's liberalism seemed to fail his own key test for a workable conception of justice: that it be self-supporting. Having abandoned Reason as the basis for his conception of justice, it is not clear why or whether anyone would commit herself to the two principles that Rawls's agents choose in the Original Position.[19] When the principles were said to be the choice dictated by Reason, the basis of the decision was clear: the principles reflected the way that a properly ordered mind thought about the world. To express deviation from either of these principles was, after due reflection, literally irrational.

For the postmetaphysical Rawls, however, the principles he identifies are simply ones that he thinks are implicit in the public culture of liberal democracies and to which, he thinks, citizens will give their allegiance. Whether this would actually be the case is, however, a largely empirical, not theoretical, matter, and Rawls failed to provide any evidence to suggest that his principles would indeed be the ones chosen.[20] Nor, furthermore, is there any evidence to suggest that if these principles were chosen that they would generate sufficient public support. Indeed, Michael Sandel and Charles Taylor both suggest quite convincingly that the Rawlsian liberalism is parasitic on a liberal culture that it not only does not support but that it may actually undermine. Both argue that liberalism's excessive focus on the individual erodes the community values essential to the successful working of the liberal system. Perhaps recognizing this problem, Rawls simply asserted his hope that justice as fairness might begin as a "mere *modus vivendi*" but would "change over time, first into a constitutional consensus and then into an overlapping consensus."[21] Rather like an aged suitor in a Victorian novel, Rawls expressed his hope that the nubile citizenry would in the first instance respect his theory and in the second grow to love it, in the process transforming some of their most deeply held feelings to coincide with the tenets of his procedural liberalism.

Stripped then of their metaphysical underpinnings, it is not immediately clear why anybody would choose Rawls's principles of justice. This is not to say that *no one* would choose them, simply that Rawls's theory lacks any attempt to justify the principles independently of the claim that they reflect ideas implicit in the public culture. Furthermore, despite having abandoned the metaphysical underpinnings of his two principles, Rawls seems unable to abandon the notion that they are, in some sense at least, neutral and/or objective. He seeks, it might be argued, the objectivity of Reason without the supporting metaphysics or, indeed, without any convincing alternative source of support. As such, it is hard not to conclude with the feminists, Marxists, and communitarians, that Rawls— like Kant before him—has simply prioritized his own values and sought to justify them on the grounds of their apparent self-evidence. This leaves his attempt to reconstruct Reason without metaphysics prey to those critiques that suggest that it is atomistic, elitist, and patriarchal. Rawls had, it seemed, failed to provide either a convincing *philosophical* or *political* defense of his theory.

Martha Nussbaum has, however, made a bold attempt to show how Reason—traditionally conceived—*is* capable of taking onboard alternative social perspectives in a way that negates many of the *political* criticisms leveled against Rawls's theory. Indeed, much of her work on literature—as we shall see in chapter 2—is aimed at showing how Enlightenment Reason can incorporate these alternative perspectives without abandoning what makes it distinctive: its neutrality and objectivity. Such work is part of Nussbaum's even more daring attempt to expand the horizons of what we traditionally conceive of as "Reason" by finding a place in rational thought for the influence and complexity of human emotions.[22] It is by incorporating alternative perspectives through a careful use of emotion that Nussbaum believes she is able to overcome the difficulties of Rawls's approach. Indeed, she outlines an approach that she calls "Aristotelian Social Democracy" consisting of a basic liberal framework—derived and defended by Reason traditionally conceived—but enhanced by a deeper understanding of human needs and capabilities. Most obviously she expands Rawls's list of "Basic Social Goods"—that which is provided to all citizens in Rawls's account as the very minimal basis of a good life—to include a list of "Basic Human Functional Capabilities." The latter are, she suggests, derived from the insights gained by incorporating various emotions—including the empathy gained from reading—into philosophical Reason.[23]

Philosophically and methodologically Nussbaum has made a *partial* literary turn. She seeks to use literature simply to *augment* philosophical Reason traditionally conceived. The extent to which emotions, even those "rational emotions" that she believes can be identified through philosophical deliberation, are indeed sufficient to overcome the political criticisms of Rawlsian liberalism is—as will be argued in chapter 2—highly debatable. For now it will simply be noted that Nussbaum's work is still predicated upon a form of metaphysics and that as such her defense of Reason does not go far enough. She neither defends Reason and metaphysics on their own terms nor does she distinguish her account from a metaphysical approach whose benefits—such as certainty—she seeks but whose costs—such as abstraction—she is not prepared to embrace. She offers a problematic *political* defense of Reason, one that suggests it can incorporate multiple perspectives, but not a *philosophical* one. The discussion of her use of literature in the next chapter will show why her position—though perhaps initially appealing as an attempt to synthesize two key philosophical traditions—is untenable.

It would then appear that, rather like the man in the old joke whose brother thinks he is a chicken but who will not take him to see a psychiatrist because he needs the eggs, the attempt to rehabilitate reason has been largely unsuccessful and half-hearted. Advocates of philosophical Reason seem willing to concede the problems of their position—not least its ontological implausibility—but do not appear willing to give up the benefits that this position would bring them if it could be shown to be valid, benefits such as objectivity, neutrality, and certainty. As such, their position appears to lack either a philosophical or a political justification. Having conceded that liberalism is a conception of the good—one that has to be defended in nonmetaphysical terms—they do not appear to want to justify it as such. It is, perhaps, the failure of these thinkers to rehabilitate Reason that paved the way for the rejection of philosophy and the turn toward literature and literary criticism as a source of insight into the political.

STRONG WORDS, WEAK ARGUMENTS

Judith Butler and Richard Rorty are two American thinkers who like many of their European colleagues and predecessors seem to have equated the death or decline of Enlightenment Reason with the death or decline of philosophy. In the absence of Reason, they seem to suggest, all that remains is *language*, and for the analysis of language, literary criticism seems ideally suited. The use of the word "seems" here is, however, deliberate, for claims about the death or decline of philosophy bring with them a number of other claims about the death, decline, or irrelevance of *argument*. As such, positions such as Rorty's and Butler's are not so much *argued for* as assumed or stated. Rorty does offer a justification for his position, but it is one based on a *reading* of certain philosophical texts, one that eschews the value of *argument*. Tracing the origins of these thinkers' claims about language, philosophy, and the world is therefore a matter of offering a genealogy. Rorty's position emerges from a *reading* of the work of a number of American pragmatists and from a *reading* of the work of the later Wittgenstein and Butler's from a *reading* of Hegel, Nietzsche, and Heidegger. In addition, both thinkers' work demonstrates the influence of the wave of French theory that crashed onto American academic shores in the late 1970s and early 1980s.

Despite their somewhat different origins, Butler's and Rorty's positions are in many ways quite similar. Both thinkers appear to reject philosophy, to embrace language, to dismiss argument, and to adopt *reading* and *redescription* as critical modes. As far as embracing language is concerned, both Butler and Rorty appear to predicate their claims—if this is not too much of a philosophical term—upon one of two theses about language and the world. The first is the weaker linguistic thesis:

(1) Language, by shaping our outlook on the world, helps determine the world in which we live.

The second linguistic thesis is much stronger:

(2) Language is primary: the language that we use determines the world in which we live.

As anybody who has ever stubbed her toe knows, however, the second thesis is very hard to maintain: it is, perhaps, impossible to redescribe physical pain until it goes away. Tellingly, neither Butler not Rorty makes this claim explicitly. Rather, both seem to offer some version of the first thesis: the weaker linguistic one. Both point to the ways in which the language we use helps determine our understanding of the world. Both note the ways in which language changes over time and the power of thinkers and poets—figures such as themselves—to change the way we talk about the world and in so doing to create new ways of thinking about, looking at, and acting in the world. Nevertheless, there are also times when—consciously or unconsciously—Butler and Rorty appear to conflate the theses, presenting the more plausible weaker thesis as the basis of their claims but acting as if the stronger thesis is operational. In many ways, and particularly with regard to his account of redescription, Rorty appears much guiltier of this conflation than Butler.

For Richard Rorty, author of the decidedly upbeat *Achieving Our Country* and *Philosophy and Social Hope*, the alleged death of philosophy appears to be a source of great optimism.[24] Unconstrained by representational theories of language, humanity is now free, he suggests, to "de-divinize the world": to accept its own role in creating social and political life.[25] By "representational theories of language" is meant here, of course, the suggestion that words are labels for things in the world that exist prior to language and that the structure of language reflects the logical structure of that prelinguistic world. To say that something is true or false on this account is to say something about the correspondence between the language and the world. It is the sort of thing that Wittgenstein talks about in the *Tractatus* and the sort of thing that Rorty explicitly eschews.[26] "[S]ince truth is a property of sentences," he writes, "since sentences are dependent for their existence upon vocabularies, and since vocabularies are made by human beings, so are truths."[27] From here it is only a short step—for Rorty at least—to the suggestion that all kinds of problems—philosophical *and* political—can be resolved through the power of *redescription*. "The method" he writes, "is to redescribe lots and lots of things in new ways, until you have created a pattern of linguistic behavior which will tempt the rising generation to adopt it, thereby causing them to look for appropriate forms of nonlinguistic behavior."[28] It is a claim that suggests that Rorty has moved unashamedly from the first linguistic thesis—that language helps determine the world in which we live—to the second linguistic thesis—that language is primary.

For Judith Butler, on the other hand, the death of philosophy and Enlightenment Reason seems to be a source of great pessimism. Showing a lesser tendency to conflate the strong and weak claims about language, Butler explicitly denies that she sees redescription as a political and philosophical "cure-all."[29] Rather, language for her seems to be the way in which an at least partially nonlinguistic power manifests itself in everyday life. This is, of course, a rather ugly formulation of Butler's account, but there is, perhaps, no other way to capture Butler's deliberately nonanalytic position with any degree of rigor: Butler's dense prose style is designed, in part, to avoid such summaries of her work. For Butler, this partially nonlinguistic power appears insurmountable, leaving us only with the power of words, performance, and play to subvert and resist. There is, nevertheless, no detailed account of this partially nonlinguistic power in Butler's work. Possibly taking her cue from Foucault's observation that "to imagine another system is to extend our participation in the present system,"[30] Butler seems to think it is impossible to give an account of this partially non-linguistic power that is not itself complicit with that power. In offering *argument*, she seems to suggest, one would simply be undermining one's own position by using terms that were, in themselves, already deeply problematic: always already implicated in an existing power structure that one was seeking to resist or subvert. It is for this reason that she appears to prioritize *redescription* over argument, for the former offers at least the *possibility* of a language that is not so deeply implicated or tainted by its association with power.

Both Butler and Rorty appear to hold some position between the weak and strong theses about language and the world, leading them to reject argument, to throw out reasons with a small "r" along with Reason with a big "R." It is not a position that either thinker clearly articulates, however, precisely because to do so would be to engage in *argument*. For purposes of clarification, however, we might say that their claims about *arguments* fall into one of three possible categories:

1. *Arguments* simply cannot be given for any political or philosophical position.
2. *Arguments* can be given for political and philosophical positions, but such *arguments* are simply *readings* that have gained widespread acceptance.
3. *Arguments* can be given for political and philosophical positions, *arguments* that are simply accepted *readings*, but it is more effective to give alternative *readings*.

In order to elucidate these positions more clearly, and indeed to facilitate the rehabilitated account of argument in a postfoundational world, it is now necessary to say something about the distinction that has so far been implicit between *arguments* and *readings*.

ARGUMENTS AND *READINGS*: A DISTINCTION

It might be noted that neither Judith Butler nor Richard Rorty makes the distinction being drawn here between *arguments* and *readings*, not least because both seem to regard the former as simply a version of the latter. This is because both regard the world as a kind of text and see the skills that one uses to read a text as simply interchangeable with the analytical skills that one employs as a natural or social scientist: the *portability claim*. The distinction between *arguments* and *readings* is, perhaps, somewhat intuitive and as such hard to articulate. It is, however, no less important for that difficulty. In many ways it is very much akin to a distinction between *rigor* and *creativity*, or the distinction between moves *in* a language game and moves *across* language games. Such claims merely serve, however, to beg the definitional question. It will perhaps be best simply to state the distinction and to flesh it out afterward.

The distinction is as follows. An *argument* is the marshalling of reasons in favor of claims that can be evaluated against agreed-upon standards. A *reading*, on the other hand, is a critical practice best summarized by Richard Rorty's account of Harold Bloom's work: "the critic asks neither the author nor the text about their intention but simply beats the text into a shape that will serve his purpose. He does this by imposing a vocabulary . . . on the text which may have nothing to do with any vocabulary used by that text or its author."[31] In this practice of *reading*, resolving the difficulties of apparently contradictory claims is not a matter of finding some deeper sense in which the claims can be reconciled, nor of abandoning one of the claims in favor of the one that appears stronger or more plausible; rather, it is a matter of finding some way to *describe* these claims that does not generate the same contradiction, or that makes the contradiction seem irrelevant. *Readings* on this account rely largely upon their *effect* upon the reader, *arguments* upon the validity of their internal logic.

An *argument* is, therefore, somewhat constrained by what counts as a good reason. Convincing others of the validity of one's position in an *argument* is a matter of marshalling facts and evidence within the prevailing *standards of justification* to support one's claims. "Standards of justification" means the benchmark against which the plausibility of claims is judged, be it "Objective Truth" or "beyond a reasonable doubt." An *argument* is, therefore, something to do with *reasons* and *standards*, although neither this claim nor the suggestion that *arguments* rely upon their own internal logic for veracity commits us to a representational theory of truth. A *reading*, on the other hand, is constrained only by the imagination of the person giving the *reading*, or by the imagination of the audience for that *reading*. A crucial difference between an *argument* and a *reading* is that—in any given instance—the standards of justification in an argument remain more or less fixed, whereas, a creative or performative *reading* can itself alter the standards of justification in a way that an *argument* cannot. Convincing another of the value of one's *reading* is on this account less to do with the marshalling of *reasons* against an agreed-upon standard and more to do with the power of one's language: whether or not one's *reading* "clicks" or resonates with her in a way that is pleasing, given what she already believes—or what the *reading* can lead her to believe—about the world. *Readings* resonate with readers in a way that works of art do or do not, hence the appropriateness of the turn to literature as a source of insight among those who embrace *readings* as the dominant critical mode. We might think, for example, of Sylvia Plath's poem *Stillborn*, which suggests the way in which a failed *reading* seems lifeless in contrast to the reading that resonates and captures the reader's attention and allegiance.[32]

A further important difference between *arguments* and *readings* is that—for the most part—conflicting *arguments* demand to be resolved, whereas conflicting *readings* can coexist. The standard of justification for an *argument* is, "Is it true, given what we know about the world?" The standard of justification for a *reading* is somewhat less demanding than this and certainly not as stable as that for an *argument*. It could be, for example, "Is it plausible?"; "Does it resonate?"; "Is it pleasing?"; or any manner of other criteria. This is not to suggest that literary criticism—the model for such an approach—is completely anarchic, simply that many different approaches to texts exist, and that these approaches and the readings that they engender can ultimately coexist with one another. As such, there is a difference between the depths of analysis required for *readings* and for *arguments*. "To be sure, there is justification," in Wittgenstein's famous phrase, "but justification comes to an end."[33] In the absence of a representational theory of truth, the best that we can hope for in terms of certainty is that we exhaust this process of justification. In the case of *readings* this process comes to an end far sooner and in far more ways than in the case of *arguments*, the latter demanding a more exhausting process of justification. This is because the model for *arguments* is philosophy or social science, while for *readings* it is literary criticism. The standards of justification for a *reading* or an *argument* are, that is to say, partly dictated by what is at stake in each field. Traditionally, there has been far more at stake over the questions of whether an action is just or unjust, or whether poverty causes crime—the questions of philosophy and social science—than over the questions of literature, such as who betrays Elizabeth Bennet in *Pride and Prejudice*.[34] The former have implications for the way that we live our lives, the latter—in most circumstances outside of the Academy at least—ultimately very little import at all.

Arguments and *Readings*: Butler and Rorty

Having identified the distinction between *arguments* and *readings*, it is now possible to say something about the status of *arguments* in the work of Judith Butler and Richard Rorty. Of the three possible positions identified earlier, Butler and Rorty both seem to hold some version of (2)—that *arguments* can be given for political and philosophical positions, but that such *arguments* are simply *readings* that have gained widespread acceptance—and/or position (3)—that we can give *arguments* for political and philosophical positions, *arguments* that are simply accepted *readings*, but that it is more effective to give alternative *readings*. It is hard to imagine that anybody would sincerely hold the first position simply because it is clear that people give and make arguments all the time for various types of political and philosophical positions. Butler and Rorty both seem to suggest, however, that in so doing, such people are either offering *readings* that they misperceive as *arguments*—the second position—or that they are simply wasting their time because a better strategy is open to them—the third position.

The second position suggests that *arguments* are simply made up of *readings* that have gained widespread acceptance: that *reasons* have no special ontological status but are simply accepted *readings*. *Arguments* fail, this position suggests, fail in the same way that Plath's stillborn poems fail: they do not resonate with the reader or capture her imagination, and as such they are rejected. Although Butler does not make this claim explicit, it is a position that seems to be entailed by her work. The notion that *reasons* are simply accepted *readings* correlates strongly to her dismissal of "accepted wisdom" and "common sense." For Butler these concepts are closely related to her recurrent trope of *hegemony*. "Hegemony"—especially if it is regarded as a sort of "coercion with the consent of the governed"—seems to correlate directly to Butler's Foucaultian suggestion that the language that we use is shaped by powerful nonlinguistic forces that we do not control but that nevertheless shape the way we view the world. Human beings on this account may indeed appear to make *arguments* for positions that they hold, but the impact and scope of these arguments is largely restricted by the language in which these *arguments* are formulated. It is for this reason that Butler is so anxious to abandon ordinary language.

It also appears, however, that Butler also holds some version of the third position. It is nevertheless a position that is much more closely associated with Richard Rorty. Fittingly for a thinker who often positions himself within the American pragmatic tradition, adopting this position allows Rorty to remain agnostic on whether or not it is actually possible to make meaningful *arguments*. The third position simply holds that doing so is a waste of time. A more productive alternative is, it suggests, to offer new vocabularies in which the old *arguments* simply disappear. This is done by offering a *reading* of a given situation that makes the old *arguments* seem irrelevant or obsolete. The position suggests that the language we use—though in some sense determinative of the world in which we live—is somewhat arbitrary, malleable, and easily replaced. It is a view that Wittgenstein seems to advocate when he observes that with "different training the same ostensive teaching of these words would have effected a quite different understanding."[35] Indeed, there also appears to be a clear Wittgensteinian pedigree for the activity of redescription. Asserting that one *"might* say: 'N' has become meaningless; and that this would mean that the sign 'N' no longer has a use in our language game," Wittgenstein adds in a crucial parenthesis, "(unless we gave it a new one)."[36] Rorty seems to have in mind passages such as these when he offers a *reading* of the later Wittgenstein to justify his rejection of *reasons* and philosophy. Such a rejection may, however, be somewhat premature.

POSTANALYTIC PHILOSOPHY:
THE RETURN OF *REASONS* AND *ARGUMENTS*

That the claims about the death of philosophy have been exaggerated is suggested by the existence of an alternative to the metaphysical and postmodernist and poststructuralist approaches outlined earlier, an approach that has been called "postanalytic" philosophy.[37] Establishing the validity of this postanalytic approach is not only important for the remainder of this study but also for the practice of politics in the postfoundational world. Showing that it is indeed possible to give *reasons* and to make *arguments* for various political positions— as opposed to seeking to *persuade* others through the power of one's language— has an important political corollary in that it allows us to treat others as *ends* and not simply as the *means* of our political wills. In seeking to redescribe them and/or their beliefs in the manner advocated by Rorty we are perhaps potentially guilty of treating them in the way that he treats literary texts and characters: simply beating them into shapes that serve our purposes. While this might be acceptable for literary figures, it is not yet acceptable—at least within liberalism—for nonliterary ones. In addition, offering reasons for our positions may also help us avoid what MacIntyre described as the *shrillness* of much contemporary political discourse: giving us shared grounds on which to debate important political issues with those whom we disagree rather than simply seeking to shout them into submission. In order to establish this position, and with it the continued validity of *argument* and *reasons* within postmodernity, we turn to the work of Ludwig Wittgenstein.

Ludwig Wittgenstein's influence on the linguistic turn in contemporary philosophy cannot be overstated. His impact on the literary turn in political thought and analysis is perhaps somewhat more indirect: largely the result of his influence on Richard Rorty. Rorty's turn to literary criticism is clearly predicated upon a *reading* of the later-Wittgenstein's work. There is, of course, a certain degree of circularity here: it is Rorty's adoption of *reading* as a critical method that leads to his *reading* of Wittgenstein, that which justifies his rejection of philosophy and his adoption of *reading* as a critical method.[38] Indeed, Rorty's Wittgenstein sounds an awful lot like a poststructuralist: he is concerned with the ways in which our language shapes the world and confines us, and with *redescription* and *play* as a way out of this linguistic cage.[39] As such, it is perhaps fitting that we should turn to Wittgenstein as a means of showing why the postmodernist and poststructuralist claims about language and *argument*—the claims upon which both Rorty and Butler appear to predicate their turn to literary critical methods as a source of insight—are overstated. The aim here will not be to offer an account of Wittgenstein's work that is closer to some truth about his meaning in order to win the battle at the level of textual interpretation, for to do so would be to buy into the mistaken assumption upon which the turn to literature and literary criticism is based: that there is little difference between the world and a text. Rather, it will be to suggest that Wittgenstein provides us with the philosophical resources for an account of the relationship between language and the world that shows how the philosophical *argument* is both possible and useful in postmodernity, one that seeks to temper—in important ways—the faith that thinkers such as Rorty and Butler seem to place in the power of language.

The cornerstone of Rorty's account of Wittgenstein—if this is not too foundational a term—is the latter's concept of a "language game." At various points in *Philosophical Investigations*, Wittgenstein suggests that language is structured like a game. It is a telling metaphor. Just as with a game there are rules for the use of language, but these rules are neither fixed—in the sense that they can change over time—nor exhaustive: there is, as Wittgenstein notes, no rule telling us how high to throw the ball when serving in tennis. All argument and justification, Wittgenstein suggests, takes place within such language games, and these games are how we make sense of the world. "To understand a sentence," he writes, "means to understand a language. To understand a language means to master a technique."[40] For Rorty the key passages in Wittgenstein's work are those where he points to the almost arbitrary nature of language that we use, and where he suggests that human beings are free to make up new language games and to find new meanings for old words. These passages provide the impetus for Rorty to dismiss philosophical arguments on the grounds that they are simply previously rehearsed moves in language games—the second position—or alternatively, because we can avoid arguments altogether by simply inventing new language games—the third position. It is this last aspect of Wittgenstein's work that explains Rorty's belief that it is the poet and not the scientist who is the central figure of our epoch.

Precisely because she takes so much of the literary and linguistic turn for granted, Judith Butler would never seek to establish the validity of her position in the manner of Richard Rorty. Nevertheless, as has been suggested, Butler also seems to hold some perspective akin to that of the second position: that arguments are simply moves in language games—though she would never herself use this vocabulary—and that the terms or rules of such language games are set by the powerful. In order to avoid perpetuating their power, she suggests, we should avoid using their language and focus instead upon finding new and more empowering ways of talking and being in the world, hence her concern with the value of *redescription* as a political method. Butler is, however, much more focused on the nonlinguistic aspects of power than Rorty. Her concern with "bodies that matter" and with performance indicates that although redescription remains a powerful weapon in her arsenal, she is less convinced than Rorty of the power of language alone. For this reason, her position might be better formulated as the following:

(4) We can give *arguments* for political and philosophical positions, *arguments* that are simply accepted *readings*, but it is more effective to give alternative *performances*.

That Butler clearly regards her own *redescription* and writing as performative—an argument that will be developed in more detail in chapter 5—suggests that although she does not see *redescription* as a universal panacea in the manner of Rorty, it is still part of a resistive strategy that is predicated upon a belief in the power of language, one that suggests that *arguments* are a waste of time because they are always already implicated in existing power structures.

WITTGENSTEIN, LANGUAGE, AND THE WORLD

A closer examination of Wittgenstein's work on the relationship between language and the world shows us, however, that there is much that is problematic about these thinkers' claims. It can also give us a more plausible account of the relationship, one that suggests that not only can we make *arguments* in postmodernity, but that there are also good *reasons* for so doing. Wittgenstein's work in the *Philosophical Investigations* suggests that language is indeed a powerful tool for shaping the world: the concepts that we use to describe the world are, he suggests, key determinants in shaping both our conscious and unconscious understanding of it. Rorty's *reading* of Wittgenstein nevertheless overstates the extent to which he believes that language is malleable: language on Wittgenstein's account is much less "fluid" than Rorty believes.[41] Indeed, Wittgenstein's work offers a far more plausible account of the relationship between language and the world than that suggested by Rorty or Butler, one that makes their rejection of *argument* appear somewhat premature. Language, Wittgenstein seems to suggest, while not "fixed" in the manner he set out in the *Tractatus,* is nevertheless somewhat "viscous." This "viscosity" appears to arise from a kind of linguistic structure that emerges from our usage of it, that which he calls "grammar." It is this account of "grammar" that paves the way for the return of *argument* to philosophy.

The structure of language that arises from our usage of it, Wittgenstein asserts, is in no way *necessary*. "Grammar does not tell us," he writes, "how language must be constructed in order to fulfill its purpose, in order to have such and such an effect on human beings. It only describes and in no way explains the use of signs."[42] Rather, it emerges simply from our past usage of it: because we have used language in certain ways more or less consistently in the past, we come to expect that it will be used that way again in the future. Nobody consciously sets out the rules for this use of language; rather, these rules simply emerge from our repeated usage of it. It is this grammatical structure of language that makes *arguments* possible, for the grammar of our usage serves to generate an internal logic for our language. Ways of speaking that follow this internal logic—*arguments*—are generally more valid than those that do not. It is this logic that allows us to choose between different positions and to select the position that seems most plausible given our experience of the world. It may be that this is precisely what poststructuralists and postmodernists mean when they assert that *arguments* are simply *readings* that have gained widespread acceptance. This is, however, simply a claim about the origins of *arguments*. It should not lead us to reject arguments in the manner of Butler and Rorty. It is important to note, however, that the basis of the rejection differs for each thinker.

Rorty rejects *arguments* because he believes that having identified their contingent origins, he is now free to invent the world. Butler does so on two grounds: first, because of her undeniable belief in the power of language to shape the world; second, because, for her, the widespread acceptance of arguments is indicative of the influence or hegemony of a partially nonlinguistic power that should be resisted. In neither case, however, do these seem to be good grounds for turning toward redescription and/or performance. In Rorty's case, just as recognizing the social constructedness of money does not lead us—most of us, at least—to abandon it, identifying the origins of arguments should not lead us to abandon them. In Butler's case, her rejection seems to eradicate all kinds of important distinctions between good arguments and bad ones and—as will be argued in greater detail in chapter 5—between all kinds of uses of power. Both approaches seem, furthermore, to prioritize novelty unnecessarily and to underestimate the continued usefulness of arguments. That we can and do use arguments to get around in the world is an important factor for maintaining their existence, both philosophically and politically. It is also indicative of another important aspect of language highlighted by Wittgenstein's work: that it is, in some sense, still connected to the world.

The claim that language is still connected to the world—redolent as it is of representationalist epistemologies—is, of course, enough to have postmodernists and poststructuralists shaking their heads (or whatever it is that such figures do to indicate disagreement). Nevertheless, making this claim simply requires paying attention to those aspects of the weaker thesis about language and the world—that language, by shaping our outlook on the world, helps determine the world in which we live—to which both Judith Butler and Richard Rorty appear to subscribe. Rorty approvingly quotes Wallace Stevens's observation that language is the mind pushing back against reality.[43] Here it is merely being suggested that reality might itself push back against imagination and language. On the postmodernist and poststructuralist account of the world, language merely *helps* determine the world in which we live. Neither Butler nor Rorty, for example, comes out and says *directly* that language is primary, although Rorty in particular often writes as if he believes this to be the case. Such a claim suggests, of course, that the world in which we live is—as indeed Butler appears to hold—also partly determined by other factors: by some other nonlinguistic reality intersecting with language, with both language and the nonlinguistic reality existing in a symbiotic relationship, each affecting and being affected by the other. This is precisely what is suggested by Wittgenstein's concept of a "form of life."

"[T]o imagine a language," writes Wittgenstein in the *Philosophical Investigations*, "means to imagine a form of life."[44] Although the term is never quite defined in Wittgenstein's work, it nevertheless captures the way in which the language that we use, though created by and for humans, is connected to the way that we live. Returning to Thucydides and the Greeks, we might think about the Greek concern with balance that is reflected in the ubiquitousness of binary oppositions in their poetry and prose. By presenting binary oppositions, such as in Pericles' Funeral Oration—between men and women, one and the many, life and death, and so on—the Greeks sought to find the middle ground between the two extremes. In this their language was intimately connected to their form of life and its concern with balance and harmony. Words, on this account, are tools for particular purposes. Just as a screwdriver has a particularly shaped head to fit particularly shaped screws, words are useful precisely because they fit or map onto some reality that is only partly determined by language. Indeed, if *arguments* are simply established *readings*, then it may be that this connectedness between language and the world is one of the *reasons* they resonate with us the way they do. So, although the connection between language and the world is not as fixed as Wittgenstein asserts in the *Tractatus*, it is certainly not as arbitrary as Rorty suggests. In a discussion of chess, for example, Wittgenstein declares: "When one shews someone the king in chess and says: 'This is the King,' this does not tell him the use of the piece—unless he already knows the rules of the game up to this point: the shape of the king."[45] In order to use a language, Wittgenstein suggests, we require a good deal of background knowledge about our existence in the world—the way we interact with it and so on—background knowledge that he later calls "stage-setting" information.[46] As far as the ontological status of this "stage-setting" information is concerned, Wittgenstein is somewhat ambiguous, and we can remain agnostic. At times he appears to suggest that it is simply a matter of convention; at other times he appears to have a rather more Platonic view.[47] Either way, however, Wittgenstein's concept of a "form of life" captures the way in which the words that we use are intimately connected to our actions and the way that we are in the world. It is for this reason that Rorty's third position—that we can give *arguments* for political and philosophical positions, *arguments* that are simply accepted *readings*, but that it is more effective to give alternative *readings*—and Butler's variation—the fourth position—are both overstated. The language that we use in the world is arbitrary in the sense that it might have developed differently, but it developed in the way it did in part because it serves useful functions in the world, and it does this because of the way that it maps onto and indeed meshes with the world. As such, it is undoubtedly a useful tool for getting about in it.

In these circumstances, creating a new language game through *redescription* or simply changing the language game that we are playing at any particular time is rather more difficult than Rorty seems to suggest. The new language game would have to do everything that the old language game did and more. It is also for this reason that the fourth position is overstated. Butler seems to prioritize novelty; indeed, her position is somewhat akin to buying a new car because we have a flat tire. It is because she believes that language games are loaded in favor of the powerful that we should create new ones. The language that we use is, nevertheless, useful, precisely because we use it, and we use it because of the way that we are in the world and the type of beings that we are. To abandon argument and invent new language games whenever we run into difficulty—philosophical or political—with the current one would be to undo the very concept of language itself. Language would, in these circumstances, be so fluid as to be meaningless: we too would face the linguistic chaos of the civil war in Corcyra.

Rorty may be misled into his position by his rather thin conception of language. For him it seems that language is simply a collection of words, rather as they might appear in a dictionary. In these circumstances it is easy to see how he might think that language can be so easily manipulated. The arbitrariness of words—the fact that they could have meant something different from their current meaning—suggests that changing language is simply a matter of changing the definitions of words, which is really just a matter of getting other people to agree on the new definition. For Butler, however, there is a closer connection between language and the world than for Rorty. To extend the metaphor, for Butler, words appear in the dictionary with the definitions they do because of nonlinguistic power. It is for this reason that she champions other forms of subversion, including parody and performance. Both thinkers are, however, concerned with changing the world in which we live by shifting our understanding of it through redescription, performance, or a combination of the two, for if the world is partly—or even wholly—constituted by language, then changing the world is a matter of getting others to agree on their new account of it.

The Wittgensteinian account of language offered here, however, offers a much more plausible, "thicker" conception of language: words are related to the way that human beings are in the world, and as such, they are more resistant to change than either account suggests. Rorty's account of Wittgenstein misses, it seems, a key definition in the latter's thought. "I shall," writes Wittgenstein, "also call the whole *consisting of language and the actions into which it is woven*, the 'language game.'"[48] Once language is conceived of in this way, the claim that changing the world is simply a matter of changing the language that we use to describe it is rendered much more complex than Rorty and less necessary than Butler seem to believe. Language, on this account, is much more viscous than fluid. As such, it is much less likely to change with the frequency and manner suggested by the rejection of *argument* and the turn to *redescription* in Rorty's work. It is also much more useful than Butler's work seems to suggest. It is certainly capable of being employed in ways that might undermine the nonlinguistic power with which Butler is concerned, not least because her concern with creating new ways of speaking often seems to create a complexity that might itself serve to undo the concept of an intelligible language. Wittgenstein's account of language being "woven into" the world also suggests why nonfictional human beings are much less easily manipulated than fictional ones: they often answer back and refuse to be beaten into the shapes that certain theorists require. Consequently, this Wittgensteinian account of the relationship between language and the world shows us why adopting a literary view of the world as a text for political purposes may well be a mistake: language is much less flexible and arguments much more useful than either Rorty or Butler seems to suggest.

PHILOSOPHY IN A POSTFOUNDATIONAL WORLD

It has been suggested then that the work of the later Ludwig Wittgenstein provides us with the intellectual resources for a defense of philosophy that while accepting the prerequisites of postfoundationalism nevertheless allows room for *arguments* and *reasons*. The "grammar" or structure of language that arises from our use of it is what makes *arguments* possible. There are, however, moments in Wittgenstein's work where he appears to reject philosophy altogether: where he suggests that philosophical thinking is a mistake that needs to be cured. "It is," he says memorably, "like a pair of glasses on our nose through which we see whatever we look at. It never occurs to us to take them off."[49] Such comments are, however, focused on one-sided thinking—the sort of thing that, according to Thucydides, led to Athens' downfall—not philosophy per se. It is one-sided thinking that, he suggests, makes us unable to see or think our way out of a problem. As Hanna Pitkin memorably observes in *Wittgenstein and Justice*: "Wittgenstein's special genius lies in being able to hold . . . conflicting themes in balance, and teaching us ways of doing so for ourselves."[50] Overcoming such "philosophical thinking" is a matter of adopting a multiplicity of perspectives, though this is much harder than it is sometimes presented by Butler and Rorty.

Butler and Rorty both focus to too great an extent on language's undeniable capacity to help shape the world in which we live. Rorty in particular does so at the apparent expense of a nonlinguistic reality that also helps shape that language. Whether this is a rhetorical and political strategy or simply a philosophical mistake is perhaps unknowable. Wittgenstein's concept of "philosophical thinking" and the work of Butler and Rorty should, however, alert us to certain dangers inherent in doing philosophy in a postfoundational world, *political* philosophy in particular. Foremost among these is one-sidedness, the sort of thing that leads these thinkers to prioritize novelty and thereby possibly to undo the concept of language. Ironically it is precisely to avoid this one-sidedness that a number of thinkers in this study turned to literature in the first place. Nevertheless, Wittgenstein's work offers us an account of philosophy that might permit us to avoid such an approach.

In the *Philosophical Investigations*, Wittgenstein gives an account of a philosophical method predicated upon his conception of language and its relationship to the world:

> Our investigation is therefore a grammatical one. Such an investigation sheds light on our problem by clearing misunderstandings away. Misunderstandings concerning the use of words, caused among other things, by certain analogies between the forms of expression in different regions in language. Some of them can be removed by substituting one form of expression for another; this may be called an "analysis" of our forms of expression, for the process is sometimes like one of taking a thing apart.[51]

Here Wittgenstein might, perhaps, be thought to be advocating precisely the sort of redescriptive method championed by Rorty and Butler. The key phrase in this passage is, however, "some of them," as this indicates that Wittgenstein is not—as Rorty would have us believe—advocating this method as the *only* way to go about analyzing arguments and phenomena. Rather, he is suggesting that it is simply one of many different methods, all of which involve looking to see how language is constructed and how it functions in its actual usage. Similarly, the Wittgensteinian claim, that "at some point one has to pass from explanation to mere description,"[52] which also seems to support the position adopted by Butler and Rorty, is notable for the qualifier "at some point." Rorty seems to regard such phrases as irrelevant, but by paying attention to them suggests that Wittgenstein offers us a way to do postfoundational philosophy. The time to move from explanation to description is when explanation within a language game has been completely exhausted. This is clearly something that differs according to what is under investigation. As with Wittgenstein's example about there being no rule for how high one should throw the ball while serving in tennis, there is clearly no hard-and-fast rule about when explanation is exhausted: it changes from case to case, and the only way to decide when it has been exhausted is, in Wittgenstein's phrase, to "*look and see.*"[53]

This "looking and seeing" consists of examining the theories that are being offered within existing language games—such as philosophy—and putting those theories into dialogue with our experience of the world in which we live in precisely the same way that Wittgenstein produces lots of everyday examples and looks to see if they capture something that we feel to be true about our experience of the world. If a theorist makes a claim, for example, about the power of literature to affect its readers then we should examine that theory against our experience of literature's impact upon its readers, and assess the extent to which we regard it as plausible, given what we know about readers and texts and the world. Within this language game of philosophy we can place the theory we are examining in dialogue with our experience of the world and assess the extent to which they correlate. It may be that there is little correlation; in which case we can simply abandon the theory or look for other possible explanations—constrained by what we know of the world—within that language game. We can, that is, offer reasons and arguments *within* language games for positions that we hold and measure them against our experience of the world. It is only when there are two or more apparently conflicting phenomena that resonate with our experience of the world that we cannot reconcile, that we should then look for some alternative set of terms—or language game—in which to describe them. There is, however, much work that can be done within the existing language game before we get to that point.

The only way to put some flesh on the bones of this admittedly skeletal account of philosophy in a postfoundational world is to *show by doing* in the subsequent chapters where the claims that are made on behalf of the turn to literature in political thought and analysis are critically assessed. We start with the work of Martha Nussbaum.

Part 2

The Literary Turn
in Thought and Practice

Chapter 2

Martha Nussbaum
Literary Imagination and the Public Life

"'First of all,' he said, 'if you can learn a simple trick, Scout, you'll get along a lot better with all kinds of folks. You never really understand a person until you consider things from his point of view—'Sir?' "—until you climb into his skin and walk around in it.'"

—Harper Lee, *To Kill A Mockingbird*[1]

Of all the thinkers who have made the literary turn, Martha Nussbaum's work is notable for explicitly concerning itself with versions of all three aspects of the turn identified at the outset: the *epistemological and ontological* question, the *moral and political* question, and the *methodological* question. As far as the first question is concerned, while she does not reject philosophy in the manner of Butler and Rorty, Nussbaum nevertheless attempts to augment traditional Reason with literature, seeking to expand our conception of what might be considered valid premises in a good argument. With regard to the second, she suggests that by generating empathy in its readers, literature can enhance the practice of liberal democracy by providing a basis—in emotion—for a stable system of government. Finally, she suggests that reading certain novels can provide us with insight into the political that is otherwise absent from traditional methods of behavioral social science. Her work is an ambitious attempt to harness what she considers the emotive power of literature in both the practice and study of public life. This chapter sets out and assesses the validity of Nussbaum's claims about the power of literature to solve the philosophical, political, and methodological problems that she identifies. The very breadth and ambition of her claims about literature suggest, however, that many of these claims simply will not hold good. Even so, hers is the most systematic and rigorous of all the attempts to incorporate

41

literature into political thought and analysis, and there is much in her work that is suggestive of the ways in which political-philosophical thought might benefit from the infusion of certain literary methods. In this perhaps she is to be congratulated for having made what might be called a "pioneering sacrifice" in the study and practice of the literary turn. Although much of what follows here is critical of her claims, it should also be acknowledged that this analysis takes place in the considerable shadow cast by her work on the use of literature in law, classics, economics, and philosophy.

Martha Nussbaum and the Emotive Power of Literature

Discussions of literature played a role in Martha Nussbaum's thought long before the publication of her book *Poetic Justice: The Literary Imagination and Public Life*, but it was here that she presented the first systematic account of her theory of literature in social and political thought and analysis. Although there is some inconsistency and/or evolution in her presentation of the argument, Nussbaum's central claims about literature and the value of literary insight to social and political thought and analysis appear to be twofold. First, that reading certain novels provides insight into different ways of living useful for social and political theory; second, that certain novels develop a particular innate human capacity—which she, following Dickens, labels *Fancy*—that make their readers more compassionate citizens of liberal-democratic societies.

As far as the first claim is concerned, Nussbaum asserts that her proposal is a "... modest one, that economic science should be built on the human data of the sort novels such as Dickens's reveal to the imagination, that economic science should seek a more complicated and philosophically adequate set of foundations."[2] As it is currently formulated, she argues, economic modeling that takes as its standard of evaluation some notion of utility is simply too abstract to capture all of the various nuances of human existence. To remedy this excessive abstraction Nussbaum advocates an "approach to quality of life measurement based on a notion of human functioning or human capability."[3] In this we see the fundamentally Aristotelian nature of Nussbaum's project, seeking as it does to combine the universal with the specific. In *The Politics*, Aristotle notes that the problem with laws is that they "speak only to the universal and do not command with a view to circumstances."[4] Nevertheless, he also notes that "what is unaccompanied by the passionate element is generally superior to that which is innate. Now this is not present in law, but every human soul necessarily has it," suggesting that there is indeed value in these universal laws, especially for passionate humans who might be misguided by their emotions. He further suggests, however, that it is precisely these passions that allow humans to "deliberate in a finer fashion concerning particulars."[5] If combining literature and social science is Nussbaum's attempt to operationalize Aristotle's dual claims, then it is fitting that we see it most clearly in her discussion of economic modeling.

In order that economists might better tailor their models to the—more fully defined—needs and demands of the citizenry, Nussbaum says that they should read novels such as *Hard Times* by Charles Dickens. Reading a novel in which certain characters' overly narrow focus on utility has such disastrous consequences for its protagonists will, says Nussbaum, alert these economists to the ways in which their own models similarly ignore the demands of fully rounded human beings situated in particular contexts. Nussbaum is not, however, suggesting that novels—and by extension a concern with emotion and narrative—should *replace* such formal modeling, but simply that they act as an *additional* component in the act of social theorizing. "[S]torytelling and literary imagining are not," she says, "opposed to rational argument, but can provide essential ingredients in a rational argument."[6] In this we see Nussbaum's formulation of two of the key aspects of the literary turn: first, the *methodological* assertion that literature can give us insight into ways of living that is simply unavailable through traditional models of behavioral social science, here represented by economics; second, the *epistemological and ontological* assertion that a turn to literature can augment and correct for certain deficiencies of philosophical Reason traditionally conceived.

It is in Nussbaum's second suggestion—that certain novels force their readers to exercise their moral imaginations in such a way that they come to care about characters like those depicted in the text—that we see her concern with the literary turn's *moral and political* claim. She is not, it must be noted, simply claiming that literature will generate an uncritical appeal to the emotions—at several points she acknowledges Socrates' warning that poetry and drama might well lead citizens to generate inappropriate desires—rather, she suggests that just as rationality and Reason can be informed by the emotions generated by reading novels, these emotions are themselves to be informed by Reason and rationality in a kind of reflective equilibrium. Her inspiration for this claim is what she calls Adam Smith's "Judicious Spectator." In his *Theory of Moral Sentiments*, Smith argues that society, though made up of sovereign individuals, is nevertheless held together by what he calls "fellow feeling." This "fellow feeling," argues Smith, arises from the ability of the citizenry to imagine themselves in the situation of another. Nussbaum cites two key passages from Smith's work to support her claims about the value of reading to moral and political practice and inquiry:

> [T]he spectator . . . must endeavour, as much as he can, to put himself in the situation of the other, and to bring home to himself every little circumstance of distress which can possibly occur to the sufferer. He

must adopt the whole case of his companion with all its minutest in-
cidents; and strive to render as perfect as possible that imaginary
change of situation upon which his sympathy is founded.[7]

Emotions are, however, only the beginning of this process. The element of
rationality is injected by Smith's second claim:

> The compassion of the spectator must arise altogether from the con-
> sideration of what he himself would feel if he was reduced to the same
> unhappy situation and, what is perhaps impossible, was at the same
> time able to regard it with his present reason and judgment.[8]

In this position, Smith asserts, one is able to imagine oneself in the predicament
of another while *simultaneously* utilizing one's own judgment as a detached observer. It is, it seems, the perfect Aristotelian combination of the *rational*—that
which emerges from the detached observation and the use of traditional philosophical Reason—and the *emotional*—that which emerges from exercising the
imagination. It is this position, says Nussbaum, that is engendered by reading certain novels. Reading, she asserts, is "an artificial construction of judicious specta-
torship, leading us in a pleasing natural way into the attitude that befits the good
citizen and judge."[9] Nussbaum believes it is this combination of Reason *and*
emotion that provides her with the "more philosophically adequate" set of foundations for her social theory and the basis for a more stable liberal society.

The introduction of emotion into social theorizing and philosophy seems
perhaps contrary to the assertion that Nussbaum is an advocate of liberalism
predicated upon traditional Reason. As Stanley Fish notes, "In the vocabulary of
liberalism certain words mark the zone of suspicion—words like *conviction, belief, passion,* all of which are for the liberal mentality very close to fanaticism."[10]
Nussbaum is, therefore, very careful to temper these emotions with Reason. As
far as those emotions engendered by reading are concerned, in addition to the
reader's own rational capacities, Nussbaum provides a further constraint—
another liberal check on the power of emotions—with a process of conversational "reflective equilibrium" that she, borrowing from the ethical critic Wayne
Booth, calls "coduction."[11] "Ethical assessment of the novels themselves, in conversation both with other readers and with the arguments of moral and political
theory is," says Nussbaum, "necessary if the contribution of novels is to be politically fruitful."[12] Nussbaum suggests that certain aspects of the novels we read
might be deforming or pernicious and that we should therefore question texts as
we read them. Indeed, she asserts that there are "good reasons to criticize some
aspects of Dickens's portrayal of society," including his hostility to unions, his
criticism of formal economic modeling, and his suggestion that the poor should
be entertained rather than assisted.[13] With the potential to be swept away by

sentimentality tempered by both the position of the "judicious spectator" and the process of coduction, the reader, Nussbaum argues, will come to a properly informed, rational understanding of the situation of another. It is a position that is, she suggests, superior to both the perspective of the behavioral social scientist and, indeed, to that of the citizen being modeled. "People," she notes, "can be wrong about what is happening to them in many ways."[14]

Nevertheless, just as Nussbaum asserts that not *all* emotions are to be trusted, she is equally adamant that not *all* texts are to be trusted either. The Nussbaum of *Poetic Justice* is, for example, keen to distinguish the *novel* from music and movies, although the Nussbaum of *Upheavals of Thought* is rather more ecumenical in her choice of media.[15] She is also concerned only with a certain *type* of novel: the "mainstream realist novel,"[16] especially those "with social and political themes."[17] In *Poetic Justice*, Nussbaum identifies three such novels: *Hard Times* by Charles Dickens, *Native Son* by Richard Wright, and *Maurice* by E. M. Forster. All three will, she believes, have a positive impact upon their readers. *Hard Times* will, Nussbaum argues, alert its readers—in particular, the "person brought up solely on economic texts [who] has not been encouraged to think of workers (or indeed anyone else) as fully human beings, with stories of their own to tell"[18]—to the plight of the working classes. *Native Son* is useful, she suggests, for overcoming the "black metal fence in the law school parking lot that marks 'the line' between the world of the university and the world of inner-city Chicago," alerting readers to the problems faced by African Americans in their everyday lives.[19] Similarly, she believes *Maurice* will make its readers more sensitive to the position of homosexuals "by making it easy for them to see Maurice as someone they, or one of their friends or loved ones, might be."[20] In each instance, Nussbaum offers an account of the text that purports to show how easily the reader—who, we are to assume, is straight, white, and middle class—will come to identify with those whose existence might differ from her own. Nussbaum's account of the impact of these texts is predicated upon what might be called her "theory of the novel." It asserts that "the very form constructs compassion in readers, positioning them as people who care intensely about the suffering and bad luck of others, and who identify with them in ways that show possibilities for themselves."[21]

Literature and the Reader: Conflation and Inflation

Nussbaum's claims about literature and the public life are then: that reading certain novels provides us with insight into other ways of living useful for social theory and that reading such novels also exercises in us a certain moral capacity—*Fancy*—that is politically useful in liberal-democratic societies. There appears, nevertheless, to be a certain imprecision in Nussbaum's presentation of her argument. Most obviously we see this in her account of the way in which the alleged benefit of reading actually manifests itself in public life.

At the outset of *Poetic Justice*, Nussbaum seems characteristically clear on the matter. Reading novels will enhance the practice of what she calls "economic science" by allowing economists to make better—in the sense of being more *informed*—models of social reality. The benefits of this improved modeling will, Nussbaum suggests, trickle down to the citizenry through an elite, steering "judges in their judging, legislators in their legislating, [and] policy makers in measuring the quality of life of people near and far."[22] By the middle of the book, however, Nussbaum appears to suggest that citizens can benefit more *directly* from the benefits of the literary imagination, but only when they serve as jurors in courtrooms.[23] In a subsequent article and exchange with Wayne Booth and Richard Posner, Nussbaum inflates her claims considerably. There Nussbaum summarizes her argument in *Poetic Justice* thusly: "I argue that certain specific literary works develop those imaginative abilities in a valuable way and are therefore helpful to citizens."[24] What starts off as a "modest proposal about economic science," applicable only to those concerned with formal modeling, appears to develop into a full-fledged theory of the benefits of the moral imagination applicable to all citizens who read novels. That the normally meticulous Nussbaum should run together a number of these claims, and indeed fail to give a fuller account of the mechanism by which the alleged benefits of reading are supposed to impact upon a polity, is perhaps indicative of the extent to which her claims about novel reading and the moral imagination are inextricably linked to her broader political philosophy, that which she calls "Aristotelian Social Democracy."[25]

LITERATURE AND ARISTOTELIAN SOCIAL DEMOCRACY

The central tenets of "Aristotelian Social Democracy" are deceptively straightforward: that there should be a basic liberal framework—essentially that set out by John Rawls—but one that takes a much broader—Aristotelian—view of human flourishing. In place of Rawls's "basic social goods," Nussbaum offers a list of "Basic Human Functional Capabilities": a minimal theory of the good life that seeks to protect certain basic human capabilities.[26] The key difficulty here, of course, is how such a system should be instituted, that is, how a society should seek to draw the line between protecting basic liberal freedoms, while simultaneously redistributing resources to make Nussbaum's list a reality. The very tiredness of the liberal-communitarian debate suggests that this might be an insurmountable problem. Nussbaum appears to believe, however, that the literary imagination is a way to bridge the gap between these two competing traditions.

That bridging the gap between liberals and communitarians is indeed Nussbaum's aim is evidenced by her list of favored philosophers in *Poetic Justice*: one that mixes traditional liberals, such as Rawls, Mill, and Smith, with Aristotle.[27] In this respect, Nussbaum appears to share something in both method and outlook with Richard Rorty. In addition to his penchant for melding traditions, Rorty also holds that most of contemporary Western society's basic problems have been, or can be, solved within the liberal framework. Resolving injustice, he suggests, is simply a matter of bringing others into that framework rather than by radically altering our tried-and-tested institutions. It is this which, Nussbaum believes, is achieved by novel reading, that which allows her to absorb the various critiques of liberalism—that it is patriarchal, overly gendered, elitist, insufficiently attentive to issues of race, and so forth—while remaining steadfast in her commitment to rationality. Reading books by, or about, working-class people, African Americans, gays, lesbians, and women will, she suggests, permit liberal thinkers to incorporate the perspectives of class, gender, race, and sexuality into their thinking while remaining fundamentally committed to the structures of liberalism based on Reason. The limited radicalism of her project is perhaps exposed by her claim that the specter haunting contemporary society is not—as Marx would have it—communism but rather Jacob Marley, a ghost who "drags for all eternity a chain made of cash boxes, because in life his imagination never ventured outside the walls of his successful business to encounter the lives of men and women around him, men and women of different social class and background."[28] For Nussbaum, social justice requires neither the radical redistribution of wealth nor the overthrow of the existing political system but simply that we all read a little more widely.

As such, literature appears to do a great deal of work in Nussbaum's social and political theory. It is literature that enhances the practice of liberalism, gives social insight unavailable elsewhere, and allows traditional Reason to respond to various political criticisms. While the entirety of Nussbaum's social and political thought will not be the focus of our study, that thought's reliance upon the claim that literature is able to do everything that Nussbaum expects of it will. There are a number of problems with Nussbaum's claims in terms of both her methodology and the political implications of her approach, for although there is something intuitively appealing and phenomenologically plausible about the claim that in reading we come to care about particular characters, possibly getting a glimpse of the world from their perspective while simultaneously maintaining our own detached position—we can, despite occasionally hyperbolic book jacket claims to the contrary, always put down the book—it is not clear that this is sufficient to support the weight that Nussbaum places on literature in her work. Indeed, at times it seems that literature functions as a panacea for all sorts of difficulties that Nussbaum encounters in her work. We see this most obviously in her conflation of the claim that *seeing* another perspective is akin to *caring* about it.

READING, COMPASSION, AND TORTURE

In *Eichmann in Jerusalem,* Hannah Arendt describes the Nazi war criminal's re-action to being handed a copy of Vladimir Nabokov's *Lolita.* "After two days," recounts Arendt, "Eichmann returned it, visibly indignant; 'Quite an unwhole-some book' . . . he told his guard."[29] Similarly, Adolf Hitler is said to have ob-served that novels bored him.[30] In both instances, insensitivity toward literature appears to be correlated with cruelty toward humanity, suggesting a prima facie appeal to Nussbaum's claims about literature and the moral imagination. Nev-ertheless, in an article on Nussbaum's theory of compassion, Jeremiah P. Con-way notes that of the fourteen men summoned to the Wannsee Conference to discuss the "Final Solution," nine held doctorate degrees and all were educated at Central Europe's finest universities, suggesting perhaps that the correlation between reading and compassion is not as tight as Nussbaum would have us believe.[31] Indeed, it may well be that if reading *does* generate insight into an-other's deepest beliefs, then such insight might—as in the case of Orwell's fic-tional "Room 101"—actually serve to make such cruelty *more* effective. This is the *empathetic torturer* argument. As Alexander Nehamas points out, "There are plenty of examples of exquisitely sensitive torturers, discerning sadists, per-ceptive tormentors—many of whom were excellent readers as well. To be able truly to see the world from another's point of view may be the greatest weapon one can yield in a war against another."[32] It is an argument that poses a serious challenge to the validity of Nussbaum's claims about the role of literature in so-cial and political thought. Her response is somewhat less than convincing.

In responding to the *empathetic torturer* argument, Nussbaum draws a dis-tinction between *compassion* and *empathy.* Reading, she suggests, generates the former and not just the latter. The significance of this distinction arises from a definition that Nussbaum borrows from Aristotle. Compassion, she says, de-mands three key evaluative judgments: "that what is happening to the person whom one contemplates is seriously bad, that it is not the person's own fault (or beyond the fault, if fault is there), and that the spectator herself has similar pos-sibilities and vulnerabilities."[33] Furthermore, she continues, empathy is likely to be hooked up to compassion "only in someone who has had a good early educa-tion in childhood, one that teaches concern for others."[34] It is not clear, however, that this theory offers an adequate response to the *empathetic torturer* objection. In the first instance, regardless of what one *calls* the capacity that reading is sup-posed to engender, the fact remains that many well-read people still continue to behave in unacceptable ways, be it genocide or simple professional jealousy. "De-spite their familiarity with the classics," noted K. K. Ruthven, "professors of lit-erature do not appear to lead better lives than other people, and frequently display unbecoming virulence on the subject of one another's shortcomings."[35]

Nussbaum's second move is, if anything, even more problematic. She suggests that compassion will emerge from reading only if the reader is *already* a compassionate person, something that is inculcated in early childhood. Here she seems to be drawing on her work on the Stoics and their argument that understanding is a moral capacity that requires exercise.[36] In this vein, Nussbaum suggests that novels are—to adapt another of her images—something of a moral "Stairmaster": devices for exercising preexisting moral capacities.[37] As such, Nussbaum's claims about the moral power of literature seem to be predicated upon an undeveloped and undefended theory of human nature, one that suggests either that human beings are inherently compassionate or that they become compassionate through a process of early socialization. In itself, this is not too controversial a claim: certainly Nussbaum could offer such a theory without too much difficulty. Nevertheless, such a theory of human nature would appear to make Nussbaum's claim about literature redundant. Reading, such an account would suggest, will only generate compassion in the already compassionate. Empirically speaking, this poses enormous difficulties for the plausibility of her claims about the moral power of literature: it would never be clear, for example, whether a particular act of compassion should be attributed to humanity's basic compassion or to the compassion "pumped up" through the act of reading. In social science terms, her claims are overdetermined.

The problems involved in finding evidence to support Nussbaum's claims about literature and empathy would be less troubling if the theory itself were more obviously plausible, but it still seems to run up against the apparently intractable problem of people who are well read but nevertheless behave badly. Being well read, it might be noted, did not prevent Norman Mailer from stabbing his wife. Aware perhaps of the weakness of her response, Nussbaum falls back on an alternative explanation: People who are well read but who lack compassion have simply read the *wrong* books. "I am not aware," she writes, "that Nazis were great readers of Dickens or Henry James. And they certainly were great readers of Nietzsche and listeners to Wagner, figures whose bad influence might well have undermined the good influence of Dickens even had there been such influence."[38]

Despite Nussbaum's claim then that the *"empathetic torturer* argument is easily answered,"[39] she does not appear to have a convincing response. Rather, she simply seems to shift position in the face of conflicting evidence. Aware perhaps that her semantic arguments—about the distinction between *empathy* and *compassion*—are unconvincing, Nussbaum shifts to a claim about early education, one that undermines the emphasis she appears to place on reading literature. When this move proves problematic, Nussbaum suggests that people who lack compassion have simply not read the *right* books. Her apparently "modest proposal" has, it seems, become quite complicated. Nussbaum now appears to be suggesting that while novel reading might indeed generate *empathy*, it is only so-cially and politically useful when it generates *compassion*, and that this will only occur when two conditions have been met: one, that the reader has had a suit-able education in early childhood that teaches compassion for others; two, that the reader has read the "right" books.

Leaving aside her potentially redundant claims about compassion, educa-tion, and reading, Nussbaum's assertion that moral improvement is a matter of reading the "right" books raises two important questions about the value of her claims. First, how we are to know that we are indeed choosing the right books to read, particularly given Nussbaum's claim that "one does not need to think the politics of a novel correct in all ways to find the experience itself politically valuable."[40] Second, and more important, is the question of *how* these books af-fect their readers. Nussbaum suggests that this is something to do with the cre-ation of the "judicious spectator." Closer examination of this mechanism reveals, however, that both it and the two theories of textual impact upon which it is based are far from satisfactory.

THE PROBLEMATIC "JUDICIOUS SPECTATOR"

In her account of the "judicious spectator" Nussbaum cites two key passages from Smith. In the second of these passages, Smith notes that imagining that one is somebody else while simultaneously maintaining one's own detachment "is perhaps impossible."[41] It is a caveat that Nussbaum appears to ignore, but one that is of fundamental importance for the plausibility of her claims, for al-though liberal culture is rife with the suggestion that one should try to imag-ine how it feels to be somebody else—such as, for example, John Rawls's "Original Position"—it is not clear that this is as easy as common parlance would indicate.[42] Nussbaum might counter, of course, that it is precisely this capacity—*Fancy*—that is to be enhanced through the act of reading, but this appears to involve her in a certain degree of circularity. In order to adopt the position of the "judicious spectator," one would already have to have a fairly well-developed sense of *Fancy*: precisely that which the position of the "judi-cious spectator" is supposed to generate. Furthermore, the position of the "ju-dicious spectator" asks us not simply to imagine that one is somebody else but to imagine that we are both somebody else and ourselves *at the same time*. The personal identity issues involved here ought perhaps to be enough to convince us that the "judicious spectator" device is rife with problems. Indeed, imagining that one is somebody else to the extent that this theory requires is generally considered a sign of mental illness in our culture; imagining that one is some-body else and oneself simultaneously is likely to make that perception a reality.

As such, the "judicious spectator" seems to be a rather implausible device upon which for Nussbaum to place so much explanatory emphasis in her theory. Nor do her problems end here, for Nussbaum's claims about the "judicious spectator" are further undermined by the implausibility of the theories of textual impact underpinning it.

Two Theories of Textual Impact

Nussbaum's claims about the "judicious spectator" are themselves predicated upon her "theory of the novel." This theory suggests that the novel—by its very nature—constructs certain responses in the reader. "It tells its readers," writes Nussbaum, "to notice this and not this, to be active in these and not those ways. It leads them into certain postures of the mind and heart and not others."[43] It is an approach that suggests—somewhat implausibly perhaps—that novels have discernible *intents*. Indeed, throughout her work Nussbaum anthropomorphizes texts, granting them agency and intent: "texts of different types present human beings";[44] "[n]ovels, recognizing this, in general construct and speak to an implicit reader";[45] "my criticism (like the novel's)";[46] and so on. At times, this intent appears to be that of the author in writing the novel. Nussbaum links, for example, Ralph Ellison's comments about his reasons for writing *Invisible Man* to her account of the text's impact, and she does the same for both Dickens and Richard Wright.[47] She does so despite her claim in *Love's Knowledge* that nothing she says "implies that critical statements made by the author have any authority in the interpretation of the text."[48] The apparent contradiction in her claims notwithstanding, it seems that Nussbaum is an advocate of what might best be described as a "supply side" theory of the novel. It is a theory that suggests that the impact a text has on a reader derives from the *text itself* and not the reader, and that furthermore texts have a definite and ultimately discernible meaning, one that allows us to describe certain readings as correct and others as incorrect. Nussbaum offers two accounts of this "supply side" theory of the novel: *direct* and *indirect*.

In her reading of *Hard Times*, Nussbaum asserts that the themes of the novel are such that the reader is led to consider the condition of the working classes. "In reading Dickens' story," she writes, "we embrace the ordinary. It is made an object of our keenest interest and sympathy. We visit these places as friends concerned about what is happening in them."[49] The very *portrayal* of these themes is, Nussbaum suggests in her *direct* account of textual impact, sufficient to force the reader to consider them. There is a definite *aesthetic* aspect to this effect. "Its moral operations are not," writes Nussbaum of *Hard Times*, "independent of its aesthetic excellence. It binds us to the workers because it causes us to take pleasure in their company. A tedious novel would not have had the same moral power."[50] *Hard Times* is, says Nussbaum, particularly useful because it portrays the effects of the absence of precisely that which she believes novel reading will inculcate: *Fancy.* Mr. Gradgrind—the staunch utilitarian who forbids his children from reading creative works—is, says Nussbaum, forced to deal with the consequences of his philosophy. This portrayal will, she says, alert other would-be Gradgrinds to the dangers of their approach. In this Nussbaum does not give any thought to the practice of *reading* or the role of the *reader* in her account because, she asserts, "we know what it is to read a novel."[51]

This *direct* account of textual impact appears, however, to be an example of what Jonathan Rose has called the *Receptive Fallacy:* the attempt to discern the message that a text transmits to its audience by examining the *text* rather than the *audience.*[52] The claim that a text affects everybody in the same way—the implication of Nussbaum's claim that identifying textual impact is simply a matter of identifying the text's aims—is patently false: a novel that one person might experience as life changing may well leave another person cold. Indeed, the problem might be particularly acute in the case of would-be political novels such as *Hard Times.* As Italo Calvino points out: "It is not so much the book that is politically revolutionary as the use that can be made of it; even a work intended to be politically revolutionary does not become so except in the course of being used, in its often retarded and indirect effects."[53] Few would, for example, have predicted the impact that a conference on Kafka's work would have on the Czech intellectuals who took part in the Prague Spring of 1968, while books written with ostensible political goals clearly in mind—such as, for example, *Hard Times*—are often didactic and uninspiring. Nussbaum is not, however, unaware of the problems posed by the unpredictability of reader response for her theory. "Different readers," she says, "will legitimately notice different things about a novel. Both interpreting and assessing it in varied ways."[54] Unwilling, perhaps, to enter the postmodern labyrinth of reader-response theory[55]—to do so would be to abandon her structuring belief in Reason—Nussbaum offers, therefore, a second account of the way in which texts affect their readers: *indirectly.*

The undeniable but, for Nussbaum, theoretically inconvenient, phenomenon of multiple possible textual readings leads her to refine her theory. This phenomenon of multiple readings, she writes, "naturally suggests a further development of the idea of public reasoning as novel reading: that the reasoning involved is not only context specific but also, when well done, comparative, evolving in conversation with other readers whose perceptions challenge or supplement one's own."[56] This theory of "coduction" makes the rather plausible suggestion that we come to an understanding or an agreement on the meaning of the text in conversation with others.[57] Just as Nussbaum claims that—as judicious spectators—we evaluate our reactions to texts against our other political and philosophical commitments, here we evaluate them in conjunction with other people. It is a sort of conversational "reflective equilibrium" about books and their meaning. Nevertheless, as with John Rawls's use of reflective equilibrium in his *A Theory of Justice*, it is clear that for Nussbaum the endpoint of this process is never seriously in doubt: just as Rawls's reflective equilibrium necessarily produces his two principles of justice, Nussbaum's coduction produces a reading that is identical to the one that she identifies in her discussion of the *direct* impact of texts. Either way, it seems, Nussbaum suggests that novels have definite meanings that readers will derive, either *directly* from reading them or *indirectly* from discussing them.

It is this discovery of the novel's meaning that Nussbaum believes will make readers more tolerant, open, and compassionate. The ultimate arbiter of this textual meaning is, however, Nussbaum herself. In response to Oscar Wilde's reading of *The Old Curiosity Shop*—in which he famously declared that "One would have to have a heart of stone to read the death of Little Nell without laughing"—Nussbaum asserts that his "was not a responsive reading of the text."[58] Wilde, she suggests, simply did not read the text in the manner that it prescribes, something that she appears to regard as an act of perversity. It is an unconvincing and a politically unattractive response. Methodologically it is certainly not clear that texts have to be read in a particular way: certainly few literary critics now regard their job as discerning a text's intrinsic meaning. Politically it suggests that difference and disagreement is a product of perversity, a move that does not appear to show much toleration of alternative perspectives, nor respect for the holders of those viewpoints. In this regard at least Nussbaum's views appear to be distinctly illiberal. Indeed, at times, her work on literature appears to be an attempt to *impose* certain values on a citizenry, an attempt in which she makes literature something of a coconspirator. This aspect of Nussbaum's work becomes all the more obvious—and all the more ironic—when we examine her claims about the role of literature in liberal education.

LITERATURE AND ILLIBERAL EDUCATION

That Nussbaum sees her work in *Poetic Justice* as a complement to her work on liberal education is demonstrated by Chapter 3 of her book *Cultivating Humanity: A Defense of Reform in Liberal Education*: "The Narrative Imagination." In it Nussbaum essentially repeats, in a condensed from, the argument set out in her earlier book *Poetic Justice*. What is interesting about *Cultivating Humanity* for our purposes here, however, is that Nussbaum is setting out what she believes to be a Socratic theory of education in the contemporary Academy. Noting that there is "a common human tendency to think of one's own habits

and ways as best for all persons and all times,"[59] Nussbaum connects literature
to her Socratic approach in her suggestion that literature shows its readers
other ways of being. "There is no more effective way to wake pupils up," she
writes, "than to confront them with difference in an area where they had previously thought their own ways neutral, necessary and natural."[60] Texts that show
us different ways of living or make us sympathize with complicated characters
in complicated ways are, she suggests, very useful in generating precisely the
shift in perception that her Socratic approach demands. Where Nussbaum appears to differ from Socrates, however, is that she seems concerned to produce
definite outcomes with her approach.

Whereas Socrates pushed his questioning so relentlessly that he was eventually put to death, the limits on Nussbaum's approach are quite clear: one
should only question until one sees the value of *her* claims. "The most important
ingredient of a Socratic classroom is," she writes, "obviously the instructor."[61] In
Gorgias, Socrates famously asks whether he should be a servant or a physician
to the City, either serving her most immediate desires or curing her of her ills.[62]
Nussbaum clearly sees herself as a Socratic physician, but her bedside manner
leaves much to be desired. She is the most overbearing of physicians: her concern is not, ironically, to listen to her patient but merely to prescribe what she
considers the appropriate medicine. Indeed, her claim that literature expands the
moral imagination appears to flounder on her own example: she cannot, it appears, imagine that anybody who thinks about these issues would come to an
opinion that differs from her own. The puzzle here perhaps is why Nussbaum, a
thinker who has shown herself to be a careful, nuanced, and sensitive reader of
all sorts of texts—particularly those of the Ancient world—should prove herself to be such an insensitive and overbearing critic of the novels that she prescribes for her patients. The answer to this puzzle lies perhaps in the theoretical
needs of Nussbaum's problematic philosophical position.

THE FUNCTION OF LITERATURE
IN NUSSBAUM'S THOUGHT

"I believe," wrote Franz Kafka, "that we should only read those books that bite
and sting us. If a book we are reading does not rouse us with a blow to the head,
then why read it?"[63] Almost all of us who read books for a living and/or pleasure have experienced that most delightfully troubling of phenomena: a book
that forces us to think differently about the world and the way that we live. Literature's capacity to generate in its readers a "rigorous scrutiny of everything
they believe in and live by," what Stanley Fish called its "dialectical potential,"
can hardly be denied.[64] Martha Nussbaum makes much of this phenomenon in

her work on literature and liberal education; indeed, it seems to be this *dialectical* aspect of literary insight that motivates much of her work in the area of compassion, empathy, and politics. Nevertheless, as will be argued in greater detail in the next chapter, the process by which this dialectical impact occurs—by which literature leads its readers to reconsider their views on the world and the way they live—is somewhat fragile. It depends upon many variables, including the reader's reasons for reading, her particular needs in reading, the way she reads, and, of course, the text itself. The very multiplicity of possible readings should alert us to the fact that what inflames one reader will leave another one cold. We have all no doubt experienced the annoying friend who has browbeaten us into reading *the* book that changed her life, only to be left distinctly underwhelmed by the text in question.

For Martha Nussbaum, in contrast, the process by which texts affect their readers appears to be a somewhat straightforward matter: simply a product of the text and the properly "responsive" reading. The dialectical experience of reading is presented as a somewhat robust and predictable process capable of curing all of our ethical ills: a sort of "take Two Flaubert and call me in the morning" approach to all kinds of moral deficiencies. In order to identify a text's impact upon the reader one has simply to identify that text's intent and themes, provided, of course, that they are presented in an appropriately artistic manner. It is a suggestion that seems to be equally true for both her *direct* and her *indirect* theories of textual impact. It is, nevertheless, the latter that reveals most clearly the origins of her overly strong claims about literature.

As she herself notes, Nussbaum borrows her theory of "coduction" from Wayne Booth. As with her reading of Adam Smith's *Theory of Moral Sentiments*, however, Nussbaum's account of Booth's work is somewhat skewed by her theoretical needs. Smith, it might be noted, referred to the "impartial" not the "judicious" spectator in his work, with Nussbaum's slight misrepresentation introducing a deliberative element into the device that is notable by its absence from the original. In the case of Booth, Nussbaum's presentation of his claims about textual impact is considerably more robust than his own. "No strictly speaking scientific study will ever prove that a given story has been *the* cause of a given change in any one reader," writes Booth. "Our evidence will always consist mainly of anecdotes—most often memories or responses to stories in our early, more malleable years."[65] In sharp contrast to Nussbaum's claim that reading *Hard Times* will—*in and of itself*—make us more sympathetic to the plight of the working classes, or that *Native Son* will allow whites to understand the problems faced by African Americans, Booth is rather more circumspect, suggesting that this is a rather more delicate, multivariate process. The key difference here is perhaps that Booth is an Aristotelian, one whose ideal political community is the *polis*.[66] Nussbaum, on the other hand, though clearly sympathetic to the Aristotelian perspective, is ultimately a liberal. It is this that explains the difference between the strength of their claims.

In Booth's ideal political community—the polis—substantiating and reinforcing a definite conception of the good is a perfectly legitimate act, and there are many devices open for the state to do just that. In his political model, reading and ethical criticism are only parts of a much larger process of social-ization. In the liberal polity, in contrast, where the state is supposed to main-tain some form of neutrality, fewer channels are open for championing a particular conception of the good, and each conception has to compete with every other conception in the marketplace of ideas. In the absence of the mul-tiple mechanisms of socialization available in the polis, Nussbaum's claims become simply one voice among many in the liberal polity. It is for this reason that Nussbaum is forced to tie the connection between reading and change in the reader more tightly than even Booth—the leading ethical critic of his age—thinks is plausible.

Nussbaum turns to literature, it is being suggested, to resolve some of the theoretical difficulties of "Aristotelian Social Democracy," most obviously the problem of justifying her thicker account of "human capabilities" within a framework of liberal theory. Nussbaum's claim seems to be that through a process of Reasoning, informed by the rational emotions generated by reading specific novels, citizens will come to see the value of her perspective on human functioning. Far from offering a *solution* to these theoretical difficulties, how-ever, literature actually becomes their victim when Nussbaum is forced to make overly strong claims about its impact upon readers in order to substantiate her broader political-theoretical claims about society. It seems that much of Nuss-baum's work in the area of literature and politics is parasitic upon an experience that many readers have had: a book that changes their perspective on some as-pect of their lives. While there is indeed something highly plausible about Nussbaum's claim that texts can alter their readers' lives in the Socratic fashion that she identifies in *Cultivating Humanity*, Nussbaum herself never seems to have changed her position as a result of having read a text. Rather, texts for Nussbaum seem to confirm for her what she already "knows" to be the case. Unaware perhaps of Vladimir Nabokov's advice to readers—"Ask yourself if the symbol you have detected is not your own footprint"[67]—Nussbaum offers astonishingly unself-aware readings of the works she cites, readings that seem to correspond perfectly to her own interests. Of *Hard Times*, for example, she says: "Dickens's novel . . . persistently tracks the social origins, formations, and deformations of desire in a way that strikingly anticipates some of the most in-teresting recent criticisms of economic rationality."[68] What she does not say is that these "recent criticisms" were made by Martha Nussbaum and Amartya Sen, and that in a move that—as we shall see—is common to many of those who write about politics, philosophy, and literature, Nussbaum takes this *correspondence* between her theoretical commitments and their reflection in her reading of the text as *evidence* for the plausibility of those theoretical claims in the world outside of the text.[69]

Nussbaum's textual readings are often remarkably self-serving. As such, they are unlikely to win many converts to her cause. Although she criticizes other theorists' approaches to literature—she suggests, for example, that Richard Posner's approach "is to offer a simple plot summary"[70]—her method seems to be to show how the texts correspond to her own theoretical commitments. Ironically, although Nussbaum criticizes a number of literary critics for thinking that their skills transfer easily to the realm of philosophical thought where she suggests they lack "sophistication" and are "guilty of lapses of conceptual clarity,"[71] she never once questions whether her own skills transfer to the reading of literature. For her, interdisciplinarity is a one-way street. As a result, her readings seem unlikely to have the desired Socratic impact that she identifies in *Cultivating Humanity*. Indeed, it is not clear that having read Nussbaum one even needs to read the novels that she recommends. If such texts had any dialectical potential—and her choice of some rather pedestrian novels such as *Hard Times* suggests otherwise—then it seems that Nussbaum's readings will destroy it. Part of the impact of a dialectical text arises from the disconcerting experience of actually reading it, and this often will not occur if one knows what is going to happen in advance, or if the text has already been reduced to trite formulas or simple moral lessons. Dialectic is not, it might be noted, something that can be experienced secondhand. For this reason it is not necessarily clear why Nussbaum spends so long setting out her own accounts of the texts that she discusses. Reading about reading is unlikely to produce the impact that she seeks: it is rather like expecting to benefit from watching other people exercise, on the Stairmaster or otherwise. In this regard we can perhaps see certain political problems in Nussbaum's project arising from the disparity between the claims that she makes about texts in liberal democracies and the way that she actually uses them.

THE POLITICS OF *POETIC JUSTICE*

As we have seen, Nussbaum claims that some novels are politically useful because they allow the citizenry to expand their imagination and thus to deal more compassionately with those whose lives differ from their own. Underpinning these claims is, however, Nussbaum's firm commitment to philosophical Reason traditionally conceived. It is the latter that permits her to claim that she, as an observer, can have a better understanding of somebody's situation than the person actually in it. An expansion of her imagination and an awareness of the contingency of her own insights might, however, permit her to see that there may be certain aspects of a situation that even the most empathetic or compassionate observer might not see. To act in these circumstances would perhaps be to remove that person's agency: a distinctly illiberal move. There is also an irony in her work that appears to be lost on Nussbaum: while she claims that economic modelers should formulate their models to accommodate the needs of differently situated peoples, her own approach to texts is predicated upon the assumption that even such differently situated persons will come to an agreement on the meaning of a text. What makes this move politically pernicious is her assumption that this meaning is the one that she identifies. Nussbaum appears to consider her own reading infallible: coduction is simply the means by which others will come to see what she has already drawn from the text. As such, Nussbaum's work on literature seems to be a process of imposing her own meanings onto texts and her own ideas onto citizens. Rather than listening to alternative readings, readings that might reveal hitherto unconsidered aspects of a situation, Nussbaum champions her own readings and her own understandings of differently situated people. In this respect her work belies one of her central claims: "We should be on guard," she says in *Poetic Justice*, "against the ease with which simplified models tend to take over and begin to look like the whole of reality."[72] Nussbaum's work manages to reduce both texts and the lives of differently situated people to just such a model. In this respect, her work also seems to belie another of her claims: that literature is a way out of the ivory tower.

"Very few black students," notes Nussbaum, "take non-required courses in philosophy, and even in my current law teaching I see few black faces. I find things out mostly by reading and imagining."[73] It is this reading and imagining that Nussbaum believes allows her to understand and to speak for, the situation of those differently situated from herself. As we have seen, however, her reading of texts is often deeply unsympathetic: one could not perhaps imagine more redundant readings of texts than some of those that she offers in *Poetic Justice*.[74] Against this background one does not hold out much hope for her readings of nonfictional characters. It never seems to occur to Nussbaum to ask—and not just herself but also the students—why so few African Americans take her classes. In this regard, Nussbaum is perhaps closer to Mary Dalton, the well-meaning but ultimately naïve socialite in Richard Wright's *Native Son*, than she could possibly imagine. Just as perhaps Dalton's failure to understand the social codes that divided her from Bigger Thomas ultimately cost them both of their lives, Nussbaum's own failings may ultimately damage those she thinks her reading permits her to understand. In her critique of Judith Butler's work, Nussbaum criticizes Butler's failure to become involved in practical politics.[75] Yet it is not clear that Nussbaum's own work allows her any greater access to people beyond the ivory tower, and Nussbaum's claims are not tempered by Butler's concern with avoiding the sort of reification of which Nussbaum appears to be guilty. Indeed, one cannot help but feel when reading Nussbaum that literature functions in her work as a "meet and greet" for the fictional nineteenth-century poor, fictional African Americans, and fictional homosexuals, characters who are preferable to the real poor, real African Americans, and real homosexuals for Nussbaum because they do not answer back and thus pose a threat to her deeply held assumptions about their lives and situations.

MARTHA NUSSBAUM AND THE LITERARY TURN

Martha Nussbaum's work on literature, politics, and philosophy then embodies all three aspects of the literary turn: *epistemological and ontological*, *moral and political*, and *methodological*. The three questions are, of course, intimately connected to one another in her work, and breaking them up in this fashion necessarily obscures some of the ways in which they overlap and intersect in her work. Nevertheless, so doing also allows us to see the many ways in which her claims are overstated.

In the first instance, it is not clear that Nussbaum has convincingly shown that literature does indeed augment philosophical Reason in the way that she suggests. This is not to say, of course, that it could *never* do so, simply that Nussbaum has not shown that it does so on *this* account. Her "supply side" theory of the novel—that which suggests that the simple *depiction* of alternative perspectives is enough to generate concern for those perspectives—is insufficiently plausible to do the work that Nussbaum requires of it. In the second instance, Nussbaum's claim about the moral and political power of literature seems, as it is currently formulated, to undermine rather than to enhance the practice of liberal democracy. Her commitment to a liberal framework for society leads her to inflate the moral claims that are made on behalf of literature so that the text alone becomes the sole device through which the appropriate moral lessons are learned. Moreover, Nussbaum's commitment to deriving specific lessons from specific texts seems to deafen her to other possible readings and makes the matter of deriving moral lessons from a novel rather more one of coming to an agreement on *Nussbaum's* interpretation of the text than any genuine process of conversational coduction. It is difficult not to conclude that Nussbaum is simply seeking to impose her own textual interpretations—and, indeed, her own moral and political lessons—onto the reading citizenry. Third, as far as the methodological insights generated by literature are concerned, as with the moral lessons that are supposedly to be derived from the texts that she recommends, it is simply not clear that the insights Nussbaum derives from the text are not, in some sense, simply projected onto it by Nussbaum herself. She mistakes the experience of reading a text and finding textual evidence that resonates with something that she believes to be true with the claim that this is indeed evidence for her viewpoint. It is a confusion that, as we shall see, is common in the political and philosophical work on literature, and one that will be addressed in much greater detail in chapter 7. For now it is also important to note that despite these many problems, Nussbaum's work is also suggestive of a number of important avenues for future exploration.

Although Nussbaum's "derivation" of lessons from the novels she reads seems at times to be a distinctly illiberal way of imposing certain views on a citizenry while all the while claiming that it is the text and not the critic who is speaking, the suggestion that people should discuss texts in conjunction with others as a way of examining their moral and political beliefs is certainly one that is worth developing. Indeed, the rash of popular book clubs and city-reading projects suggests that there is something of value in Nussbaum's claim. It may well be that if we do indeed derive any moral and/or political benefit from reading, then that benefit might arise from the conversations *about* the text rather than from the text *itself.* It is a suggestion that will be picked up and developed in part 3 of this book. Similarly, the claim that literature has "dialectical" potential can hardly be denied, and much of part 3 will also be concerned with showing the ways in which we might capture what is of value here while avoiding what is obviously problematic in Nussbaum's account. Toward that end, however, we will now turn to the work of another theorist of the literary turn who attempts to make similar use of literature's potential to shock and disorient its readers: Richard Rorty.

Chapter 3

Richard Rorty
Non-Philosopher Kings
and the Literary Republic

"'Theory?' Philip Swallow's ears quivered under their silvery hatch. . . . "That word brings out the Goering in me. When I hear it I reach for my revolver.'"
—David Lodge, *Small World*[1]

It is, perhaps, no surprise that Richard Rorty, a thinker whose work has itself considerable power to shock and disorient its readers, should seek to make much of literature's power to do the same. Indeed, unlike Martha Nussbaum, who has made what has been termed a *partial* literary turn, Rorty is somebody for whom the literariness goes all the way down: Rorty describes himself as an "auxiliary to the poet rather than the physicist,"[2] and he asserts that literary criticism—not philosophy—is now the paradigmatic critical practice in bourgeois liberal democracies. He suggests, furthermore, that literary criticism does for thinkers such as himself "what the search for universal moral principles is supposed to do for metaphysicians."[3] He is, that is to say, one of the most vocal advocates of the claim that philosophy is dead, and that argument is simply another form of narrative. Having addressed this *epistemological and ontological* aspect of Rorty's work in chapter 1, the aim here will be to address his *methodological* and *moral and political* claims about literature. The two questions are, however, relatively indistinguishable in his work, with Rorty arguing that literature can give us insight into ways of living that is simply unavailable through the traditional methods of social science and philosophy, and that this insight—in and of itself—is sufficient to generate moral values in its readers that are not only of benefit to the practice of liberal democracy but that provide the only possible basis for that system of government.

The task of addressing these questions is, however, somewhat complicated by the shocking and disorienting qualities of Rorty's approach, most obviously his use of irony. It is this, perhaps, that partly accounts for the hostility generated by his work. A diverse array of thinkers, including Richard Posner and Chantal Mouffe, has lined up to attack him on the grounds of his alleged complacency, frivolity, and disingenuity.[4] Indeed, Susan Haack spoke for many when she observed that "there could be no honest intellectual work in Rorty's post-epistemological utopia."[5] For many this disingenuity is directly connected to his literariness—his apparent rejection of traditional philosophy and adoption of the method of redescription smack of a postmodern opportunism—but it will here be suggested that this is rather more to do with Rorty himself, and that even his work on literature is itself affected by his willingness to do "[w]hatever works" to achieve his moral and political ends.[6] Indeed, it will be argued that although Rorty asserts that "novels rather than moral treatises are the most useful vehicles of moral education,"[7] novels per se actually play only a very small role in his theory. As in Nussbaum's work, the theorist or the critic has a considerably larger role to play in generating the values of potential benefit to liberal democracy than the literature he or she assigns. Unlike Nussbaum, however, it will be argued that Rorty—as befits a self-confessed ironist—is perfectly conscious that his claims about literature mask his actual prioritizing of the theorist or the critic over the text. As such, he appears to be the advocate of a rather manipulative, elitist, and distinctly illiberal form of politics in which reader-citizens are treated as means and not ends. Nevertheless, it will also be argued that, somewhat paradoxically perhaps given his prioritizing of the theorist, Rorty's work also alerts us to the role of the reader—as opposed to just the text—in generating values of potential benefit to liberal-democratic societies, a role that is all but forgotten in Nussbaum's supply-side theory of the novel. It is this that suggests the beginnings of a more plausible theory of literature and public ethics.

LITERATURE AND THE
DIALECTICS OF LIBERAL DEMOCRACY

Given that Rorty is a thinker for whom the literariness goes all the way down, his *methodological* and *moral and political* claims about the power of literature are embedded in a much broader set of claims about literature and its relationship to liberal democracy. Indeed, in order to understand Rorty's *methodological* and *moral and political claims*, it is first necessary to say something about the manner in which he conceives of and understands liberal democracy and its relationship to his broader philosophical position.

Richard Rorty first sprang to public attention in 1979 with the publication of his book *Philosophy and the Mirror of Nature*, in which he eschewed much of what passed for traditional philosophy. Rorty rejected, amongst other cornerstones of the tradition, epistemology, the subject-object distinction, mind-body dualism, and the suggestion that philosophy had any special insight with which to adjudicate the disputes of other disciplines. In this book, and the ones that followed—*Consequences of Pragmatism, Contingency, Irony, and Solidarity*, three volumes of *Philosophical Papers, Achieving Our Country*, a work on leftist politics in the United States, and *Philosophy and Social Hope*, a populist collection of literary and philosophical writings—Rorty offers a more creative approach to philosophical thought. Drawing on the work of a wide range of thinkers—including Nietzsche, Heidegger, Foucault, and Derrida—Rorty moves beyond the stale debates of analytic thought and appears to take seriously those passages in the later Wittgenstein that suggest that we should abandon "philosophical thinking" in favor of a more "problem-solving" approach to life. Once we do this, he suggests, we can simply abandon certain apparently perennial philosophical questions—such as the nature of reality and the existence of objective Truth with a capital "T"—as being an unnecessary diversion from our everyday task of coping with the world. What Vladimir Nabokov might call the "Knight's move" in this process—"the shift that displaces the mirror"[8]—is the abandonment of the representational theory of truth. Abandoning representationalism—itself, he believes, the legacy of a particular way of talking—Rorty argues that we can begin to accept and embrace our own role in making the world in which we live. "Truth," he writes, "cannot be out there—cannot exist independently of the human mind—because sentences cannot exist, or be out there . . . descriptions of the world can be true or false. The world on its own—unaided by the describing activities of human beings—cannot."[9]

Politically, says Rorty, accepting this claim means that we have no criteria for judging between competing accounts of human existence; as such, we can no longer seek to justify liberal democracy with reference to metaphysics. Far from seeing this as a problem, however, Rorty sees it as an opportunity. Democracies, he says, "are now in a position to throw away some of the ladders used in their own construction."[10] Instead of trying to *discover* a justification for liberalism, he suggests, human beings are now free to *create* one. Following Judith Shklar, Rorty suggests that we should simply conceive of liberals as people for whom "cruelty is the worst thing that we can do."[11] For Rorty, then, liberalism is justified solely by its capacity for reducing cruelty; there is no deeper theory underpinning the system. Citing Joseph Schumpeter's assertion that "to realize the relative validity of one's convictions and yet stand for them unflinchingly is what distinguishes a civilized man from a barbarian,"[12] Rorty argues that we should recognize that justifying liberalism is no longer a job for philosophy but "for genres such as ethnography, the journalist's report, the comic book, the docudrama, and, especially, the novel."[13] It is precisely because literature can help reduce cruelty, Rorty argues, that it provides a basis for liberal democracy in a world without philosophy.

RORTY: LITERATURE AND CRUELTY

Literature, according to Rorty, can help reduce cruelty in two ways that are useful to the practice of liberal-democratic societies. First, it can teach us about other people, making us more sensitive to cruelty suffered by people to whom we might not normally attend, thereby cultivating the value of *solidarity*. Second, it can teach us about ourselves, making us more sensitive to the cruelty of which we ourselves are capable, thereby cultivating the value of *contingency*. For Rorty, the *methodological* and the *moral and political* questions are then collapsed into one. On his account, literature gives us insight that is unavailable through philosophy or traditional social science, and it is this insight that generates the values of contingency and solidarity that he believes are useful to a liberal-democratic society. By solidarity Rorty seems to mean something like Smith's "fellow feeling," or Nussbaum's empathy. By contingency, he seems to mean something akin to Nussbaum's suggestion that reading can alert us to the partiality of our own position, though in his case it emerges from a Nietzschean perspectivism that Nussbaum would eschew.

The first argument—that literature can generate solidarity—is largely undeveloped in Rorty's work. Rather like Martha Nussbaum, Rorty seems to assume that his argument is relatively unproblematic: that the mere depiction of difference will be sufficient to engender the values that he so desires. "Fiction like that of Dickens, Olive Schreiner, or Richard Wright gives us," he writes, "details about kinds of suffering being endured by people to whom we had not previously attended."[14] The suggestion that such novels will not have their desired effect unless—as in Nussbaum's account—the readers are already compassionate people is, however, possibly implicit in Rorty's second and much more original and interesting argument: that novels can change their readers, making them more sensitive to certain kinds of suffering and cruelty and, as such, better citizens of bourgeois liberal democracies.

Rorty's claim that novels can change who we are as readers relies on what he calls "dialectic." It is, he writes, "the sort of thing which only writers with very special talents, writing at just the right moment in just the right way, are able to bring off."[15] Given the multiplicity of variables that appear to make up this rare effect, Rorty argues that the subset of writers able to achieve it is considerably smaller than those who merely alert us to different ways of living. Indeed, he identifies only a handful of novelists whose work has the potential for such impact, among them, Marcel Proust, James Joyce, and his beloved Vladimir Nabokov. Given that this is such an important aspect of his work, Rorty is remarkably vague about his central concept. In *Contingency, Irony, and Solidarity* he defines "dialectic" as "the attempt to play off vocabularies against one another."[16] A clearer insight into Rorty's thought comes, however, from his discussion of Stanley Fish's notion of a "self-consuming artifact" in his account of textual impact upon readers. Fish argues that certain texts have the capacity to destabilize their readers, forcing them into a "searching and rigorous scrutiny of everything they believe in and live by."[17] As such, we might think of Rorty's work as an attempt to capture that most delightfully troubling of phenomenon: a book that forces us to think differently about the world and the way that we live. It is the sort of thing that Mill talks about in his *Autobiography* when he discusses the effect of Marmontel's *Memoirs* and Wordsworth's poetry on his intellectual development; or that captured by Nathan Zuckerman, Philip Roth's literary counterpart, in the novel *American Pastoral*, when he recounts the impact of John R. Tunis's baseball novels on his young self. "I was ten," he writes, "and I had never read anything like it. The cruelty of life. The injustice of it. I could not believe it."[18]

A straw poll among one's friends, relatives, and colleagues about which books most deeply affected them in the way that Rorty describes suggests nevertheless that although this is indeed a widespread phenomenon, it is also a deeply *personal* one. As was previously noted, we have probably all been urged to read a book that has changed somebody else's life, only to find that the text in question is truly turgid. Alternatively, we have had the experience described by Mill in his account of Wordsworth's impact on his thought. "I had," he writes, "looked into *The Excursion* two or three years before and found little in it; and should probably have found as little, had I read it at this time. But the miscellaneous poems, in the two-volume edition of 1815 . . . proved to be the precise thing for my mental wants at that particular juncture."[19] We have only found a particular text useful at a specific moment because of our needs and/or concerns at the time of reading. What both of these phenomena suggest is that—as Rorty himself notes—dialectic is somewhat fragile, depending both upon the skill of the author and the needs or concerns of the reader. It may be, therefore, that Rorty's work is an attempt to capture and employ an experience that is simply too fragile or unpredictable to have the impact he desires. It is somewhat telling that Rorty does not offer an extended discussion of this dialectical experience, beyond gesturing to Fish's account. Rather, he simply identifies certain texts that he believes will make their readers more attentive to others, or more self-aware. Foremost among the former are works by Dickens and Orwell's *1984*; among the latter, Vladimir Nabokov's dual masterpieces, *Lolita* and *Pale Fire*. It is Rorty's account of Nabokov that is most revealing about the role of literature in his thought.

"THE *DOPPELGÄNGER* SUBJECT IS A FRIGHTFUL BORE": RORTY AND NABOKOV

In the many pages of photographs that adorn *The American Years*—the second volume of Brian Boyd's marvelous biography of Vladimir Nabokov—are two portraits of Nabokov taken in the same October 1968 session by Latvian photographer Philippe Halsman. In one, a serious-looking Nabokov is leaning lightly upon his right hand, his brow furrowed, his eyes fixed firmly on the viewer. In the other, Nabokov leans into the frame, with eyebrows raised and an impish smile upon his lips. In combination, the pictures suggest Nabokov's playfulness, the sense that we can never quite be certain that he is being serious. It is but one quality that he shares with Richard Rorty. Indeed, the latter's political values—that which he labels "postmodernist bourgeois liberalism"—are closely echoed by Nabokov. "Since my youth," he declared, "my political creed has remained as bleak and as changeless as old gray rock. It is classical to the point of triteness. Freedom of speech, freedom of thought, freedom of art. The social and economic structure of the ideal state is of little concern to me. My desires are modest. . . . No torture and no executions."[20] As with Rorty, it is a political creed underpinned by a concern with cruelty. Describing himself as a "mild old gentleman who loathes cruelty,"[21] Nabokov identified himself as "an old-fashioned liberal."[22] Indeed, those Nabokov novels that lend themselves most readily to "political" readings— *Invitation to a Beheading* and *Bend Sinister*—novels that even Nabokov—an author who continually claimed that "a work of art has absolutely no value whatsoever to society"[23]—was prepared to admit bridged the "esthetic distance" between his life and the political events surrounding it are, in a sense, concerned with the institutional cruelty of the Soviet and Nazi regimes.[24]

Additionally, Rorty and Nabokov also share a distinctly pro-American attitude. Foreshadowing Rorty's call in *Achieving Our Country*[25] for a more patriotic perspective, Nabokov declared:

> Rightly or wrongly, I am not one of those perfectionists who by dint of hypercriticizing America find themselves wallowing in the same muddy camp with indigenous rascals and envious foreign observers. My admiration for this adopted country of mine can easily survive the joys and flaws that, indeed, are nothing in comparison to the abyss of evil in the history of Russia.[26]

Philosophically too, both appear to have a great deal in common. In much the same way that Rorty rejects the philosophical underpinnings of the representational theory of truth, Nabokov—in response to an interviewer's question on the "nature of everyday reality"—asserted that "the term 'everyday reality' is utterly static since it presupposes a situation that is permanently observable, essentially objective, and universally known. I suspect that you have invented that expert on 'everyday reality.' Neither exists."[27] Similarly, although Nabokov denied the influence of Wittgenstein—and indeed, just about everybody else—on his work, it is clear that he, like Rorty, dealt with what might be considered Wittgensteinian themes.

In *Culture and Value*, Wittgenstein describes the experience of being troubled by an apparently insolvable philosophical problem as akin to being stuck in a room because it does not occur to one to pull rather than to push the door. Nabokov's protagonists in *Look at the Harlequins!* and *The Defense* suffer from similar afflictions. In *The Defense*, Nabokov describes his protagonist's nervous breakdown in Wittgensteinian terms: "His vision became darker and darker and in relation to every vague object in the hall he stood in check. He had to escape; he moved, the whole of his fat body shaking, and was completely unable to imagine what people did in order to get out of a room—and yet there should be a simple method."[28] There are perhaps few other authors for whose work the Wittgensteinian term *language games* is a more apt description. Beyond Wittgenstein, both Rorty and Nabokov seem to share an affinity for the scientific ideas of Thomas Kuhn.[29] In *Bend Sinister*, Nabokov seems to anticipate Kuhn's theory of "paradigm shifts" when the philosopher Krug observes: "The nearest star is Alpha Centauri. The sun is about 93 millions of miles. Our solar system emerged from a spiral nebula. . . . We can easily imagine people in 3000 A.D. sneering at our naïve nonsense and replacing it by some nonsense of their own."[30] Not least among these philosophical similarities between Rorty and Nabokov is the emphasis that both place on the role of human agency and language in creating the world in which we live. Indeed, Baroness Bredow's instructions to her great nephew Vadim Vadimovich in Nabokov's *Look at the Harlequins!* might serve as a summary of both Nabokov's and Rorty's positions. "Play!," she said. "Invent the world! Invent reality!"[31]

Against this background, Rorty's choice of Nabokov's work seems both fitting and puzzling: fitting because of the close affinities between the work of the two men; puzzling because of Nabokov's oft-repeated assertion that he regarded politically motivated literature—what he called "the literature of social intent"—as an anathema to his aesthetic outlook. Typically Rorty—a figure whose work cuts across many traditional categories and approaches—seems to choose Nabokov, precisely because he believes that the sort of private self-reflection that Nabokov's work engenders in the reader will have beneficial political effects.

In reading *Lolita*, argues Rorty, we become so enamored of the charmingly vicious Humbert Humbert that we momentarily forget about the eponymous heroine of the text: the little girl who has lost her father, her mother, and her brother, and who seems destined never to be heard, not by her mother, not by Humbert, nor even ultimately by her deaf husband. We forget, writes Rorty, "because Nabokov *arranged* for us to forget temporarily. He programmed us to forget first and then remember later on—remember in confusion and guilt."[32] Our ability to forget, argues Rorty, draws our attention to a particular type of cruelty that we ourselves are capable of—the cruelty of incuriosity—and it is this that, he says, makes us better citizens of postmodernist bourgeois liberal utopia. Similarly, he suggests that in reading *Pale Fire* our interest in the peculiar but poetic Kinbote blinds us to the Shades' pain: both that of John and Sybil over the death of their homely daughter Hazel, and indeed of Hazel herself, a figure whose centrality to the text is all but forgotten as Kinbote beats Shade's reflective poem into his more compelling tale of Zembla, a distant foreign land. The impact of both texts is, says Rorty, dialectical: we "emerge from the final pages of [the] novel rubbing our heads, worrying about whether we are all right, wondering whether we like ourselves."[33] The outcome of this direct and personal dialectical experience seems clear: "The reader, suddenly revealed to himself as, if not hypocritical, at least cruelly incurious, recognizes his *semblable*, his brother in Humbert and Kinbote. Suddenly *Lolita* does have a 'moral in tow.'"[34]

Tensions in Rorty's Thought

Collapsing the *methodological* and the *moral and political* claims into each other then, Rorty appears to hold that simply by virtue of reading and experiencing the dialectical impact of *Pale Fire* and *Lolita* readers will become better citizens of his postmodernist bourgeois liberal utopia. In this, perhaps, Rorty sounds a lot like Nussbaum, not least because his approach to the texts seems—like hers—to map directly onto both his political commitments and his theoretical needs. We should read, he says, because reading will help us become less cruel people, thereby alerting us not only to the suffering of other people but also to our own capacity for harming others. Furthermore, as with Nussbaum, there seems to be something of a tension in Rorty's work between his claims about literature, reading, and texts, and the way that literature actually functions in his theory.

In the first instance there seems to be a disparity between Rorty's highly plausible suggestion that dialectic is fragile and unpredictable, and his rather robust claims about the impact that certain texts will have on their readers. In his preface to the Everyman edition of *Pale Fire*, for example, Rorty posts the following warning: "This introduction not only gives away the plot of *Pale Fire* but presumes to describe the reader's reactions in the course of a first reading of the book—reactions that will not occur if the Introduction is read first. The first-time reader may wish to postpone the Introduction until he or she has finished the Index."[35] The tension here is clear. On the one hand, Rorty seems to suggest that texts can have definite impacts upon their readers, something which itself seems to suggest, à la Nussbaum, that textual impact arises from the simple experience of reading the text: the robust claim. On the other hand—what we might call the "fragile claim"—Rorty suggests that this dialectical impact will be destroyed if the reader has advance warning about the text—a point that seems lost on Nussbaum—an indication perhaps that dialectic is far more precarious than the robust claim suggests and is dependent, at least partly, upon the nature, aims, and needs of the reader.

Similar tensions exist elsewhere in Rorty's thought. His rejection of the representational theory of truth and his celebration of human agency in the creation of meaning would seem to commit him to some form of reader-response theory; briefly, that which suggests that poems are made and not found, and that textual meaning is defined by the interpretive communities, not by the text itself.[36] Certainly this seems to be the implication of his claim that textual coherence "is no more than the fact that somebody has found something interesting to say about a group of marks or noises—some way of describing those marks and noises which relates them to some of the other things we are interested in talking about";[37] or that the reader's relationship to the authors of such texts such as *In Search of Lost Time*, *Finnegans Wake*, or *Postcards* "depends largely upon her being left alone to dream up her own footnotes."[38] Such claims seem to contradict his surprising use of the trope of authorial intent in his assertion that Nabokov "arranged" for his texts to have the impact that he describes. Indeed, his suggestion that such texts will have the same impact, *regardless* of who reads them seems to contradict his assertion that, for those like himself who are pragmatic functionalists in matters of interpretation, "it is no surprise that some putatively great works leave some readers cold, functionalists do not expect the same key to open each heart."[39]

THE TENSIONS RESOLVED

The tensions in Rorty's thought between his claims about the fragility of literature's dialectical impact, his apparent commitment to some form of reader response theory, and the claims he makes about the impact two of Nabokov's novels will have on their readers can be resolved by identifying three key aspects of his work: first, his approach to textual interpretation; second, the inherent elitism of postmodernist bourgeois liberalism; and third, the important role of the theorist in achieving Rorty's political goals.

As far as the first of these is concerned, Rorty's approach to matters of textual interpretation was identified in the first chapter. It is, nevertheless, perhaps worth repeating his central claim—borrowed from Harold Bloom—here:

> The critic asks neither the author nor the text about their intention but simply beats the text into shape which will serve his purpose. He makes the text refer to whatever is relevant to that purpose. He does this by imposing a vocabulary . . . on the text which may have nothing to do with any vocabulary used by the text or its author.[40]

For Rorty, interpretation is a *creative* act. His model for this mode of interpretation is Charles Kinbote—the scholar at the heart of Nabokov's *Pale Fire*—a figure who perhaps, somewhat tellingly, Rorty regards as an exemplar of cruelty.[41] As it is applied to texts, of course, it is hard to make the argument that this approach is cruel or illiberal—despite the expansion of rights to trees, animals, and communities in recent years we have, as yet, no notion of "textual rights"—but when combined with Rorty's elitism, and his observation that "the difference between people and ideas is . . . only superficial,"[42] politically this approach begins to look very suspicious indeed. There is an important moral difference between using texts as a means to an end—beating them into a shape to serve one's purpose—and in manipulating people in the same way, not least because deliberating misinterpreting a person can itself be an act of immense cruelty. Not only does Rorty fail to acknowledge this difference between fictional and nonfictional persons, but we also see him advocating a world in which there are interpreters and interpreted. It is a distinction that—perhaps somewhat worryingly for Rorty's liberal aspirations—breaks down along intellectual lines.

"In an ideal liberal world," writes Rorty, "the intellectuals would still be ironists, although the non-intellectuals would not."[43] In Rorty's ideal polity there is a distinction to be drawn between those—the intellectuals—who are to be trusted with the secrets of postmodernity—the end of Truth, objectivity, and metaphysics—and those—the masses—who are to be permitted and even *encouraged* to believe in such quaint ideas in the interests of social cohesion, or what Rorty calls "solidarity." This distinction—between intellectuals and the masses—is central to Rorty's overall project and one whose inherent elitism poses certain political problems for a professed liberal. Liberalism, no matter how one conceives of it—as the product of metaphysically derived principles or simply the best way to reduce cruelty—demands certain basic commitments. Foremost among these is perhaps that we treat people as *ends* and not as *means*.

In his concern to impose his own readings of texts onto a citizenry in order to establish his preferred—albeit relatively benign—outcome, Rorty—like Nussbaum before him—seems to forget this central tenet of liberalism. In this we see perhaps a version of an old Rousseauian paradox, with both Nussbaum and Rorty forcing the citizens of their polities to be free. Neither seems to allow much room in his or her theory for alternative perspectives on the texts that they recommend. For both thinkers there are right and wrong readings of certain key texts. Rorty, furthermore, seems to regard the facts of others lives as material for reinterpretation rather than experience that is to be respected, hence his frightening claim about there not being much difference between people and ideas. It is a move that is justified for Rorty by his very literariness.

As was argued in chapter 1, for Rorty, in the absence of any external criteria of validity, all arguments are readings, and such readings are simply stories whose worth is to be judged by the extent to which they promote certain values, in this case, those of postmodernist bourgeois liberalism. In this, it might be argued, Rorty provides a further counter-example to Nussbaum's claim that reading leads one to look beyond simple models of society. Rorty's range of literary references suggests that he is incredibly well read, and yet he seems to replace the economists' utility standard with a cruelty standard, thereby replacing one oversimplified model of the world with another. It is, furthermore, a model in which he alone appears to be the ultimate arbiter. Liberalism has, of course, always had a certain streak of elitism and patriarchy—from John Stuart Mill's claim that despotism is by far the best form of government for savages (gaudily painted or otherwise),[44] to John Rawls's assertion that the choosers in the "Original Position" should be heads of households[45]—and Rorty's version is clearly no exception. It is for this reason that he prioritizes the intellectual: whether that intellectual is a philosopher, a political theorist or, most preferably in Rorty's account, a literary critic. The role of the intellectual in these circumstances is to tell stories that promote liberal values, regardless of their veracity. In this perhaps Rorty's literary utopia echoes that of Socrates' Ideal City in a literal reading of Plato's *Republic*, with literary critics acting as Non-Philosopher Kings shaping the polity, their knowledge emerging not from the Forms but rather from "proper readings" of literary texts, their position maintained by the "Noble Lie" of correct literary interpretation.

Given Rorty's commitment to the role of the intellectual, his selection of Nabokov as his novelist of choice is both pertinent and misleading. Just as Nabokov inserts himself in the text, sometimes obviously, as in the Hitchcock-like cameos he makes in *King, Queen, Knave* or *Pnin*, sometimes surreptitiously, only hinting at his presence with an apple core or a peach pit in *Lolita*, it is clear that he is behind the scenes attempting to orchestrate an elaborate fiction.[46] Drawing attention to himself—or "baring the device," as it has been called—

is Nabokov's way of alerting the "careful reader" to the work's status as fiction. In Rorty's case, he too stands behind the scenes attempting to orchestrate the reactions of his readers but—significantly—without "baring the device." Indeed, Rorty goes out of his way to hide himself. It is an act that seems politically justified for him by its potential impact: the shoring up of his liberal utopia. Noting that there is a "haze [that] surrounds writers who are not associated with any particular discipline, and are therefore not expected to play by any antecedently known rules,"[47] Rorty—whose name, as Terry Eagleton tells us, means "fond of amusement and excitement"[48]—joyfully jumps between disciplines, priding himself on his syncretism. Noting furthermore that one is "let off a lot of bad questions" because of the "numinous haze which surrounds the 'creative artist,'"[49] Rorty draws a very tight connection between the artist and the theorist. In the miasma that results, he is able to blur a lot of distinctions and avoid some hard questions. In this, his literariness seems to be something of a mask.

Rorty's assertion that he sees himself as an auxiliary to the poet rather than the physicist is, for example, something of a false dichotomy, for it is clear that in his broad definition of "poet," as "one who makes things new,"[50] even physicists can fall into this category; indeed, Rorty identifies Galileo as one such figure.[51] Similarly, in shifting around between disciplines, Rorty seeks to avoid being pinned down on the nature of his claims: questions about philosophy lead to a lexical shrug of the shoulders and a denial of his status as philosopher, while questions about literature often produce the same result. It is little wonder that David L. Hall once referred to Rorty as the "Cheshire Cat" of contemporary theory,[52] though given his views on redescription, we might also see him as something of a latter-day Humpty Dumpty.[53] Hiding behind such obfuscations and Hazes (and here we might think about the first name of the doomed Ms. Shade from *Pale Fire*),[54] Rorty has so far managed to avoid a close examination of the exact role of literature in his thought, something that the disparity between his philosophical commitments, and the claims he makes about literature's impact, certainly seems to demand.

RORTY'S THREE-PRONGED LITERARY STRATEGY

There is, it seems, something disingenuous in Rorty's account of the role of literature in his thought, for although he claims that it is the *content* of certain novels and the effects that these novels have on their readers that is responsible for the cultivation of values beneficial to the practice of liberal democracy, it would appear that literature is actually rather more a tool of the literary intellectual than a self-originating source of politically useful values. Indeed, Rorty himself appears to use literature to draw different groups of people into the "ongoing conversation of humankind" that constitutes his postmodernist bourgeois liberalism. In this he appears to be the architect of an almost-Straussian ironic political strategy, one that uses different aspects of the same approach to appeal to different groups. It seems to be a three-pronged strategy.

The first prong is meant for those readers "left cold" by a difficult, allusive, and highly literary novel such as *Lolita*. Rorty's account of the text tells such people how to react, or how they *should* have reacted had they been better readers. He presents his interpretation of the text as anything but contingent. Unlike Nussbaum, however, who seems to believe that only *her* account of the text is valid, Rorty is aware that different readers will legitimately have different reactions, so his concern is simply to shape the readers' reactions in beneficial ways. His apparent confidence that *everybody* who reads the text will have the *same* reaction is not then the product of a dubious theory of "textual intent," in the manner of Nussbaum, but rather a masterful rhetorical device. Flattering to deceive, Rorty seems to treat all of his readers as equals, suggesting that they too will have the insights that he had, putting those readers who were unable to read the text as brilliantly as he did, on a par with himself.[55] Rorty tells such people how to read the text and then acts as if it was their reading all along, making them, in the process, "one of us," thereby creating his sought-after solidarity through a combination of manipulation and flattery. It is a strategy that relies in part upon the uncertainty of the reader and upon the cultural power of the "Great Author" device in which, for reasons that are not entirely clear, the plausibility of an argument can appear to be enhanced by being shown to have been held by an important writer.

The second prong of Rorty's strategy appeals to those readers who—far from being left cold by *Lolita*—are destabilized by the novel: those who found themselves being drawn in by Nabokov's prose and simultaneously horrified by their pleasure in a novel whose ostensible subject matter is pedophilia; those who believed Humbert's claim that it was Lolita who seduced him, but who are, nevertheless, unable to accept the novel's central relationship; and those readers who "emerge from the novel, rubbing their heads, wondering whether they like themselves." For these readers, Rorty is there—like his namesake Mr. R. in Nabokov's *Transparent Things*—to say "Easy, you know, does it, son." Like the good therapist, he assures these readers that their reactions were perfectly normal and then seeks to channel this unease into support for his brand of liberalism. In effect, he seeks to truncate the dialectical process—the rigorous scrutiny of everything they believe in and live by—in favor of a quick commitment to his outlook. This is, of course, the quintessential Rortian position: a commitment to a set of ideas without the difficult thinking that is often required to get there, what Rorty, following Wittgenstein, calls "kicking away the ladders of justification." For this group of readers, Rorty does indeed seek to capitalize upon the destabilizing impact upon literature with a kind of literary opportunism, one that seeks to shape the outcome of the dialectical process in the interests of promoting his own political agenda.

The third prong of Rorty's strategy spears intellectuals: people such as Rorty himself who recognize the folly of metaphysics and the nonsense of the representational theory of truth. For these people Rorty presents interesting readings of exciting texts as the basis of an attractive political philosophy. Given the choice between wading through the diagrams, equations, and occasionally obscure arguments of say, *A Theory of Justice*, and reading Nabokov's playful, flowing, and allusive prose, many might readily turn to a Rortian world in which reading novels is a sound basis for liberalism. In this process, intellectuals too are hopefully flattered into solidarity, although for them "one of us," Rorty's telling phrase, means something quite different than it does for the masses: a position among the Elect as a Non-Philosopher King. This is not to say that a literature-based liberalism cannot also be attractive to nonintellectuals: there is definitely an incentive for them here too, as Rorty notes, "we have to tempt young adults into our classrooms before we can start bending their flexible young minds to our political purposes."[56] What might also attract intellectuals is, however, the opportunity to bend those young minds to their own purposes.

In Rorty's work, then, literature appears to be something of a tool of the theorist-intellectual rather than a direct source of moral insight for the citizenry. These theorist-intellectuals are, however, literary critics or thinkers who utilize the methods of literary criticism in their own disciplines. This suggests that literature might still have a role to play in Rorty's thought, albeit not the one he initially claims. Nevertheless, examining Rorty's work on literary criticism suggests that even here literature has little role to play, at least in terms of generating insight, for it would appear that a critic's status among the Non-Philosopher Kings has much more to do with the *kind of person* she is rather than *the kind of books* she has read.

THE PREEMINENT DISCIPLINE

For a discipline that he regards as preeminent within the modern Academy, Richard Rorty seems to have a remarkably narrow conception of literary criticism. He identifies only three approaches, two of which appear merely as caricatures before being dismissed in favor of the third. The first of these is an approach that is concerned with some foundational value such as "textual meaning" or "authorial intent." Given his rejection of such absolute concepts as "Truth" and "Reality" it is obviously no surprise to find Rorty asserting that in reading we must "firmly reject questions about the 'aim of the writer' or the 'nature of literature,' as well as the idea that literary criticism requires taking such gawky topics seriously."[57] The second type of literary criticism—"methodological reading"—is, says Rorty, produced by people who lack "an appetite for poetry." It is, he says, "the sort of thing you get, for example, in an anthology of readings of Conrad's *Heart of Darkness* which I recently slogged through—one psychoanalytic reading, one reader-response reading, one feminist reading, one deconstructive reading, and one new-historicist reading."[58] The approach seems to be to bring a theory to the text and then look to that text for evidence of the value of the theory, the sort of thing, it will be argued in the next chapter, of which Terry Eagleton often appears to be guilty. Such readers—fictionally personified in Lotaria, the graduate student in Italo Calvino's *If on a Winter's Night a Traveler* who uses a computer to read texts[59]—are clearly disdained in Rorty's account, as are those who offer them. His accolades are reserved for the third type of literary critic identified in his work: the "Strong Poet."

In his book *The Anxiety of Influence*, Harold Bloom sets out a theory that suggests that poetry is a struggle against influence: poets must, he says, overcome their predecessors if they are to create new and original art.[60] His archetype is Shakespeare who was, says Bloom, able to learn from then overshadow Christopher Marlowe in a poetic struggle fraught with Freudian overtones of parricide. Rorty, also an admirer of Freud, embraces this figure—the "Strong Poet"—as his preferred literary critic, one who is able to impose his own meaning onto a text in such a way as to obliterate all previous interpretations. It is for this reason that we see him prioritizing Kinbote over Shade in *Pale Fire*, arguing that, "Kinbote is absolutely right when he concludes his foreword to 'Pale Fire' by saying 'Without my notes Shade's text simply has no reality at all.'"[61] The connection between the poet and the literary critic is very tight in Rorty's thought. He sees both figures as being engaged in the same practice, hence his broad definition of "the poet" as "one who makes things new."[62] Literary critics "make things new," he suggests, by recontextualizing the works that they discuss. "Influential critics," he writes, "the sort of critics who propose new canons—people like Arnold, Pater, Leavis, Eliot, Edmund Wilson, Lionel Trilling, Frank Kermode, Harold Bloom—are not in the business of explaining the real meaning of books, nor of evaluating something called their 'literary merit.' Rather, they spend their time placing books in the context of other books, figures in the context of other figures."[63] This approach, he suggests, transfers quite easily to social and political theory where "the method is to redescribe lots and lots of things in new ways, until you have created a pattern of linguistic behavior which will tempt the rising generation to adopt it, thereby causing them to work for appropriate forms of nonlinguistic behavior."[64] Although Rorty gives no specific examples of how this might happen, it is an approach that correlates to his optimism about the power of language and his conception of the world as a text identified in chapter 1.

The role of the theorist in Rorty's thought is then to redescribe people's lives in such a way that they might adopt certain patterns of "nonlinguistic behavior," preferably those of postmodernist bourgeois liberalism. It is, however, as has already been noted, an approach that seems to treat people as *means* and not as *ends*. It seems to draw no distinction between real people and fictional characters. The *political* implications of this confusion are somewhat disturbing, especially for a theorist—such as Rorty—who considers himself a liberal. Once one has removed respect for other persons from liberalism—precisely that which reading is supposed to engender for theorists such as Rorty and Nussbaum—it is not clear what is left of the theory. In Rorty's case, it seems, we are left with a—distinctly nonliberal—literary republic in which certain critics and theorists prescribe moral and political values for the public at large by offering interesting interpretations of literary texts. Rorty's justification for this republic—his explanation of why literary critics should have this position—is, unsurprisingly perhaps, both politically and philosophically unconvincing.

NON-PHILOSOPHER KINGS: RICHARD RORTY'S LITERARY CRITICS

As we have seen, Richard Rorty's claim, that certain novels will have a *direct* impact on their readers, leading them quite naturally into certain attitudes that are befitting to citizens of liberal democracies, is a misleading one. Literature is rather more a tool of an intellectual elite to use in shaping their ideal polity. These intellectuals are, however, literary critics, or at least theorists who use the methods of literary criticism, which raises the issue of why literary critics are to be granted this privileged status in Rorty's thought. Their ability to recontextualize people and texts is certainly part of any answer to this question; nevertheless, it cannot be the only aspect. Nietzsche is, for example, a fine example of the "strong poet," and few—including Rorty himself—would be comfortable in taking him as a moral advisor for liberal democracy. So it is perhaps something more than their powers of redescription that gives such figures their privileged status in Rorty's thought. Rorty suggests, in fact, that literary critics are to be so prioritized because of their *moral* insights. "Ironists read literary critics, and take them as moral advisers," he writes, "simply because such critics have an exceptionally large range of acquaintance. They are moral advisers not because they have special access to moral truth but because they have been around."[65] This, then, is what he means by his claim that literature is supposed to do for thinkers such as himself what the search for universal moral principles is supposed to do for metaphysicians: it offers them an alternative perspective and in so doing generates moral insight.

For all of the elaborateness of Rorty's approach to literature, his literariness, and his turn to narrative, his theory seems to come down to the problematic assumption underpinning Nussbaum's work: that somehow reading novels will generate moral insight, albeit among intellectuals and not the masses. Unlike Nussbaum, however, Rorty makes no such attempt to justify this basic claim. His claim about literature and moral insight for ordinary or "lay" readers is, it has been argued, largely rhetorical, part of a much more complex political strategy that relies more on the theorist than on literature for its impact. As far as intellectuals are concerned, however, Rorty takes it as a given that somehow reading lots of novels makes these intellectuals suitable guardians for his polity. It is an assumption that runs into both significant empirical and theoretical difficulties.

In the first instance, in addition to K. K. Ruthven's observations about literary critics not appearing to lead better lives than other people, Rorty's approach also runs into the "empathetic torturer" problem, not least because Rorty himself notes that there "can be sensitive killers, cruel aesthetes, pitiless poets—masters of imagery who are content to turn the lives of other human beings into images on a screen, while simply not noticing that there are other people suffering."[66] The claim that having read lots of texts is what makes such people capable of prescribing for the masses then does not seem terribly plausible or attractive. Rorty nevertheless offers a further argument for the role of literary critics in his polity. "They have," he says, "read more books and are thus in a better position not to get trapped in the vocabulary of any single book."[67] It is not clear, however, that this claim resolves any of Rorty's difficulties. Not only is there the danger that such figures could be so abstracted from the world beyond the text that they become capable of the sort of cruelty that Hannah Arendt ascribes to Martin Heidegger, but it is also somewhat implausible to suggest that reading a large number of books will in and of itself prevent one from becoming caught up in a final vocabulary. Indeed, it might well be argued that this rather weak argument simply reveals the problematic assumption underpinning Rorty's argument about the moral role of literary critics.

Given Rorty's commitment to the contingency of all things, becoming "caught up in a final vocabulary" is—after cruelty itself—one of the greatest possible sins in his liberal utopia. Indeed, becoming caught up in such a final vocabulary seems to be a precursor to such cruelty. Metaphysics, logic, and representationalism are, for Rorty, examples of such final vocabularies. They are language games that reify themselves into hard-and-fast claims about the world. Such claims, says Rorty, produce the sort of incommensurable moral conflicts that arise when conflicting vocabularies overlap but cannot reconcile. Rorty's way out of such impasses is to find new ways to describe the same situations, ways that permit both sides to look at the situation anew, and thus to overcome their differences, thereby creating the solidarity that is—for want of a better word—the "foundation" of his theory. It is for this reason that Rorty sometimes seems to regard the capacity for redescription as a *moral* capacity: the reason for his prioritizing of literary critics over all other types of theorists. It is they, he suggests, who demonstrate the greatest capacity for redescription, and they who should, therefore, be permitted to redescribe the citizenry and their lives in the interests of postmodernist bourgeois liberalism. The plausibility of this claim is, however, undermined by the existence of literary figures whose work one might admire but whose lives leave much to be desired, a position pithily summarized in D. H. Lawrence's famous maxim, "Never trust the artist. Trust the tale." Rorty seeks to excuse himself from this problem with his firm public/private distinction. "We do not care," he writes, "whether these writers managed to live up to their own self-images. What we want to know is whether to adopt those images—to recreate ourselves in whole or part in these people's image."[68] And yet, such figures are given a certain elite position in Rorty's thought. It is their job to mold the citizenry. For this reason, it might be legitimate to seek to inquire into their personal qualities, not least because it seems that at base, Rorty's argument is not an argument about how much such people have *read* but rather *the kind of people they are* in and of themselves.

The claim that Rorty's literary critics are chosen by him because of *the type of persons* they are or, rather, the *type of readers* they are is justified by his preference for only one type of literary criticism: that of the "Strong Poet." In his discussion of literary criticism, Rorty identifies three different types of literary critics: those concerned with authorial intent or intrinsic textual meaning, methodological readers, and Strong Poets. Of these three, only the strong poets are to be regarded as moral exemplars, because they have read a lot of novels, or because they are gifted redescribers, or because of some combination of the two: Rorty is ambiguous on this point. Where Rorty is not ambiguous is in his assertion that literary critics of the first and second kind are to be shunned precisely because they do get caught up in final vocabularies. In the case of literary critics of the first kind, the final vocabulary is one in which texts have specific meanings, often correlated to some notion of authorial intent. In the case of the "methodological readers" it is a final vocabulary dominated by whatever grid they choose to lay over a text, be it Marxism, Freudianism, or feminism. Clearly such critics have read a large number of texts—witness, for example, the breadth of literature covered by Terry Eagleton in the next chapter—so it is not the *reading per se* that prevents them from becoming caught up in the final vocabulary. The only possible difference between these critics and those prioritized by Rorty is, therefore, *not what they have read* but *who they are*, people who do not get caught up in a final vocabulary, people such as Rorty himself.

CONCLUSIONS

Rorty's work on literature and politics is in effect an argument suggesting that people such as himself—"paunchy professors . . . zipping off to interdisciplinary conferences held in pleasant places"[69]—should be the non-philosopher kings of a liberal-democratic republic. It is for this reason that Rorty draws a distinction between his private philosophical views and his public commitments. It is the latter that are meant to help shape the liberal polity. It is why we see Rorty making the strongest claims about the impact of literature in those works with the potential to reach the widest audiences—such as his introduction to *Pale Fire*—claims that, as we have seen, conflict with his private philosophical beliefs. Although Rorty suggests that literature has some role to play in generating critical insight—in either the masses or the intellectuals— neither argument holds good to the extent that his theory requires. It is not literature that affects the masses in Rorty's work but, rather, the theorist working *through* literature. Similarly, although Rorty seems to believe that reading lots of texts permits such theorist-intellectuals to avoid becoming caught up in final vocabularies, his discussion of three types of literary critics and his assertion that two of them do just that suggest otherwise. The *methodological* and *moral and political* claims about literature in Rorty's work seem to be either disingenuous, or simply misplaced.

What remains of Rorty's literary strategy is simply his claim that all arguments are forms of narrative, and that convincing others of the validity of one's position is simply a matter of imposing an interpretation of the world and its events onto such people. His suggestion that the ends of such an approach should be liberal institutions and an end to cruelty are merely additions; they cannot in any sense be *derived* from his broader claims. As Rorty himself notes, "The connection between ironism and liberalism is very loose."[70] In this respect, literature appears to function in Rorty's theory much as myth does in a literal reading of Plato's *Republic*: even down to its classification of people into three different groups. Literature, like myth in Plato, is supposed to bind people to the state, creating solidarity. In Rorty's case, of course, this is solidarity that he seeks to create through flattery, making people "one of us" not through their status as readers of the same texts but through a three-pronged strategy that seeks to draw different groups into the ongoing conversation of liberal society: people "left cold" by difficult texts; people destabilized by them; and finally, intellectuals such as himself, with "an appetite for poetry." Indeed, much of *Achieving Our Country* can be read as an appeal to intellectuals or "philosophical types" to keep, as Stephen Macedo suggested in another context, "their big mouths shut"[71] in the interests of establishing and maintaining liberal institutions.

Nevertheless, there is also much in Rorty's work that is suggestive of a role that literature might play in a more coherent conception of political philosophy—one *influenced* but not *dominated* by literary insights—and, indeed, in a more stable liberal society. First, it is clear that there is something to the suggestion that literature has dialectical potential: it can make us think differently about the world and the way that we live. There is even evidence to suggest that it can make us aware of problems faced by people to whom we would not normally attend. Reading books about African Americans, homosexuals, and the working class might—and often does—lead us to pay attention to these groups of people, possibly for the first time, though the process by which this happens is not as dependable, or necessarily replicable, as he suggests. There is, however, no evidence to suggest that we would come to *care* for them in the way that Rorty—and Nussbaum before him—suggests. Rorty's claims are simply too strong here: they are, as befits his approach, part of a rhetorical strategy and not a philosophical argument. Rorty's theory simply suggests that way in which reading such novels might bring these problems to our attention; as such, he provides, perhaps, the beginnings of a theory about how literature *might* be used to generate solidarity in a liberal-democratic society. Rorty's work also draws attention—in part at least—to the role that the reader plays in her own reaction to the text. While this is often not conscious, it suggests that we should begin to look toward the reader rather than just the text when we come to think about how such solidarity might be formed. Rorty's work is furthermore also suggestive of a problem that seems to plague the current work on politics and philosophy and their relationship to literature: the tendency to confuse the world of the text with the world in which that text was created. Such a tendency was common in the characters of nineteenth-century fiction—such as Catherine Morland in Jane Austen's *Northanger Abbey* and, of course, Flaubert's eponymous *Madame Bovary*—and continues to be a problem for those theorists who seek to use literature to enhance their political or philosophical position. Rorty's work alerts us to this tendency, which we see particularly clearly in the work of Terry Eagleton, a literary critic whose pioneering work in literary criticism provides a model for those political theorists who have turned to literature and literary criticism for inspiration and methodology.

Chapter 4

Terry Eagleton:
Is There a Class in This Text?
Literary Criticism and Social Theory

"'Well, it's not normal. It's like one of them gory stories, it's something people have quit doing—like boiling in oil or being a saint or walling up cats,' she said. 'There's no reason for it. People have quit doing it.'
'They ain't quit doing it as long as I'm doing it.'"
—Flannery O'Connor, *Wise Blood*[1]

In a book that is concerned with the introduction of the literary into the political, a discussion of Terry Eagleton's work might seem a little puzzling, not least because Eagleton appears to have an entirely different perspective from the other thinkers under study: he is (in)famous for his political approach to literary problems, not his literary approach to political ones. Eagleton would, furthermore, certainly balk at his inclusion in a study that appeared to lump him with liberal-democratic theorists such as Richard Rorty and Martha Nussbaum, especially given their claims about the alleged *moral* power of literature. Indeed, even the suggestion that his work was the obverse of the literary turn would probably draw his—apparently considerable—critical wrath: far from seeing his work as *introducing* politics into the study of literature, Eagleton clearly regards it as an attempt to expose and overcome the objectionable politics already implicit in that enterprise. "There is," he writes, "no need to drag politics into literary theory: it has been there from the beginning."[2]

EAGLETON AND THE LITERARY TURN

Eagleton's own self-conception notwithstanding, there are a number of reasons his work is important to this study. Foremost among these is that he is one of the leading advocates of the *methodological* claim about literature and politics. Indeed, he argues that literary theory is "less an object of intellectual enquiry in its own right than a particular perspective in which to view the history of our times,"[3] going so far as to assert that the aesthetic is "a way of gaining access to certain central questions of modern European thought . . . light[ing] up, from that particular angle, a range of wider social, political and ethical issues."[4] As such, he appears to have been practicing—for some time—what advocates of the literary turn have only just begun to preach: that literary analysis can give us useful insight into the political. Indeed, Eagleton's work is an audacious attempt by one of Europe's most influential cultural critics to expand the frontiers of literary analysis. Although the current study evinces serious reservations with the *type* of politics that literary study sometimes engenders, Eagleton is nevertheless to be congratulated for helping open up literary study to previously marginalized voices and overlooked areas of study. As Valentine Cunningham observed: "Who would not be happy with the way in which theory has not just given a voice to former marginal interests and persons in texts, but has given an affirming voice to critics from, or identifying with, those margins."[5]

Despite being one of the most vocal proponents of the claim that literary theory can give us insight into the political, Eagleton never sets out his methodological claims in the manner of a Nussbaum or a Rorty. He appears, however, to have two key claims. First, he offers a version of the *privileged observer* claim, arguing that literature and literary theory offer us a critical perspective on the world outside the text that is unavailable elsewhere. Second, he takes the *portability* claim as a given: he regards his skills as a literary critic as being equally applicable to all areas of study, textual and nontextual, literary and political. In this, Eagleton seems to provide a model for much of the work on literature now being done in political science and philosophy departments. The extent to which the work of the literary turn *consciously* mimics Eagleton's work is unclear. Certainly, few—if indeed any—of its key thinkers cite Eagleton in their work. Nevertheless, his indirect influence can perhaps be detected in the ways in which many of these figures have adopted his methods and/or his underpinning assumptions about literature and politics. They are, however, assumptions and methods that, this study will argue, are rife with problems.

Foremost among them is the confusion between the *written* and the *unwritten* worlds—between the world of the text and the world in which that text was written—and the *standards of justification* that pertain to the study of each. Eagleton, it will be argued, seems unclear on the differences between these two worlds. It may be, however, that such confusion is deliberate, part of a broader political strategy in which Eagleton accepts the political benefits of a method that he knows to be flawed. Certainly he seems more concerned with achieving his practical political goals than with setting out and justifying his theoretical underpinnings. In this he might share something with Richard Rorty's "[w]hatever works" approach to politics.[6] Militating against this "pragmatic" interpretation is, of course, Eagleton's hostility to Rorty and his methods. Contextualizing his work and identifying his specific claims about literature and politics will allow us to untangle Eagleton's methodological confusions. His motivations for employing them are, however, likely to remain hidden, not least because Eagleton constructs a complex rhetorical persona as part of his method.

A MAN OUT OF TIME?: MARXISM, POLITICS, AND LITERATURE

In his book *The Future of Theory*, Jean-Michel Rabaté notes the prevailing concern with *urgency* among the practitioners of literary theory: the sense that they are, in some sense, already too late.[7] Eagleton, in contrast, seems to revel in his apparently anachronistic status. "I must confess," he writes, that "I belong to that dwindling band who still believe that the base/superstructure model has something valuable to say, even if this is nowadays a proportion smaller than those who believe in the Virgin Birth or the Loch Ness monster."[8] As his comment suggests, Eagleton's literary criticism is predicated upon a firm commitment to Marxist theory as a basis for social and political analysis. Noting the decline in popularity of Marxist theory in recent years, Eagleton asserts that contemporary critics have, nevertheless, "a responsibility to attend a little more closely to what it is that Marxists have been arguing for the last century or so."[9] It is, he says, "not as though anyone actually *disproved* the doctrine."[10]

As befits a thinker who holds such an explicitly Marxist position, Eagleton asserts that "literature" is a social practice constructed by human action, in this case the act of theorizing. "[W]ithout some kind of theory," argues Eagleton, "however unreflective and implicit, we would not know what a 'literary work' was in the first place, or how we were to read it."[11] It is a claim about the importance of "stage-setting" information that reflects the influence of Ludwig Wittgenstein on Eagleton's work. It is an influence that we also see in his assertion that there is "no 'essence' of literature whatsoever."[12] Combining his readings of Marx and Wittgenstein, Eagleton argues—in a claim that would undoubtedly find favor with Butler—that this social practice of theorizing is directly connected to the dual forces of power and ideology. "Literature, in the meaning of the word we have inherited, *is*," he writes, "an ideology."[13] The latter is defined as "the ways in which what we say and believe connects with the power-structure and power-relations of the society in which we live."[14] Although "power" is never explicitly defined in Eagleton's work—in part perhaps because he is a literary theorist rather than a philosopher or a social scientist—it is possible to infer from his historical account of the development of "literature" that he is talking about power predicated upon a Marxist understanding of class. It is this that generates the historical analysis that is at the core of his theory.

The social category "Literature" developed, according to Eagleton, in England in the eighteenth and nineteenth centuries. Initially, he notes, the term did not simply refer to *creative* works but, rather, to the whole body of valued writing in society, including history, philosophy, essays, and poems. "The criteria of what counted as literature were," he writes, "frankly ideological: writing which embodied the values and 'tastes' of a particular social class qualified as literature, whereas a street ballad, a popular romance, and perhaps even the drama did not."[15] Over the course of the nineteenth century, Eagleton argues, this ideological construction became increasingly more important to capitalist society. "As religion ceases to provide the social 'cement,' affective values and basic mythologies by which a socially turbulent class-society can be welded together, 'English' is," he writes, "constructed as a subject to carry this ideological burden."[16] For Eagleton, the process by which "English" was constructed to fulfill this need appears to be fairly straightforward and draws on Marx's earliest formulations of his theory. In "The German Ideology," Marx asserts that a group of ideologists appeared from within the dominant class to do the job themselves: "inside this class one part appears as the thinkers of the class (its active, conceptive ideologists who make the perfecting of the illusion of the class about itself their chief source of livelihood)."[17] Likewise, Eagleton says of the origins of "literary study": "From the outset, in the work of 'English' pioneers like F. D. Maurice and Charles Kingsley, the emphasis was on solidarity between the social classes, the cultivation of 'larger sympathies,' the installation of national pride, and the transmission of 'moral' values."[18] In the twentieth century, this conscious construction of ideology was further encouraged by the nationalistic demands of two World Wars when, according to Eagleton, Britain's leading literary critics turned their skills toward the production of propaganda.[19]

"Literature" is, then, on Eagleton's account, a flexible ideological tool, useful for generating class solidarity and nationalistic sentiment and for resolving—at the level of ideas—tensions inherent in the material base of society. Indeed, so tight is the connection between literary criticism, literary theory, and class interest in Eagleton's work that he characterizes E. D. Hirsch's concern with "authorial intent" as being part of a defense of capitalism, aimed at protecting private property—the author's meaning—from the rampaging hordes.[20] Ignoring perhaps the political turn that he himself has helped engender, Eagleton even goes so far as to suggest that departments of literature in higher education—concerned as he believes they are with abstracting the text from its basis in social reality—are still "part of the ideological apparatus of the modern capitalist state."[21] Eagleton is not, then, an advocate of "art for art's sake," nor

even "criticism for criticism's sake." His objection is to the political *values* he regards as implicit in literary criticism as it has been historically practiced. "It is
not," he writes, "the fact that literary theory is political which is objectionable,
nor . . . the fact that its frequent obliviousness of this tends to mislead: what is
really objectionable is the nature of its politics."[22] His response is to offer an alternative approach to literary theory, one he believes is neither deliberately illu-
sory nor troubled by distasteful values. This approach, while clearly divorced
from the sort of concerns Eagleton ascribes to his forebears, nevertheless recognizes that there is some role—albeit a limited one—for the aesthetic. "If," he
writes, "a work of literature chooses to highlight images of human degradation
then it would seem futile to denounce this as somehow incorrect. But there are
surely limits to this aesthetic charity. Literary critics do not always accept the
world view of a text 'on its own terms'; they sometimes want to say that this vision of things is implausible, distorting, oversimplifying."[23] In an echo of
Socrates and a foreshadowing of Nussbaum, Eagleton asserts that we should
not take a piece of literature's worldview on its own terms; rather, he suggests,
we should put it into critical dialogue with what we know about the world in
which we live.

   For Eagleton, however, what we know about the world is shaped by another set of texts: the works of Marx and Engels. Consequently, for Eagleton,
putting texts into critical dialogue with the world seems to be a matter of holding up the texts to the claims and standards of Marxist theory. In this perhaps
he sounds rather like Rorty's "methodological reader": one who simply lays his
theory over the text like a grid and reads off the appropriate response.[24] It is an
impression that is strengthened by his dismissal of the suggestion that literature
might have any transformative or dialectical potential. Indeed, Eagleton seems
to regard this claim—so central to the work of Nussbaum and Rorty—as
something of a liberal-humanist ideological fiction.[25] Eagleton's work, nevertheless, appears to display two aspects of the approach to literary criticism that
we later see employed by Martha Nussbaum and Richard Rorty.

   In the first instance, Eagleton appears absolutely certain of his reading of
literary texts; in the second, he seeks—consciously or unconsciously—to make
those texts speak with the critic's voice. Of *Wuthering Heights* we learn that, for
example, "Heathcliff is an indirect symbol of the aggressive industrial bourgeoisie of Emily Brontë's own time, a social trend extrinsic to both classes, but
implicated in their fortunes."[26] While in a manner that further foreshadows
Nussbaum's reading of literary texts, Eagleton states that any reading of *Jude the
Obscure* that sees the book as a tale of a working-man's quest for education is
simply "false," the product of a reading "biased by ideological preconceptions."[27]
Indeed, all of his readings are replete with claims about "truth," "falsity," "symbolism," and "representation." Eagleton's ideal novel or literary work appears to

be one in which class politics is at the forefront, and the symbolism is unambiguous, something akin, perhaps, to his own novel *Saints and Scholars*.[28]

If Eagleton's approach were, however, merely confined to reevaluating canonical novels against a Marxist standard then we could perhaps simply regard his work as a well-intentioned but nevertheless somewhat idiosyncratic, and potentially reductive, approach to literary texts, one with little import beyond the literature-faculty lounge. That Eagleton's bold claims on behalf of his method are now being replicated in both literature and political science departments suggests that it is well worth examining the reasoning that underpins his claims.

LITERARY THEORY AND CRITICAL INSIGHT

Combining both the *privileged observer* and the *portability* claim, Eagleton argues that literary theory offers him a perspective from which to gain valuable critical insight into social and political phenomena. He offers a number of critiques of such formations. Fascism, we learn, was a "desperate, last-ditch attempt on the part of monopoly capitalism to abolish contradictions which ha[d] become intolerable, and it d[id] so by offering a whole alternative history, a narrative of blood, soil, the 'authentic' race, the sublimity of death and self-abnegation."[29] While in 1980s' Britain, the aim of Thatcherism was "converting the moderately pleasant people who populated the country when Thatcher first arrived in Downing Street into a thoroughly nasty bunch of self-seeking oafs."[30] Eagleton also uses the perspective afforded by literary theory to critique the work of other theorists. Almost all—with the notable exception of Raymond Williams—are found wanting. Even the New Historicists, thinkers concerned with the materialist conditions of literary production and its impact upon what is produced—thinkers with whom Eagleton might be thought to have an affinity—are rejected. Indeed, in a move not dissimilar to the dismissal of the Judean People's Front by the People's Front of Judea in *Monty Python's The Life of Brian*, Eagleton asserts that the work of the New Historicists "has a good deal to do with a peculiarly American left defeatism, guilt stricken relativism, and an ignorance of socialism."[31] Indeed, just as he holds literary texts up to the standards provided by his Marxist theory, Eagleton judges the work of other theorists by the same standard. "We hear very little," he writes, "about why exactly Stanley Fish has not rushed to espouse the theory of surplus value, or what Richard Rorty thinks of neo-colonialism, or the precise nature of Jonathan Culler's views of feudal absolutism."[32]

There is, nevertheless, something of an irony in the fact that Eagleton, a theorist deeply influenced by Karl Marx and Ludwig Wittgenstein—thinkers who drew repeatedly on specific material examples—should make his own criticisms at such a high level of abstraction. As far as his *political* analysis is concerned, such is his apparent belief in the *portability* claim, Eagleton simply offers a—possibly performative—*reading* of political events. There is no attempt to understand phenomena such as Fascism or Thatcherism beyond his own reading of them: to identify their causes through, say, a detailed historical or sociological analysis. Eagleton *reads* these phenomena the way that he *reads* texts; and, given his apparent predilection for methodological reading, the events unsurprisingly seem to confirm his theory. Despite his claims about "aesthetic charity," there appears to be little—if any—room for a critical reflective equilibrium between the world and the claim. The reading of the literary text becomes evidence for the validity of a claim about the world beyond the text.

In making such a criticism of Eagleton it is, however, important to acknowledge the possibility of the *genetic fallacy*. It is—as Richard Posner notes in response to criticism of his penchant for finding politically conservative messages in great literature—always possible that such messages are indeed a part of the text, and that it is critics such as this one who are guilty of fallacious reasoning.[33] Given the very malleability of literary texts, there is of course no clear test for the existence of a genetic fallacy. Nevertheless, the onus seems to be on Posner—and, in this case, Eagleton—to explain what it is about their method that secures their work from such error. It is they who, after all, are making the strongest claims about what literature is supposedly saying. Neither, however, provides much elaboration on their method beyond the stridency of their prose, nor much in the way of self-critique. As such, even if one is being charitable, it is hard not to suspect that theirs are examples—albeit highly sophisticated ones—of methodological reading, not the genetic fallacy.

In his reading of other theorists, however, Eagleton himself shows little such interpretive charity. As with his readings of political events, his criticisms of these theorists are pitched at a similarly high level of abstraction. His standard approach seems to be to offer a *redescription* of the other theorist's work, followed by a dismissal of the very account he has just given. His response to Richard Rorty's theory of "solidarity" is illustrative of his method. In *Contingency, Irony, and Solidarity*, Rorty argues that solidarity is a product not of universal notions such as "human nature" but of closer, more local ties. Rather than engaging with this argument, say, by showing how the local ties that Rorty identifies are themselves actually the product of some underlying feature of our existence called "human nature"—the sort of thing Norman Geras attempts, albeit unsuccessfully, in *Solidarity in the Conversation of Humankind*[34]—Eagleton chooses instead simply to dismiss the argument with a rhetorical flourish. "Personally," he writes, "I only ever manifest compassion to fellow graduates of the University of Cambridge. It's true such credentials aren't always easy to establish; indeed, I have occasionally tossed a coin towards some tramp whom I thought I dimly recognized as a member of the class of '64, only to retrieve it again furtively when I recognized my mistake."[35] It could be that this highly amusing response is simply Eagleton taking on Rorty at his own game, but it is a method that we see employ repeatedly, less humorously, and regardless of his target. He is, furthermore, absolutely unapologetic about his reluctance to become engaged in the details of alternative positions or objects of inquiry. In his "Preface" to *The Illusions of Postmodernism*, Eagleton notes that "there is not much discussion of particular works of art" or "particular theorists either" in his book,[36] while in *The Ideology of the Aesthetic* he elevates this reluctance to engage with specifics into a principle. "Those trained in literary critical habits of thought are," he notes, "usually enamored of 'concrete illustration'; but since I reject the idea that 'theory' is acceptable if and only if it performs the role of humble handmaiden to the aesthetic work, I have tried to frustrate this expectation as far as possible by remaining for the most part resolutely silent about particular artifacts."[37] It is, however, not only the details of the theoretical intricacies of others' work that Eagleton passes over in silence; he is similarly silent about the details of his own position.

A MARXIST LITERARY CRITICISM?

Although Eagleton notes in *Literary Theory: An Introduction* that "there are indeed Marxist and feminist theories of literature, which in my opinion are more valuable than any of the theories discussed here,"[38] he refuses to say anything about them, arguing that to do so "might encourage the reader to make what philosophers call a 'category mistake.'"[39] Eagleton seems to regard this potential "category mistake" as arising from the belief that "political criticism" is something different from the other theories he has set out and critiqued, theories that are—on his account—also inherently political. It is not immediately clear, however, why the claim that all theories are political excuses Eagleton from the need to set out and defend the standard against which he is judging them. If all literary theories are indeed political—as he claims—then there seems to be no reason he should "expose" the interests behind these other theories and not his own. His reluctance to do so stems perhaps from certain difficulties inherent in using Marxist theory to discuss literature.

As Raymond Williams pointed out in *Marxism and Literature*: "Hardly anyone becomes a Marxist for primarily cultural or literary reasons, but for compelling political and economic ones."[40] Indeed, as Eagleton and Williams both note, Marx and Engels rarely talked about art or the relationship between it and politics. For this reason, much of Williams's work in *Marxism and Literature* is made up of an attempt to articulate what he calls "the indissoluble connection between material production, political and cultural institutions, and activity and consciousness."[41] Marx's reticence on this point is not, however, the only problem for Eagleton, Williams, and other would-be Marxist literary critics, for when Marx *does* talk about the relationship between the material base and artistic formations, his comments are hardly conducive to articulating the clear relationship that these theorists desire and, it will be argued, seem to *require*. In the "1859 Preface," for example, Marx declares that when studying periods of revolutionary transformation, it is

> "always necessary to distinguish between the material transformations of the economic conditions of production, which can be determined with the precision of natural science, and the legal, political, religious, artistic, or philosophic—in short, ideological forms, in which men become conscious of this conflict and fight it out.[42]

Whereas changes in the conditions of production can be determined with the "precision of a natural science," art is considered ideological and, as such, part of the superstructure. Eagleton acknowledges the validity of both of Marx's claims about art—that it is ideological and, that it is part of the superstructure[43]—and yet, in so doing, he creates enormous theoretical difficulties for himself, for it is not clear how these claims are to be reconciled with, first, Eagleton's approach to art and, second, with his obvious and much-asserted commitment to the Marxist theory of base and superstructure.

Eagleton seems to hold that his reading of literary texts—that which he uses as a model for his historical and political analysis—allows him to read off class interests and strategies from cultural formations: to say something about the base by talking about the superstructure. In order for him to do this and remain consistent with the Marxist theory that provides the benchmark for all his judgments about texts, society, and politics, Eagleton needs to elucidate a conception of the base-superstructure relationship that allows him to make such direct connections between the two. He must, that is, show how the base *determines* the superstructure in such a way that he is able to trace backward from the *effect* to a *cause*. Raymond Williams resolves this difficulty—to his own satisfaction at least—by placing such ideas in the base, showing how they can determine class behavior in much the same way as material formations. There are strong textual and theoretical reasons for rejecting this solution to the base-superstructure problem, and it is telling perhaps that Eagleton does not adopt it.[44] It is more telling, however, that Eagleton never once attempts to elucidate such an account of the base and superstructure relationship in his work, despite his observation that it is "one of the most important questions which Marxist literary criticism now has to confront."[45] Instead, Eagleton merely alludes to

John Berger's *Ways of Seeing*, suggesting that Berger's work contains some hint as to the way Marxist literary criticism should progress in its attempt to articulate this relationship.[46] Berger's book, however, lacks any such mention of this relationship, let alone the sort of rigorous, theoretically satisfying account that Eagleton needs to enhance the plausibility of his claim, and we are simply left to wonder about this lacuna at the heart of both theorists' work. Even in his most recent article on the subject—"Base and Superstructure Revisited"—Eagleton simply defends the conceptual distinction as it appears in the work of Marx and Engels, but never explains how he is able to cut through the multivariate determinants of the superstructural formation that is literature or culture to identify "with the precision of a natural science," the exact elements of the base that produced this formation. His approach is somewhat like trying to determine the mathematical problem armed only with the solution. His work does suggest two possibilities for this relationship between the base and the superstructure, but neither seems terribly convincing.

TWO THEORIES OF BASE AND SUPERSTRUCTURE

The first possible explanation is the *instrumentalist* one. This account suggests that the superstructure—in this case, the artistic elements thereof—is *deliberately* constructed by the ruling class to subordinate the masses. The major problem with this suggestion is that it seems to require near omniscience on the part of the ruling class, something that Marx rejected in the *Eighteenth Brumaire* when he noted that the "skill, knowledge, mental insight, and intellectual resources" of the average member of the bourgeoisie "reach no further than the end of his nose."[47] A further problem for this account of the base-superstructure relationship for Eagleton's theory is that he explicitly rejects it. "I do not really intend to suggest," writes Eagleton in *The Ideology of the Aesthetic*, "that the eighteenth-century bourgeoisie assembled around a table over their claret to dream up the concept of the aesthetic as a solution to their political dilemmas, and the political contradictions of the category is itself testimony to the mistakenness of such a viewpoint."[48] The very implausibility of this theory is, it seems, a stumbling block to its articulation as the causal mechanism.

Nevertheless, as we have already seen, Eagleton makes a number of causal claims that sound suspiciously instrumentalist. In addition to his comments about Matthew Arnold's and Walter Raleigh's deliberate attempts to shore up class power through the creation and sustenance of "English" as an academic subject, Eagleton suggests that New Criticism was "the ideology of an uprooted, defensive intelligentsia who reinvented in literature what they could not locate in reality."[49] Indeed, he suggests, once again, that the desire among New Critics to focus on textual meaning was a cover for something more sinister. "The aim of all this policing" was, he writes, "the protection of private property."[50] Of course, it would be a very odd structuralist theory that never provided room for the agents working under the influence of those structures to relish some of their behaviors. In the case of literary criticism, Matthew Arnold was clearly conscious of his desire to subordinate and subdue the masses. Nevertheless, it is unconvincing to suggest that this causal mechanism *explains* the base-superstructure relationship. The superstructure is influenced by so many factors and granted so much autonomy in its development in Marx's work that a theory of causality that relies solely on instrumentalism is always going to be highly implausible. It is probably for this reason that when pushed, Eagleton—for the most part—eschews this approach. There is, however, a certain disingenuousness to this eschewal. Having openly dismissed the theory, Eagleton—as we have seen—nevertheless continues to write as if it were true. He might do so for two reasons: first, because it would resolve a number of his theoretical difficulties; second, because his alternative—the functional explanation—is no more satisfying than his first.

The suggestion that the base-superstructure relationship is a functional one is made by G. A. Cohen in his book *Karl Marx's Theory of History: A Defence*.[51] Cohen argues that when Marx says that the superstructure reflects the base he means that it emerges because it is appropriate to the latter and functions to maintain its existence. This is, says Cohen, akin to the Darwinian claim that birds have hollow bones because hollow bones facilitate flight. Eagleton appears—at times—to speak this functional language. "As British capitalism became threatened and outstripped by its younger German and American rivals," writes Eagleton in his history of the twentieth century, "the squalid, undignified scramble of too much capital chasing too few overseas territories, which was to culminate in 1914 in the first imperialist world war, created the urgent need for a sense of national mission and identity."[52] Having noted the need, Eagleton then goes on to show how that need was fulfilled by the emergence of a literary criticism that promoted these very values, without once explaining the causal mechanism that led such critics to fulfill the needs of capitalism. In this regard, Eagleton's history suggests that literary artists and literary critics are simply the unwitting agents of destiny. Such determinism might have found favor with some of the more mechanistically inclined theorists of the Second International, but it simply does not do justice to the complexity of Marx's thought, to social reality, or to literary texts. Indeed, both Williams and Eagleton note that one of Marx's chief criticisms of capitalism is that it serves to stifle the human creativity at the core of his theory. "At the very center of Marxism," writes Williams, "is an extraordinary emphasis on human creativity and self creation."[53] Similarly, Eagleton himself criticizes E. D. Hirsch for failing to do "justice to the detail, complexity, and conflictive nature of literary works."[54] As such, it is hard to believe that Eagleton sees literary texts as a simple manifestation of the base in the way that the functional explanation requires. When he talks this way we might, once again, think of his work as being concerned more with political outcomes than with theoretical consistency.

Even if, however, Eagleton did see the superstructure as a simple manifestation of the base, his problems would be far from over, for such a view simply serves to make his analysis of cultural artifacts redundant: it has nothing to tell us that a close examination of the base would not. Furthermore, the virtue of the functional explanation, as far as Cohen is concerned, is that it does not require too detailed an analysis of the base-superstructure relationship; it simply notes that the superstructure fulfils its function, without saying how or why. Eagleton's politically inspired literary criticism is, however, concerned to trace back from the *effect*—the literary formation—to the *cause*—the economic base—in such a way that he connects the latter to the former. As it stands, Marx's argument has the structure: if b, then s, where b is the base and s is the superstructure. Eagleton seems, however, to make the invalid inference, s therefore b. As such, he cannot tell us how or why the critical analysis of art—which is *superstructural* in nature—will tell us something about the *base*.

Although this account of the base-superstructure relationship might appear to be an arcane discussion of an obscure aspect of Marxist theory, it actually goes to the heart of the literary turn. The difficulty of this relationship in Eagleton's work is simply a variation on a much larger issue for the political thought and analysis of and through literature: the problematic relationship between the *written* and *unwritten* worlds.

THE *WRITTEN* AND THE *UNWRITTEN* WORLDS

Although Eagleton never quite sets out his vision of an acceptable literary criticism, in one of the few hints he does give about what such a criticism might look like, he suggests that there should be a limit to what he calls "aesthetic charity."[55] That is, while Eagleton accepts that there may be some things that are acceptable in literature that are not so acceptable in the world outside the text, there are, nevertheless, limits to this tolerance. At some point, he seems to be suggesting, we should begin to critique the text for what it implies about the nontextual world. His approach poses, however, a number of theoretical difficulties, not least among which is how far we are to extend this aesthetic charity: Should we allow Nabokov his tale about a pedophile? Or should we criticize him for promoting the degradation of young girls? Or even, as seems more likely in Eagleton's case, for failing to address the class position of Louise,

Charlotte Haze's African American maid? That it is difficult to implement such a theory does not, of course, mean that it is without value. Nevertheless, this problem is only a minor one compared to the more fundamental difficulty with Eagleton's approach, one that is indicated by his struggles—or lack thereof—with the base-superstructure relationship. Eagleton, like many theorists of the literary turn, never explains the relationship between the *written* and the *unwritten* worlds that would allow him to use criticism of the former as criticism of the latter.

The distinction between the *written* and *unwritten* worlds is borrowed from anarchist theorist Paul Goodman.[56] It is used here to distinguish between the fictional world of the literary text—the *written* world—and the world in which that text is written—the *unwritten* world—the world in which we live, work, and engage in Eliot's trinity of birth, death, and copulation. Using T. S. Eliot to help distinguish between these two worlds is, of course, a way of acknowledging that the two worlds do indeed stand in some relationship to one another. The exact nature of this relationship is, however, elusive and hard to define. It clearly shifts, for example, according to the aims and nature of the literature under discussion. We might think of Truman Capote's "nonfiction novel" *In Cold Blood* and Ursula K. Le Guin's science fiction novel *The Dispossessed*, each of which stands in a different relationship to the distinction.[57] Consequently, any attempt to use one world to support claims about the other requires some account of the relationship between the two. In classical studies, for example, archaeological digs in the *unwritten* world are used to verify the *written* world of Homer and Hesiod.[58] Such evidence has, of course, little to tell us about the *literary* qualities of these poets, but it may tell us something about the value of their work as *history*. Details of everyday life or great historical events discussed in the poems are examined against archaeological findings, or archaeological findings against poetic details in order to establish what is known about the Ancient world. Here the two worlds—*written* and *unwritten*—are examined against each other in a sort of "reflective equilibrium." This work is, however, clearly complicated by the nature of poetic license: the *written* and *unwritten* worlds do not stand in direct mimetic relationship to one another. Very few archaeologists, one suspects, believe that the Ancient world was populated by goat-rearing, one-eyed giants. Indeed, even the most journalistic accounts of the *unwritten* world are selective and biased: we turn to artists and poets precisely for their subjectivity and creativity. For this reason—as will be argued in more detail in chapter 7—we should be at least a little cautious about using evidence from the *written* world to support claims about the *unwritten* world.

Eagleton, however, fails to demonstrate any such caution. He treats the relationship between the two worlds as if it were entirely unproblematic, as if one could simply read back from the fiction to the world in which it was created, despite his own assertion that "it is naïve to imagine that there is some direct expressive relation between a life and the work it produces."[59] In this his work appears to be a precursor to much of the work that we now see on literature in philosophy and political science departments across North America. It is a disturbing trend, not least because it appears to confuse two different *standards of justification* appropriate to two different disciplines.

Two Standards of Justification

Literary texts are open to multiple possible interpretations. This does not, however, mean that *all* interpretations are equally valid: some are clearly more attractive, intuitively pleasing, or more plausible than others. What makes one *reading* more pleasing or plausible than another is, however, a complex question for which there is no formulaic answer. For the methodological reader, for example, a *reading* that captures more of the nuances of a particular worldview—be it Marxism, Freudianism, or feminism—is likely to be regarded as superior to one that does not. For the reader motivated solely by aesthetic concerns, in contrast, a *reading* that highlights the ways in which a text achieves certain aesthetic effects is likely to be more attractive than one that does not. The criteria for a good literary critical reading of a text are multiple and depend, to a large extent, on one's aims in reading the text and one's beliefs about such texts. The process by which those criteria are fulfilled is equally difficult to capture or to quantify. In reading or making a claim about a literary text, *correspondence* might, for example, be considered a suitable basis for an interesting claim. Noting the recurrence of a symbol, a theme, or an image in the same or a different text might be a basis for theorizing about a connection between them, and a series of these connections might be woven into an interesting, effective, or convincing interpretation of a text. In order to make such a claim about a text, however, one does not need to show a *causal* relationship between the elements of correspondence. One might ask "was this the author's intent?" or some such question that linked the elements, but a negative answer to that question might not serve to make the interpretation any less *plausible*.

This aspect of *written* world analysis may have something to do with the acceptance of subjectivity in artistic interpretation. Whatever the cause, it suggests that the criteria for a plausible interpretation of a literary text are looser than those of science, where accuracy and rigor are so important. More significantly, this aspect of *written* world analysis also suggests that the criteria for the study of the *written* world are looser than for social science, the study of the *unwritten* world. Here there has to be an agreed-upon set of criteria for measurement—some benchmark or standard—even if there is debate over its epistemological status.

This is not, of course, to suggest that the standards of justification in literary interpretation are anarchic, or that the standards of justification for social science are fixed, simply that the standards of justification in literary analysis are more flexible than those of social science or philosophy. Nor is this to suggest that people never argue vehemently over what a literary text means, or that such debates are a waste of time. Nevertheless, the vehemence with which certain people hold and protect their views on a text's meaning or interpretation does not alter the fact that the criteria for a good interpretation of a text are less defined and less rigorous than for something like a scientific experiment, a social scientific study, or, as was argued in chapter 1, a philosophical argument. Indeed, it may well be that the vehemence of some of the arguments over literary meaning might be a product of precisely that lack of agreed-upon standard: in the absence of shared criteria for agreement, arguments might become increasingly shrill.

This less rigorous standard for validity in literary interpretation is, nevertheless, entirely appropriate, for although we can probably all imagine elaborate hypothetical situations in which the reading of a literary text is crucially significant for the well-being of society, whether or not Jude Fawley is working class or bourgeois on Eagleton's criteria, really does not matter any more in the *unwritten* world than whether Piggy's glasses could actually be used to start a fire as they were in *Lord of the Flies*.[60] In most cases, there is less at stake for the *unwritten* world in such questions than about whether HIV causes AIDS or whether poverty is a cause of crime. Consequently, it is only fitting that there should be less rigorous standards of justification for such interpretations than for social theories that *do* attempt to address such questions. A central problem of the literary turn—and we see this clearly illustrated in Eagleton's work—is that this more lax standard of justification from the study of the *written* world seems to be crossing over into the analysis of the *unwritten* world. The consequences of this confusion between the two standards of justification appropriate to the different forms of analysis—of the *written* and the *unwritten* world—are severalfold. Almost all can be seen in Eagleton's approach to political and social theorizing.

EAGLETON'S QUIXOTIC SOCIAL THEORY

The eponymous hero of Cervantes' *Don Quixote* was, of course, noted for his confusion of the *written* and the *unwritten* worlds, a tendency that we also see in Terry Eagleton's work on politics and literature. Although Eagleton believes that literary theory is a perspective from which to "view the history" of our times, this possibly Quixotic—possibly deliberate—tendency to confuse the *written* and *unwritten* worlds has serious consequences for the value of his account as social theory or political analysis.

The first—and most significant—problem for Eagleton's work is that the weaker standards of justification appropriate to the study of the *written* world simply do not travel well to the study of the *unwritten* world. At times, Eagleton talks as if *correspondence* is *causality*: because he is able to spot what he considers elements of class politics in artistic and cultural formations, he seems to take this as evidence for the claim that these elements were generated by the economic base. In effect, Eagleton reads texts in light of his theory of politics and society, and then he uses these readings for evidence of the plausibility of the initial theory, using evidence from the *written* world to support claims about the *unwritten* one. The potential circularity problem here is clear, and strongly reminiscent of Richard Rorty's work: Eagleton's theory justifies his readings, and his readings justify his theory. It seems, furthermore, that in a manner not dissimilar to Martha Nussbaum, Eagleton actually uses literature to resolve the tensions inherent in his theory, in particular, the problematic base-superstructure relationship. Unlike Nussbaum, however, it is not clear whether Eagleton is simply using this approach as part of a broader political strategy or whether it is a genuine conceptual confusion. In either case, in using the more lax standard of justification appropriate to study of the *written* world to justify his claims about the *unwritten* one, we see a clear instance of the confusion of these two worlds, and the way in which this confusion can undermine the plausibility of social and political analysis in the literary turn.

The consequences of this confusion are clear. Reading *Alice's Adventures in Wonderland* might lead one to conclude that the *unwritten* world is inhabited by talking cats and playing-card soldiers, but such a conclusion would clearly be misplaced. In order to justify such a claim about the *unwritten* world, one would have to test that claim against that world: to put it into the sort of "reflective equilibrium" advocated (though apparently not utilized) by Martha Nussbaum. As Shakespeare's shipwreck in landlocked Bohemia illustrates, just because an author chooses to portray events in a certain way in the *written* world does not mean they are exactly the same way in the *unwritten* one. It is a confusion that is made all the more pernicious in Eagleton's work, because he—like Nussbaum—appears to lack a meaningful self-critique.

READ MY LIPS:
EAGLETON AND TEXTUAL VENTRILOQUISM

In the study of the *written* world, singular, deeply subjective readings can often serve as the coin of the realm: a good critic is perhaps one who makes her reader feel differently about the text through a process of redescription, or by pointing out hitherto unseen details and drawing them together in an interesting way. This is certainly the case for readers—such as Eagleton and Rorty—who reject notions of artistic merit or authorial intent as a standard for criticism. When a literary critic offers a reading of a text, then, we do not ask her how she knows whether her reading is valid to the extent that we do in science, philosophy, or social science: there are simply no agreed-upon criteria for this beyond the *effect* of that *reading*. In social science and social theory, on the other hand, such questions—given the more demanding standard of justification that pertains in the *unwritten* world—are absolutely crucial. Given his status as a literary critic and literary theorist, Eagleton is—in a move reminiscent of Rorty's "haze"—able to avoid such questions about the lack of self-critique in his social theory. In Marxist theory, of course, the critical perspective on society is generated by the conditions of the new socialist society emerging in the womb of the old. Such an approach is, however, dependent on a determinist theory of history to which few, if any, contemporary thinkers would be willing to subscribe. In the absence of such a perspective, it is not clear that Eagleton's claims about society are any less subjective than his readings of texts, something that his rather simplistic accounts of Fascism and Thatcherism would seem to suggest. Eagleton—possibly for reasons of political strategy—seems to regard his position as so self-evidently correct that he does not require any such mechanism for self-critique. Rather, he presents his claims as simply true: their veracity guaranteed by his own honesty and lack of self-delusion. Stanley Fish's critique of New Historicism seems pertinent here. In response to the New Historicist suggestion, that they are "more open" to historical factors than their less methodologically sophisticated colleagues, Fish observes: "One cannot wake up in the morning and decide, 'today I am going to be open'—as opposed to deciding that today I am going to eat less or pay more attention to my children or get my finances in order."[61] If political literary criticism is, in Eagleton's approach, a matter of ventriloquism—making the texts speak with the critic's voice—then Eagleton mistakenly seems to find virtue in drawing attention to his moving lips. This may be genuine methodological error, or something more performative.

By constantly drawing attention to the political and theoretical presuppositions of his work—his commitment to Marxist theory and social change—Eagleton perhaps seeks to avoid close scrutiny of those presuppositions. He is, in effect, hiding in plain sight. He achieves this goal by constructing a rhetorical persona: a plain-speaking "Terry Eagleton" who is concerned about the struggles of the working class and has little time for the excesses of French theory. "Jacques Derrida and his progeny," notes this Eagleton with distaste, "are primarily interested in the sliding of the Mallarmean signifier, rather than in what gets said during the tea-break in the Hilton kitchens."[62] What might, however, be considered an idiosyncrasy of style in other theorists' work takes on enormous theoretical and political significance when we see Eagleton use his plain-speaking persona to gloss over important theoretical questions that pose significant problems for his thought. It is a recurrent device in his work:

> To suggest that someone *ought* to adopt a particular position may sound peculiarly patronizing, dictatorial, and elitist. Who am I to presume that I know what is in someone else's interest? Isn't this just the style in which ruling groups and classes have spoken for centuries? The plain fact is that I am in full possession of my own interest, and nobody can tell me what to do, I am entirely transparent to myself, have an utterly unmystified view of my social conditions, and will tolerate no kind of suggestion, however comradely and sympathetic its tone, from anybody else. I do not need telling by some paternal elitist about what is in my "objective" interest, because as a matter of fact I never behave in a way which violates them. Even though I eat twelve pounds of sausage a day, smoke sixty cigarettes before noon, and have just volunteered for a fifty percent wage cut, I resent the idea that I have anything to learn from anyone.[63]

The question that Eagleton raises at the outset of this passage is a legitimate one, and yet his failure to answer it is indicative of his overall method: one that relies on rhetorical flourishes rather than rigorous argument for its force. Although many of us would indeed agree that the fellow whom Eagleton pretends to be by the end of the paragraph may well be a victim of certain ideological misconceptions, it is certainly not clear that this is true for everybody, nor even, if this were so, that *Eagleton* would be in a position to alert us in more marginal, and more plausible, cases. Eagleton appears to use his rhetoric to elude close scrutiny of his own—largely undefended—position. His work is replete with such rhetorical devices. Noting, for example, the tendency among postmodern thinkers to state their own political beliefs as a means of avoiding self-critique, Eagleton notes: "Such coyly self-referential pronouncements should alert us against the now fashionable belief that for the subject to reckon himself into his utterances is inevitably a progressive move."[64] This claim, however, seems to be something of a smokescreen for Eagleton's own use of precisely the same device as part of his own plain-speaking persona. "I write," he says, "as one born into and brought up within a working-class socialist tradition, one who has been reasonably active in such politics since adolescence, and who believes that any form of political radicalism today which attempts to bypass that lineage is bound to be impoverished."[65] Indeed, it is interesting to note that at a time when he sees some of his radical ground being removed by identity politics—politics of which he has serious criticisms[66]—Eagleton should choose to highlight his Irishness as a source of insight.[67]

For Eagleton, it is being suggested, the personal attack is political in a way that stems *directly* from his attempt to use the methods of literary criticism as a source of insight into the politics of the *unwritten* world. His subjectivity, which can be a source of insight and even pleasure in his readings of literature, simply does not travel well to social and political analysis.[68] There is a greater onus on critics of the *unwritten* world to justify their claims intersubjectively and to put those claims about texts into dialogue with our experience of the world, precisely because there is more at stake in the question of whether poverty causes crime than over whether Heathcliff is a murderer.[69] Eagleton simply puts his claims about the *written* world into dialogue with a *reading* of other texts: in this case the works of Marx and Engels. In this we see, perhaps, a double confusion of the *written* and the *unwritten* worlds, with Eagleton holding Marx's and Engels's written world up as a substitute for that *unwritten* world about which they were writing. Marx and Engels, of course, reviewed their claims about the *unwritten* world in light of world events; Eagleton seems to take their account as unproblematic and simply true. For this reason, perhaps, Eagleton's social and political commentary tends to rely on the word "surely" or upon claims to "self-evidence" that he himself would not accept in, say, the Declaration of Independence. Far from the double movement of Marxist theory, he seems to have something of a double standard as far as his own claims are concerned. Whereas he holds up the work of other theorists to intense—though often undeveloped—criticism, his own work is to be taken at face value. This move is, it is being suggested, a *direct* consequence of adopting the standards of literary theory for the more rigorous demands of criticism in the *unwritten* world. "It is," says Eagleton, "always worth testing out any literary theory by asking: How could it work with Joyce's *Finnegans Wake*?"[70] Such a standard is, however, simply inadequate for social theory, not least because the malleability of texts makes correspondence between the theory and the text more or less certain.

Conclusions

This chapter has argued that the plausibility of Eagleton's attempts to utilize literary methods of study for social and political analysis is undermined by a confusion between the *written* and the *unwritten* worlds. It is a confusion that is either a genuine methodological mistake or the product of a deliberate attempt to blur the distinction as part of an overarching political strategy. Given Eagleton's intelligence, rhetorical skill, and aptitude for literature, the latter seems more plausible than the former, though it is a question whose definitive answer is beyond the scope of this study. Neither answer would, however, seem to flatter Eagleton: he is either guilty of a glaring conceptual error or much closer in outlook and method to Richard Rorty than would probably make him comfortable. Either answer would, nevertheless, place him at the heart of the literary turn. In this regard, Eagleton's work—though flawed—is useful, for it draws attention to certain problems that need to be overcome if we are indeed to champion a political reasoning and analysis inspired, but not replaced, by the methods of literature and literary criticism.

As far as the *written* and *unwritten* world distinction is concerned, it would, of course, be absurd to suggest that the two worlds do not stand in *any* relationship to each other, just as it is absurd to suggest that the relationship is so unproblematic that we might use claims about one as evidence for claims about the other. There exists some middle ground between the two positions that is worth exploring. Eagleton's work suggests that he is not unaware of this problem in his theory; nevertheless, he fails to elucidate this relationship in any convincing manner. Indeed, the confused relationship is itself utilized to resolve his own theoretical problems—particularly about the relationship between the base and the superstructure in Marxist theory—problems that need independent elucidation, justification, and resolution. The political turn in literary criticism appears to take little rigor from the study of politics; rather, it merely applies the subjectivity of literary analysis to the study of social and political phenomena. It is for this reason perhaps that we see such archness in Eagleton's work, especially with regard to other theorists. In the absence of any agreed-upon standards for literary appreciation beyond the effect on the audience, Eagleton cannot engage in details with other theorists' work and is instead reduced to constructing a rhetorical persona as a basis for critique. In the next chapter it will nevertheless be suggested that the subjectivity of this method may, under certain circumstances, be a potential source of insight that is worth incorporating in a more compelling account of the role for literary analysis in the study of the political.

Chapter 5

Judith Butler
Politics, Literature, and Radical Democracy

"The question 'What is your book about?' has always puzzled me. It is about itself and if I could condense it into other words I should not have taken such care to choose the words that I did."
                                        —Jeanette Winterson, *Art Objects*[1]

"The complexity of gender," wrote Judith Butler in the preface to the tenth anniversary edition of her book, *Gender Trouble*, "requires an interdisciplinary and postdisciplinary set of discourses in order to resist the domestication of gender studies within the academy and to radicalize the notion of feminist critique."[2] It is a claim that is at once both a challenge to traditional methods of philosophy, social science, literary analysis, and political theorizing, as well as an apt description of her own approach to the questions posed by gender, politics, and sexuality. She is, it might be noted at the outset, a professor of rhetoric and comparative literature who was trained as a philosopher.[3] It is perhaps this prodigious syncretism, along with her complex writing style and her commitment to undercutting orthodoxies—of friends, would-be friends, and foes alike—that has made Butler such a controversial figure in the modern Academy. Recalling Richard Rorty's observation about the "haze" that "surrounds writers who are not associated with any particular discipline, and are therefore not expected to play by any antecedently known rules,"[4] explains perhaps why Butler has often proved so maddening to those who seek to engage with her work.[5] Similarly, Butler's writing style is notoriously difficult, filled as it is with allusions, reversals, ellipses, neologisms, and complex sentences with multiple clauses, to say nothing of occupatio, litotes, irony, and hyperbole. Indeed, even Butler appears to have trouble summarizing her work. "The relation between drag performance and gender performativity in *Gender*

101

Trouble," she writes in *The Psychic Life of Power,* "goes *something like this.*"[6] About this aspect of her work, Butler is absolutely unapologetic. "Who," she writes, "devises the protocols of 'clarity' and whose interests do they serve? What is foreclosed by the insistence on parochial standards of transparency as requisite for all communication? What does 'transparency' keep obscure?"[7] Furthermore, Butler is as tenacious and trenchant in her approach to those with whom she might be considered to have an affinity, as with those whose work she rejects.[8] As such, Butler's work appears to have divided the Academy. Critics of her work—including Martha Nussbaum[9]—have tended to focus on what they consider Butler's lack of clarity and her apparent disregard for practical politics, whereas acolytes have tended to mimic and build on her approach, producing complex texts of their own. This controversy has created something of an in-group and an out-group: with the in-group, led by Butler, offering a—possibly understandable—self-defensiveness and the out-group offering increasingly shrill attacks.[10]

This chapter seeks to avoid both of these problematic perspectives, for neither seems to cast much critical light on Butler's work. It seeks to do so first by recognizing that Butler is a public intellectual for only a subsection of the public. This may, of course, be a deliberate political tactic—with Butler embracing, and possibly exaggerating, her own marginality as a rhetorical strategy—but it is also possible that the issues and questions that Butler raises in her work are not necessarily those of this author, or even of traditional political and social theory, something that Butler herself has acknowledged in her more recent work.[11] What follows, therefore, will seek to recognize and acknowledge that Butler may be addressing an audience with concerns outside the boundaries of traditional political thought, those who are seeking a language in which to express their claims.[12] It will seek to do so in a way that does not fetishize such difference, though this is, to some extent, probably inevitable.[13] Second, the chapter seeks, nevertheless, to offer a critique of this work, in terms of its methodology, the quality of its insights, and its implications for political thought and practice. It will do so by characterizing Butler's work as an example of the literary turn and by examining her work from that perspective. This chapter will begin, therefore, with a discussion of what it considers the merging of the literary, the philosophical, and the political in Butler's work. It will seek to justify her inclusion in this study, setting up an argument that suggests that this perspective will be a fecund source of insight into both Butler's work and into the costs and consequences of the literary turn for political thought and analysis.

BUTLER AND THE LITERARY TURN

One of the many ways in which Butler's work differs from that of the other theorists whose work is discussed here is that she, unlike Nussbaum, Rorty, and

Eagleton, feels no need to justify her merging of the literary, the political, and the philosophical. Whereas Nussbaum and Rorty seek to justify the turn to literature in their political thought, and Eagleton, the concern with politics in his literary criticism, Butler has exhibited no such anxiety, even though she has recently begun to reflect on her position within the Academy and the status of her work.[14] This is perhaps evidence of the way in which the merging of these once separate fields—and, indeed, the three questions *epistemological and ontological, moral and political,* and *methodological* raised by the literary turn—has become commonplace and the extent to which Butler's work is influenced by continental philosophy, in particular that of Michel Foucault. Just as Foucault declared "that the possibility exists for fiction to work within truth, and for fictive discourses to induce effects of truth,"[15] Butler identifies what she considers "the essential role of fiction and false belief in the quest for philosophical truth"[16] in her reading of Hegel's *Phenomenology.* Foucault's intricate and often idiosyncratic work seems to provide Butler with a precedent for her approach to social analysis and political theory. Several features of her writing indicate what might be called the "literariness" of this work, not least among which is Butler's underpinning concern with *reading* and with the power and the impact of *texts.*

As early as *Subjects of Desire,* Butler was concerned with the *literary* qualities of the philosophers whose work she discusses. Hegel's work is, she says, "Like a line of poetry that stops and forces us to consider that the way in which it is said is essential to *what* it is saying."[17] In order to experience his work properly, she says, we need to read "for multiple meanings, for plurivocity, ambiguity, and metaphor."[18] Indeed, a central concern of that work is what it means to read Hegel's text: "To know the meaning of [a] sentence is to know the meaning of Hegel's system, and that meaning cannot be known once and for all by any living subject."[19] Furthermore, she writes, "Hegel's sentences send us forth, as it were, into a journey of knowledge; they indicate what is not being expressed, what must be explored for any given expression to acquire meaning."[20] This concern with philosophical writing—by which is meant the way in which *what* is being said is directly connected to *how* it is being said—and indeed with how philosophy ought to be *read* are persistent themes in her work. We see this in her dialogue with Žižek and Laclau, where she notes that her "approach to Hegel draws upon a certain set of literary and rhetorical presumptions about how meaning is generated in his text."[21] It is even more evident in her work on *Antigone,* where her concern is with multiple readings of the same text and with the context of her own reading of Sophocles' play.[22] We also see her interest in the way philosophy is written and read in her ongoing commentary on her own work: in both her self-conscious style and her concern with the reception of her work. All theorists are, of course, to a greater and lesser extent, concerned with the way in which their work is read and received, however, it might be suggested that Butler is *acutely* so, something that is evidenced by the frequent self-referentiality of her writing.[23] This is not meant as a criticism, for it is, as shall be argued later, intimately connected to her concern with contingency, a concern that has a clear political corollary in her work.

In addition to Butler's concern with what has been termed the *literary* qualities of philosophical writing and reading—both that of herself and of others—her work also makes frequent use of literature and other cultural texts. These texts, which range from the work of Emily Dickinson to that of Ice-T, are cited and discussed not just by way of illustration of preexisting claims—though clearly that occurs too—but also as investigations into contemporary political problems.[24] *Antigone* is used to discuss the issue of kinship during a time when, she says, "the family is at once idealized in nostalgic ways within various cultural forms, a time in which the Vatican protests against homosexuality not only as an assault on the family, but also on the notion of the human, where to become human, for some, requires participation in the family in its normative sense."[25] Here the text provides Butler with the opportunity to investigate different notions of kinship, to engage, perhaps, in a kind of dialogue with the work as a means of examining her own thoughts on these issues. Much the same might be said of Butler's readings—in *Bodies That Matter*—of the fiction of Willa Cather and Nella Larsen and of Jennie Livingston's movie *Paris Is Burning*. In Butler's readings, each specific point is perhaps less important than the sum of those points and its impact on the reader. This may explain why Butler—clearly a gifted reader of a multiplicity of texts and styles—sometimes offers us what appear to be, on the surface at least, shockingly pedestrian readings of certain texts. In response to a snake taking on the appearance of the letter "W" in Cather's *My Antonia*, for example, Butler suggests that this might "signify 'woman,' the term most fully dissimulated by Cather's narrator."[26] Similarly, she suggests that a character's name of "Bellew" in Nella Larsen's *Passing* is "like bellow, . . . itself a howl, the long howl of white male anxiety in the face of the racially ambiguous woman whom he idealizes and loathes."[27] These readings are not, however, offered in and of themselves as the "lessons" we should take from the texts, in the manner of Nussbaum, or to shore up an empirically problematic assertion with fictional evidence, as in the case of Eagleton, but rather as part of a broader performance that seeks to impact upon an audience's way of conceiving of certain issues. This "dialectical" approach may be easier to illustrate when it is more successful though, as suggested in chapter 3, the extent to which such "success" is generalizable is highly questionable—dialectical impact is a product of both the text and the reader—nevertheless, there are clearly cases where this impact is more likely than in others. We see such an example in Butler's use of Tennessee Williams's work in the preface to her book on Hegel.

There is, it seems, little intrinsic connection between *A Streetcar Named Desire* and Butler's use of it. Butler merely appropriates the text for her own

rhetorical purposes. The effect of Butler's account of Blanche Dubois's confused attempts to reach Elysian Fields may be, however, to force the reader to
think about or to reconceptualize her notion of desire. "When she [Blanche
Dubois] hears that her present dismal location *is* Elysian Fields, she is sure that
the directions she received were wrong. Her predicament is implicitly philosophical. What kind of journey is desire that its direction is so deceptive?"[28]
Here the conceptualization of desire as a journey rather than perhaps as something innate or an involuntary impulse, rocks the reader back on her conceptual
feet.[29] In this moment of reader instability, Butler may create a space for rethinking an established concept, what Arthur C. Danto called "the transfiguration of the commonplace."[30] The effect is artistic. "When we let ourselves
respond to poetry," writes Jeannette Winterson, "to music, to pictures, we are
clearing a space where new stories can root, in effect we are clearing a space for
new stories about ourselves."[31] It is precisely the sort of effect that Foucault's
discussion of Velasquez's *Las Meninas* creates, or seeks to create, at the beginning of *The Order of Things*.[32] At the outset of a book that purports to be "An
Archaeology of the Human Sciences," Foucault's in-depth discussion of a
painting draws us into his account of his subject matter, paving the way, perhaps, for his "Archaeology of the Human Sciences" to be as compelling and as
deeply subjective as his artistic appreciation. It is an arresting beginning that
may (or may not, of course) force the reader to reconsider how she had conceived of such ostensibly historical projects as Foucault's "Archaeology" in the
past, to put aside her initial objections—even momentarily—and to consider
Foucault's radically new approach. Butler's work shares much with these passages in Foucault. It relies on many such transfiguring moments for its effect:
Butler's work is often not so much an argument as a *performance*, one aimed at
generating a transformative experience for the reader.

BUTLER'S PERFORMATIVITY

The notion of performativity is very strong in Butler's work. It takes many
forms. Most obviously there is a good deal of hyperbole in her claims. In, for
example, her discussion of legal attempts to regulate harm to women, Butler asserts that "*the state produces hate speech*."[33] It is a shocking claim whose "hyperbolic mode"[34] she readily acknowledges. Similarly, she responds to what she
calls the "speculative excess of Plato" by offering her own reading of his work.
"To the extent that I replicate that speculative excess," she says of this reading,
"I apologize, but only half-heartedly, for sometimes a hyperbolic rejoinder is
necessary when a given injury has remained unspoken for too long."[35] The aim
of such hyperbole is, as she says in *Excitable Speech*, "to shed some light on the

problem"[36] she is addressing. It is a creative moment that may open up possibilities for new ways of thinking about old issues. It is also a strategy that is replete with risks, not least of which is that of being taken literally, by friends and foes alike. There are, however, several ways in which Butler seeks to overcome this problem. The first is "baring the device": identifying oneself as the author of one's own claims and alerting the reader to the work's status as if not quite fiction then certainly performance. Butler does this over and over again. In the examples just given, she alerts the reader to the hyperbole of her claims. Similarly, the self-referentiality of her work—which sometimes takes the form of an unbecoming self-defensiveness—also has the same effect. Elsewhere she uses humor—something that is often overlooked by her critics—to undercut her bold claims. She starts a chapter titled "The Lesbian Phallus and the Morphological Imaginary" with the observation that "After such a promising title, I knew I could not possibly offer a satisfying essay; but perhaps the promise of the phallus is always dissatisfying in some way."[37]

In addition, Butler's own style is such that—imitators notwithstanding—her work constantly draws attention to itself as the product of a particular voice addressing particular concerns, even when she is discussing the work of other writers. Indeed, the subjectivity of Butler's readings of other philosophers' work and other writers' texts is similar to Rorty, Nussbaum, and Eagleton, such that the reader often cannot tell whether the views being discussed are those of Butler, the philosopher or author in question, or Butler's account of the views of the philosopher or author in question. Unlike Nussbaum and Eagleton, however, and much more consistently than Rorty, Butler acknowledges that her reading *is* subjective. She, for example, acknowledges, along with Laclau and Žižek, that she "makes use of [Hegel] to inquire into the necessary limits of formalism in any account of sociality,"[38] just as she later acknowledges that she is reading *Antigone* for a particular purpose. "It seemed to me," she writes, "that Antigone might work as a counterfigure to the trend championed by recent feminists to seek the backing and authority of the state to implement feminist policy aims."[39] This acknowledgment of the subjectivity of her own readings of particular texts, along with her unique writing style, her use of hyperbole and humor, and her continual baring of the device are, however, only part of a much larger concern for Butler, one that has a stylistic and political corollary in her work: *contingency*.

BUTLER AND CONTINGENCY

"The unified subject," writes Butler in her book on Hegel, "with its unified philosophical life, has served as a necessary psychological premise and normative ideal in moral philosophies since Plato and Aristotle."[40] Much of Butler's work in that book and since has been concerned with rupturing this notion of a unified subject. Butler is concerned with the ways in which the subject—as an object of theoretical inquiry and political action—is created by, and implicated in, particular social and political structures, and in the ways that what appears natural or prediscursive is actually a product of social and political relations. In *Subjects of Desire*, Butler uses a particular reading of Hegel and his subsequent interlocutors to call into question that notion of a preexisting subject. Similarly, in *Gender Trouble*, she asks the "speculative question of whether feminist politics could do without a 'subject' in the category of women."[41] Her creative approach to the questions she addresses draws on a reading of "drag": the practice of imitating, in parodic form, the social constructions of gender. "*In imitating gender*," she writes, "*drag implicitly reveals the imitative structure of gender itself— as well as its contingency*."[42] Crudely put—summarizing Butler is, given her dense style, rather like trying to summarize a poem—she argues that gender, like the notion of a prior subject, is a construction. She likens it to the sort of performance given by drag artists, all the time noting that there is no "essence" to that which is being performed. "The notion of gender parody," she writes, "does not assume that there is an original which such parodic identities imitate."[43] In *Bodies That Matter*, Butler appears to go even farther. "Thinking the body as constructed," she argues, "demands a rethinking of construction itself."[44] In both cases Butler is calling into question the established categories of social and political life and our attempts to analyze them. She is concerned not just with the dominant societal conceptions of gender, sexuality, and the subject but also with the feminist responses to these categories.[45]

Despite her thoroughness of approach, and her apparent reluctance to replace these problematic categories with more congenial alternatives, Butler is not simply a skeptic. "[T]he childish and stubborn pleasure that the skeptic takes in watching another fall, turns," she writes, "into a profound unhappiness when he is, as it were, *forced to watch himself* fall into endless contradictions."[46] Butler is—as will be argued later—clearly concerned with certain social and political issues, not simply with undercutting others, or—as Nussbaum argues—playing and theatricality for its own sake. Furthermore, it is not clear that Butler believes in the sort of contradictions that skeptics identify: she is more prone to seeing tensions and impasses than the contradictions engendered by hard Reason. Butler's belief in contingency goes "all the way down." It appears to be—if this is not too paradoxical a notion—the underpinning conception of both her literary-philosophical method and her political project. This commitment to "contingency" takes many forms.

In the first instance, like many of those who reject Enlightenment Reason and argumentation, Butler is clearly concerned not to reify her own claims: she wants to maintain their contingency even as she critiques the formulations of others. "At stake," she writes, "is how this 'contingency' is theorized, a difficult matter in any case, for a theory that would account for 'contingency' will doubt-less also always be formulated through and against that contingency. Indeed, can there be a theory of 'contingency' that is not compelled to refuse or cover over that which it seeks to explain?"[47] More succinctly, she notes, that it is the "last word . . . that is most important to forestall."[48] It is this overriding concern with contingency that perhaps explains some of the complexities of her style. In ad-dition to drawing attention to herself as the author of her own work as a means of highlighting the subjectivity and contingency of her positions, and undercut-ting her claims with irony and humor, Butler also seeks to keep everything open with her use of conditionals and qualifiers. Bold claims are often prefaced with "if." "If gender is constructed," she writes, "it is not necessarily constructed by an 'I' or a 'we' who stands before that construction in any spatial or temporal sense of 'before.'"[49] Similarly, such claims are peppered with largely unqualified qual-ifiers such as "in some ways"; "in a sense"; "something like"; and "in many ways."[50] There is a vagueness in her work that is directly connected to her quest for contingency, and that stands in direct contrast to her use of the word "pre-cisely" to indicate a vehemence of belief rather than an actual commitment to a position.[51] Butler's concern with contingency is also evidenced by the ubiqui-tousness of the "re" prefix in her work: she is committed to "rearticulation," "re-signification," "recasting," "reiteration," and "rethinking."[52] Indeed, she constantly reworks her own approach: no two performances are ever the same. *Bodies That Matter* is, she says, "offered . . . in part as a rethinking of some parts of *Gender Trouble*,"[53] and—in an essay entitled "The Question of Social Trans-formation"—she has even sought recently to recontextualize both of these works by connecting them to elements of her biography.[54] Her work, she suggests, is always meant to be open. "[A]ny analysis," she writes, "which pretends to be able to encompass every vector of power runs the risk of a certain epistemological imperialism which consists in the presupposition that any given writer might fully stand for and explain the complexities of power. No author or text can offer such a reflection of the world, and those who claim to offer such pictures be-come suspect by virtue of that very claim."[55] It is for this reason that *Gender Trouble*—a work Butler describes as a "theoretical inquiry"[56]—ends in a ques-tion. It is also the reason her work is so difficult to summarize.

In *The Psychic Life of Power*, Butler prefaces a claim about the U.S. military's regulation of homosexuality with the words "Consider—as a parting shot,"[57] capturing the way in which all of her work is something of a "parting shot," for even as Butler offers the claim, she is moving away from it.[58] To extract some "fixed" position from Butler's work would then be to offer a necessarily blurry snapshot of something always in motion. In this regard, Butler's work on Hegel, in which she argues that his work must be read in a way that recognizes the continual displacement of a final interpretation, is something of a primer for the way in which we are to approach her work: recognizing that each individual claim is part of a whole whose impact upon us, the readers, is less to do with the veracity of each particular point and more to do with the effect of the text on our thought and practice. "By reading Hegel's (and Butler's) prose carefully and painstakingly," writes Sarah Silah about Butler's work on Hegel, "the reader will actually *experience* what the philosophers are describing."[59]

A Literary Philosopher

In his book *Nietzsche: Life as Literature*, Alexander Nehamas argues that Nietzsche looked at the world "as if it were a literary text . . . he arrives at many of his views of the world and the things within it, including his views of human beings, by generalizing to them ideas and principles that apply most intuitively to the literary situation, to the creation and interpretation of literary texts and characters."[60] In his concern with the "most multifarious art of style," his use of hyperbole and litotes, irony, and humor, Nehamas suggests that Nietzsche was a distinctly "literary" philosopher. It is a claim that Butler makes—albeit indirectly—about Hegel, and a claim that can be made about Butler herself. Tracing the genealogy here is not too difficult: Foucault was deeply influenced by Nietzsche, and Butler by Foucault. Like Nietzsche, both Foucault and Butler find a certain intellectual freedom and stimulus in the *written* world of the literary text that motivates their social and political critique. Foucault notes that he belonged "to that generation who, as students, had before their eyes and were limited by a horizon consisting of Marxism, phenomenology, and existentialism. For me the break was first Beckett's *Waiting for Godot*, a breathtaking performance."[61] Butler—who also uses the Godot motif in her discussion of Hegel[62]—is a similarly "literary" thinker, one for whom the dialectical potential of literature and the interpretive freedom offered by certain kinds of literary criticism prove to be a wellspring of creative thought about politics and society. Literature offers her the contingency she seeks both philosophically and, as will be argued later, politically.

Butler engages in a sort of dialogue with literary texts as way of examining her own thoughts, and she uses literary motifs and devices in an attempt to shift her readers' perspective on what appear to be the "established" categories of social life and political analysis. She uses philosophers' texts in a similar way: reading them in a literary fashion for the thoughts and alternative perspectives that they engender rather than for the careful arguments offered therein. Finally, Butler's work is replete with literary references and would-be dialectical moments predicated upon the discussion of various cultural texts: from Aretha Franklin to Wallace Stevens and Mr. Magoo. The sum total of these effects is to place Butler's work in the category of thinkers who have turned to or who use literature and the methods of literary criticism as a source of insight into politics. The question of the *value* of this approach—both as political analysis and, given Butler's prescriptive approach, as political strategy—remains to be answered.

BUTLER AND THE PRACTICAL

"If," writes Butler in her book *Excitable Speech*, "there can be a modernity without foundationalism (and perhaps this is what is meant by the postmodern), then it will be one in which the key terms of its operation are not fully secured in advance, one that assumes a futural form for politics that cannot be fully articulated: and this will be a politics of both hope and anxiety, what Foucault termed a 'politics of discomfort.'"[63] Butler's politics are, she suggests, closely tied to her philosophical commitment to contingency: that which finds its fullest expression in her creative and playful readings of texts, philosophical and literary. In her readings and responses to feminist theory, Butler is concerned with the way in which feminist politics appears to presuppose the very categories that—and here we see the influence of Foucault in her thought—she believes are responsible for or complicit in women's subordination. We see this most clearly perhaps in *Excitable Speech*, where Butler responds to Catharine MacKinnon's attempts to use law to regulate pornography and hate speech.

MacKinnon's use of legal categories—her attempt to classify and prohibit whole areas of speech—is, of course, an anathema to Butler's overriding concern with contingency. Butler's reading of MacKinnon identifies what appears to be a contradiction at the heart of MacKinnon's work. On the one hand, MacKinnon appears to be suggesting, writes Butler, that certain types of speech—in this instance, pornography—are always harmful, that they cannot be anything else. On the other hand, she notes, MacKinnon's work is itself predicated upon the notion that language—in this case, legal language—is malleable and open to multiple uses. The contradiction comes when MacKinnon seeks to recontextualize law and legal language while simultaneously arguing that the language of hate speech is always only harmful.[64] Butler, in contrast, looks to the creative and resistive potential of any possible harm. "[T]he injurious address," writes Butler, "may appear to fix or paralyze the one it hails, but it may also produce an unexpected and enabling response."[65] Butler is not, however, opposed to this sort of regulation simply because of the linguistic or philosophical contradiction at the heart of MacKinnon's work: there is a definite political corollary to Butler's philosophical concern with contingency. Butler argues, for example, that state regulation of speech

[c]omes to represent one of the greatest threats to the discursive operation of lesbian and gay politics. Central to such politics are a number
of "speech acts" that can be, and have been, construed as offensive
and indeed injurious conduct: *graphic self-representation*, as in Map-
plethorpe's photography; *explicit self-declaration*, such as that which
takes place in the practice of coming out; and *explicit sexual education*,
as in AIDS education.[66]

Despite Nussbaum's claim that Butler is not concerned with practical politics,
she here shows herself to be concerned with the potential impact of legal regulation upon an oppressed minority. Furthermore, she also makes clear that she
is "not opposed to any and all regulations,"[67] but is simply concerned to show
that political action that is insufficiently self-reflexive may end up generating
unintentional—and potentially harmful—consequences. The corollary to her
philosophical position here is clear: given her belief in the power and unpredictability of language, the impact of such regulation cannot be foreclosed and
may continue to resonate in harmful and unintended ways; furthermore, what
might appear harmful may ultimately be empowering. Butler is concerned to
show that what might be considered beneficial from one perspective can also
prove harmful, and vice versa. Much the same can be said for her apparent hostility to extending marriage rights to homosexual couples or to allowing gays to
serve in the military.

"The naturalization of the military-marriage goal for gay politics," writes
Butler, "also marginalizes those for whom one or other of these institutions is an
anathema, if not inimical."[68] Although she suggests that allowing gays to serve in
the military and to enjoy the legal rights of marriage might further marginalize
certain groups, Butler may not ultimately be *against* either of these goals: she is
simply concerned to keep such discussions open. This is perhaps the aim of her
account of kinship in her book on *Antigone*. The discussion of alternative famil-
ial formulations in that work may be a way of calling the gay marriage rights
movement into question, pointing out that there are many other potential groups
around which society might organize, such as the Gay Men's Health Clinic in
New York.[69] In this way, Butler does indeed appear to be engaged with the practical matters of social and political life, but in a way that is outside the legal-
political battles of feminists such MacKinnon and Nussbaum. Certainly Butler
seems to see her work as having practical implications. As she says of her book
Gender Trouble, "The writing of this denaturalization was not done simply out of
a desire to play with language or prescribe theatrical politics in the place of 'real'
politics, as some critics have conjectured (as if theatre and politics are always distinct). It was done from a desire to live, to make life possible, and to rethink the
possible as such."[70] Her methods and concerns might not be those of traditional

feminism or political theory, but this is what was meant at the outset when it was suggested that Butler might be a public intellectual for only a subsection of the public: those excluded by the dominant social and political perspectives on matters such as sexuality and gender. The creativity of Butler's thought—her application of literary critical analysis to philosophy as well as to the categories of social existence—opens up these apparently closed categories, showing us their contingency and exclusionary nature. Nevertheless, to those who suggest that such an approach is akin to nihilism, or largely impractical, Butler responds by asking whether "'use' [is] the standard by which to judge theory's value to politics?"[71] It is a masterful rhetorical flourish that—in true Socratic fashion—forces the question back onto the questioner. Butler is not denying that her work has useful practical implications, but she is denying that this should be the standard by which her work is judged.

The use-value of theory is, of course, something of an empirical matter: in order to assess its impact, we need to look and see how it is being used in practical politics. In lieu of undertaking the—perhaps impossible—task of assessing the multifarious ways in which a theory—let alone a theoretical approach as complex as Butler's—plays itself out in social practice, we can, nevertheless, look and see how Butler's work plays out theoretically. We can do so by examining the concept of the political in her work and by assessing the value of her critique of other theoretical formulations, in particular her critique of liberalism.

BUTLER AND THE POLITICAL

"It is true," wrote Michel Foucault in response to criticism of his book *Discipline and Punish*, "that certain people such as those who work in the institutional setting of the prison . . . are not likely to find advice or instructions in my books to tell them 'what is to be done.' But my project is precisely to bring it about that they 'no longer know what to do,' so that the acts, gestures, discourses that up until then had seemed to go without saying become problematic, difficult, dangerous."[72] Like Butler, Foucault appears not to be concerned with setting out a program for others to follow; rather, he is more concerned with "rethinking" what we already know, or what we think we know. Like Butler, Foucault brought a certain literary sensibility to the study of fields that had previously not encouraged such a creative approach: brushing off criticism of the accuracy of his work in favor of a concern with its effect.[73] Foucault's influence, as Butler's work shows, cannot be denied: the creativity of his approach to social and political questions has opened up numerous new avenues of thought. Butler has similarly sought to do the same, seeking out her own individual voice—separate from that of Foucault—with her unique style and set of concerns. It is in this that we see the creativity of the literary turn: the power of Bloom's "Strong Poet" to reconceptualize existing institutions and categories as a means of beginning to rethink those aspects of our social and political life that we might seek to change.

Butler's political action is therefore intimately connected to the power of redescription, performance, and the malleability of language. "If we are formed in language," writes Butler with a typically conditional qualification, "then that formative power precedes and conditions any decision we might make about it, insulting us from the start, as it were, by its prior power."[74] Her response to the suggestion that we might be formed in language is—like that of Richard Rorty—to offer alternative accounts of oppressive social and political categories in a new and more complex language that seeks to disrupt the apparent fixedness of the current categories. It is for this reason that the "re-" prefix is so prevalent in her work and why she is interested in the performative and parodic aspects of drag. By redescribing and rearticulating, Butler hopes to open up previously closed categories and to highlight the many alternative possibilities: opening up new political horizons. "It is," she writes, "what opens the signifier to new meanings and new possibilities for political resignification. It is this open-ended and performative function of the signifier that seems to be crucial to a radical democratic notion of futurity."[75] Here the notion of resignification is directly connected to a set of political values, which she terms "a radical democratic notion of futurity." Her work is political, she seems to be suggesting, in both the way in which it shows into sharp relief the interests and assumptions behind prevailing norms while simultaneously refusing to prescribe what Marx called "recipes for the cookshops of the future." This is made explicit in her preface to *Gender Trouble*, where she says that "the aim of the text was to open up the field of possibility for gender without dictating which kinds of possibilities ought to be realized."[76] Here her method of resignification is directly connected to her concern with "radical democracy": so radical a democratic is Butler that she does not wish to impose her own categories on social and political life. The result is, however, a potentially empty conception of politics that is manifested in sometimes shallow or problematic critiques of other political traditions.

Butler is, it seems, well aware of what she refers to as "the limits of resignification as a strategy of opposition."[77] The criticism here is not meant to repeat Laclau's criticism of her work: that she sees redescription as a sort of political cure-all.[78] Indeed, elsewhere she suggests that such resignification should be tied to "rallying mass numbers in favor of a cause."[79] Nevertheless, it is the end of this resignification that seems problematic. Butler's criticism of other political traditions is predicated upon a conception she labels "radical democracy," but she nowhere sets out or defends it. Of course, the notion of radical democracy is such that one cannot—as befits her ongoing concern with contingency—set it out: it is for others to decide what it should be and how it should work. Nevertheless, it is clear that Butler uses this conception as something of a benchmark against which to judge other political formulations and find them wanting. In discussing the work of Rawls and Habermas, for example, work that relies on a notion of procedural abstraction, Butler notes that "Although the procedural method purports to make no substantive claims about what human beings are, it does implicitly call upon a certain rational capacity, and attributes to that rational capacity an inherent relation to universalizability."[80] It is a method she seeks to recontextualize through a discussion of the Hegelian critique of Kant's formalism, "mainly because Hegel called into question whether such formalisms are ever really as formal as they appear to be."[81] Her method, she suggests, allows us to see that "Universality in its abstract form thus requires cutting the person off from qualities which he or she may well share with others, but which do not rise to the level of abstraction required for the term 'universality.'"[82] "Abstraction," she continues, "is thus contaminated by the concretion from which it seeks to differentiate itself."[83]

Foucault, it was once said, talked about power as if it were a surprise. The comment captures the sense in which his work appears to be a grand "unveiling" of previously hidden power relations. Much the same might be said of Butler's criticism of Rawlsian and Habermasian universality. It would certainly be no surprise to these thinkers to learn that abstraction involved divorcing human beings from certain qualities that they may hold in common: it is implicit in the notion of "abstraction." Furthermore, we do not need a complex reading of Hegel to see this, nor indeed do we need to abandon traditional modes of philosophy. Michael Sandel identified the exclusionary nature of the liberal subject and the problems that it generated for liberal political thought in *Liberalism and the Limits of Justice*, and there has been a fruitful subsequent debate.[84] Liberal abstraction attempts to find commonality—albeit in the thinnest form—between competing visions of the good. Finding commonality is clearly a concern of Butler's too. "Indeed, it seems to me," she writes, that one of the tasks of the present Left is precisely to see what basis of commonality there might be among existing movements, but to find such a basis without recourse to transcendental claims."[85] Here she seems to have commonality with the later Rawls, who denies that his political liberalism is transcendental; nevertheless, Butler would reject Rawls's account because it involves abstraction: "And whereas this can appear as the necessary and founding violence of any truth-regime, it is important to resist the theoretical gesture of pathos in which exclusions are simply affirmed as sad necessities of signification."[86] Butler, it seems, wants some thicker notion of commonality, based upon a non-abstraction: this is, perhaps, the aim of her project of "hegemony." Nevertheless, she also asserts that her notion of "hegemony" stands in some relationship to liberalism. "My understanding of hegemony," she writes, "is that its normative and optimistic moment consists precisely in the possibilities for expanding the democratic possibilities for the key terms of liberalism, rendering them more inclusive, more dynamic, and more concrete."[87] It is simply not clear, however, that Butler's theoretical approach renders her capable of deciding when a term is *more* inclusive, *more* dynamic, or *more* concrete. At times, her conception of politics appears to be remarkably empty. Her comments about not accepting signification as the necessary violence for the founding of any regime suggest a vision of a world where everything is open, a world of boundless possibilities: in short, the *written* world. There are numerous problems with using this world as the basis of a political critique.

Politics and the *Written* World

In the *written* world, it might be noted, the scarcity of resources and power and the clash of values that marks, and generates politics are completely absent. This is not to suggest, of course, that novels cannot *depict* politics but simply that tensions between characters can always be resolved and scarcity always overcome—the unexpected large inheritance is only a few keystrokes away—in the *written* world, in a way that they cannot always be in the *unwritten* one. In Butler's concern with futurity, and in delaying (or, more accurately perhaps, *foregoing*) comment upon what radical democracy might look like, she is illustrating the extent to which her conception of the world and politics is deeply influenced by the literary: sequels can always be written, the deceased can always return, new hopes can emerge. Sherlock Holmes can always return from Reichenbach Falls. Everything remains open because it is yet to be written—no avenues are foreclosed—or it can be reinterpreted in new ways. In the *unwritten* world, however, people cannot always wait for relief from the issues that they turn to politics to address. In her world of openness and contingency, Butler appears untroubled by such issues. She is thus free to use this future, "radical" (and thus we are to presume "better," suggesting that the *moral and political* question is alive and well in Butler's thought) democracy to judge the current formulations and find them wanting. Furthermore, untroubled by the actualities of the *unwritten* world, Butler does not have to evaluate whether a given signification—such as that which leads some feminists to use the courts for relief—is more or less effective than simply accepting hurtful speech or pornography: any attempt is likely to be less effective than an Ideal whose articulation we must always postpone.

Butler appears to be holding up the formulations of the *unwritten* world to the standards of the *written* world as a form of political critique. Holding up such a mirror is a common trope in political theory as well as literature: we see it in Plato's *Republic* and Thomas More's *Utopia*, as well as in political or satirical literature such as *Gulliver's Travels*. This is the creative possibility of the literary turn for political thought, and we see how Butler uses it to throw existing institutions and categories into sharp relief. This is, however, only the beginning of political work, not political work in itself. Such an approach is considerably less useful for engaging with specific political problems in the *unwritten* world, because the freedom and the contingency of the world of fiction simply do not travel. Indeed, as Polybius noted in his account of Plato's *Republic*, using this fictional standard as the one against which to judge existing formulations seems deeply problematic:

> [T]he notion of bringing [the Ideal City] into comparison with the constitutions of Sparta, Rome, and Carthage would be like putting up a statue to compare with living and breathing men. Even if such a statue were faultless in point of art, the comparison of the lifeless with the living would naturally leave an impression of imperfection and incongruity upon the minds of the spectators.[88]

The object of Plato's exercise may be, however, simply to force his reader to think critically about justice, showing us a method for doing so in the process; certainly the difference between two fictional examples in *The Republic*—the Ring of Gyges and the allegory of the Cave—suggests that, as will be argued in chapter 7, Plato is more than aware of this problem. Butler implies that her work is in a similarly Socratic vein when she suggests that all of her claims are contingent and open to resignification. Nevertheless, it is clear that Butler is holding up current formulations to an idealized conception of "radical democracy" that she never sets out nor defends: suggesting the ways in which the *written* world often seems to replace the metaphysical world in the work of the literary turn. If Plato's work is performative in that it seeks to impact upon the reader in a particular way—to force her to reconsider her conceptions of justice—not to critique existing structures against an idealized standard,[89] then Butler's work is performative in that it uses literary techniques to force the reader to rethink her notions of society's established categories. In addition, however, Butler's work also brings with it a standard against which she judges other formulations: the *written* world is not used just for the dialectical moment but rather as a standard against which to judge the politics of the *unwritten* world. The performativity here is a substitute for a justification that political reasoning demands: to make a political argument we need to know the standard against which formulations are being said to be better or worse. Rorty uses cruelty as a standard, something that may merely postpone rather than resolve

such problems. Nevertheless, his identification of a standard at least provides
the possibility for an evaluation of competing accounts and visions of the political. In her refusal to state her position—a refusal that emerges from her concern with radical democracy—Butler appears to render her critique potentially
vacuous. This is particularly evident in *Bodies That Matter*, where she attempts
to justify certain claims with claims such as "for feminist reasons";[90] "for democratic reasons";[91] and, most vexingly, "for politically significant reasons."[92]
Without any account of what these "reasons" might be, or even what is meant
by the words "democratic," "feminist," or "politically significant," it is simply
impossible to know whether Butler's political criticisms and formulations
deserve serious consideration.

CONCLUSIONS

In her essay "Can the 'Other' of Philosophy Speak?"—a sort of Butlerian version of Rorty's "Trotsky and the Wild Orchids"—Butler describes her experience of lecturing on feminist philosophy at Yale:

> I noticed a few rather disturbed figures at the back of the hall, adults
> pacing back and forth, listening to what I had to say and then abruptly
> leaving, only to return again after a week or two to repeat the same
> disturbed ritual. . . . They turned out to be political theorists who were
> enraged that what I was teaching took place under the rubric of phi-
> losophy. They couldn't quite come in and take a seat, but neither could
> they leave. They needed to know what I was saying, but they couldn't
> allow themselves to get close enough to hear. It was not a question of
> whether I was teaching bad philosophy, or not teaching philosophy
> well, but whether my classes were philosophy at all.[93]

It is an apt description of the reaction that her work provokes in many. Sitting
still long enough to consider her claims, however, reveals that it is more the
question of the *type* of philosophy or *type* of political reasoning that Butler is
utilizing, along with the *type* of politics such reasoning is likely to engender,
that is at stake in her work.

On the one hand, Butler's work has proven to be useful to many, opening
up all kinds of new avenues for thinking about previously fixed categories such
as gender, class, and race. It is useful for generating uncertainty in the reader: a
sense of contingency and the potential recognition of the partiality of the
reader's own position that both Nussbaum and Rorty also seek. It is in this
space perhaps that uncertainty is created and the potential for political thought

occurs. On the other hand, Butler seems to be something of a "tease": she promises rather more than she can deliver, something that is perhaps not surprising given the self-acknowledged "hyperbolic mode" of some of her claims. Indeed, at times her work simply reinvents the wheel, often less effectively—as in the case of her critique of the abstraction of liberalism—or simply obfuscates what is already clear. There is, for example, very little difference between Butler's response to MacKinnon's anti-pornography legislation and Mill's defense of free speech in *On Liberty*. When it is not shrouded in the complex language that she employs as a political strategy, Butler's political critique can sometimes also seem surprisingly banal: her discussion of the difference between anti-Semitism and criticism of Israel in her book *Precarious Life: The Powers of Mourning and Violence* is a particular case in point.[94] Such apparent banality may, however, be a product of her method, something that is in itself both the strength and weakness of this performative aspect of the literary turn.

Butler's work relies for its effect largely upon *dialectic*. As such, it can leave the reader deeply moved, forcing him or her into a rigorous scrutiny of everything he or she believes in and lives by, or simply cold, either because the reader already takes what the dialectic seeks to reveal as a given, or because the dialectical impact that the author intends simply does not occur, relying as it does upon the proper alignment of the author, the text, and the reader. It is perhaps this overreliance on dialectic that accounts for some of the shrillness of the political debate engendered by the literary turn in political thought. As will be discussed in greater detail in the final chapter, dialectic is revelatory—it is, in effect, seeing the world through new eyes, being born again perhaps—thus it generates claims that seem simply "self-evident" to those affected by the dialectic, and simply false or even crazy to those who are not. In this perhaps it is likely to generate debates from incommensurable positions, as some of the debate surrounding Butler's work itself testifies. As a result, what seeks to remain open and ongoing may simply generate entrenchment and defensiveness. At the same time, such an approach may indeed generate new ways of seeing that render such previously incommensurable debates obsolete or transformed. What might be needed is a way to capture both the creativity of dialectic with some of the rigor of philosophy and social science, and it is to sketching an outline of what this might look like with regard to the *moral and political* and the *methodological* questions that we will now turn.

Part 3

The Future of the Literary Turn?

Chapter 6

How to Read a Novel in a Democracy
Literature and Public Ethics

> There was a certain innocence with which we read those books; we read
> them apart from our own history and expectations, like Alice running after
> the White Rabbit and jumping into the hole. This innocence paid off: I do
> not think that without it we could have understood our own inarticulateness.
> —Azar Nafisi, *Reading Lolita in Tehran: A Memoir in Books*[1]

The frequency with which the claim that reading is somehow "good for us" is
made by both professionals and amateurs alike—as much by liberal theorists
intent on enhancing democratic practice as by exasperated parents who hope
that their children will turn off the television and pick up a book—suggests that
its *prima facie* appeal remains strong. In the language of philosophy, the suggestion seems to correspond to some of our deepest intuitions about literature
and democracy. As we have seen, however, the attempts to theorize or operationalize this claim on behalf of liberal democracy—what is here being referred
to as the *moral and political* claim—run into two key problems: one methodological, the other political.

In the first instance, the suggestion that particular books will have definite
and predictable impacts upon their readers is an impossible one to maintain.
Both Nussbaum and Rorty seem to be guilty of what Jonathan Rose has called
the "Receptive Fallacy": attempting to describe the response of readers by talking about the text rather than the readers.[2] Furthermore, that both Nussbaum
and Rorty feel the need to champion their own readings of the texts that they
recommend—rather than simply assigning the texts and sitting back to watch
as liberal democracy flourishes—suggests that they too have less than complete
faith in this aspect of their claims. The methodological problems implicit in

this aspect of their enterprise—the fallacious suggestion that reading about reading will inevitably produce the effects that these theorists desire—play themselves out in the political problems also implicit in their approach. By telling their would-be readers what lessons they should derive from the texts that they read, thereby seeking to shape—consciously or unconsciously—these readers' reactions, both Nussbaum and Rorty seem to be guilty of a distinctly illiberal form of manipulation, one that treats these reader-citizens as *means* and not *ends*. Persuasion and argument are, to be sure, perfectly legitimate forms of engagement in liberal democracy, but as we have seen, Nussbaum and Rorty seem to be relying more on the authority of their status as cultural critics and literary intellectuals to support their readings—readings that are often presented as more or less self-evident—than they do upon marshalling reasons or arguments for their position. As such, their claim that such reading will enhance the practice of liberal democracy seems to be somewhat undermined by the disingenuousness of their approach.

Nevertheless, the appeal of the suggestion that literature can change who we are as people, potentially forcing us to think differently about the world and the way that we live and generating moral feelings toward others, remains a strong one. Reversing Immanuel Kant's well-known dictum that what may be true in theory might not be so in practice, it seems that the *moral and political* claim about literature might indeed be true in practice but not in theory. Understanding that practice theoretically may, however, allow us to utilize literature more effectively to enhance liberal democracy by identifying the real origin of whatever moral and political improvement we do see arising from reading. Indeed, examining the work of all of the thinkers in this study—not just those explicitly concerned with the *moral and political* question—suggests that there is a conceptual problem at the heart of this work. It is one that arises from the failure to recognize that any moral and political improvement that we see arising from the sort of literary encounters described by these theorists is more likely to come from the *discussions about* literature rather than from the literature itself.

SOLIPSISM AND LITERATURE

The suggestion that literature can lead us to pay attention to people to whom we had previously not attended is a plausible one. Indeed, just as we have probably all had the experience of reading a book that forces us to think differently about the world and the way that we live, we have probably all had the experience of a text that sparks some hitherto unknown interest in us, be it about fourteenth-century architecture or the plight of the twenty-first-century poor. Nussbaum and Rorty both seem to suggest, however, that this experience is, in and of itself, enough to generate some kind of compassion or concern with cruelty being perpetrated on others. As we saw in chapter 2, however, the "empathetic torturer" argument suggests otherwise: understanding a person's deepest needs and aspirations might well be the best weapon a sadistically minded individual could use against her. This is not to say that literature can *never* generate compassion or concern in its readers, simply that there is no guarantee that it will *always* do so. As such, Nussbaum's and Rorty's claims are overstated.

Much the same can be said about the suggestion that literature can change who we are as people. Obviously many of us have had the experience of reading a text that has affected us in significant ways, even to the point of feeling that we are no longer the same person after having read it. Nevertheless, it has been argued that this is a somewhat delicate and unpredictable experience, one that depends on the text, the reader, the reader's needs and life experience, and, indeed, the way in which she reads a particular text. The last point is particularly important in determining the likelihood that a book is going to have the transfiguring or dialectical effect described by Rorty. Reading a book with the specific intent of having it change one's life is unlikely to produce the desired effect: dialectic cannot be forced. Similarly, reading it with the express intent of expanding one's moral imagination—or because one has been told that the book will expand one's moral imagination—is equally unlikely to produce the desired effect. There is, furthermore, the methodological problem involved in trying to identify the origin or source of a dialectical impact after the fact. If reading does indeed change who we are as people, then trying to identify the ways in which a book affected us involves a paradox. The person identifying the origin of the change is—in some sense, at least—no longer the same person who was changed; as such, she is effectively trying to identify which aspects of an experience were most important to somebody else. Thus it is not clear whether her claims about the importance of the *text* to this transfiguration are entirely trustworthy. For all of these reasons, the claims that are currently made on behalf of the *moral and political* power of literature are simply too strong to be plausible.

It seems a key problem here is that these theorists are relying on literature to lift individuals out of their own solipsistic worlds and to pay attention to others. Reading is itself, however, a largely solipsistic act. The work of Nussbaum and Rorty, and indeed that of Eagleton and Butler too, suggests that there is a distinct tendency—among even the most sophisticated of readers—to perpetuate this solipsism by seeing in a text only that which they wish to see and ignoring that which contradicts their worldview. For all of their claims about the dialectical power of literature, none of these thinkers provides an account of a text that has fundamentally shaken his or her perspective on the world. The frequency, furthermore, with which these readers read texts in light of their own needs and concerns—be it conscious or unconscious—suggests that turning to literature as a way out of solipsism is itself something of a mistake. Indeed, it may be that using literary characters as stand-ins for real people actually cultivates an inability to listen to the voices of real people, because such readers already "know" about them from their reading. Martha Nussbaum's Mary Dalton-esque discussion of the paucity of African Americans in her law classes is not the only example. Valentine Cunningham notes that another proponent of literature and "Othering," Gayatri Chakravorty Spivak, "can't ever avoid thinking about herself in these thoughts about Others. And her namings of Third World women usually involve the loud naming of herself."[3] There is a tendency for such thinkers to treat real people as fictional characters about whom one speaks rather than listens, and no matter how skilled these readers are as interpreters, liberalism seems to demand that we also pay attention to what people *say* about their situations.

All of this is not to say, however, that the posited connection between literature and liberal democracy is nonexistent—far from it. Rather, it simply suggests that we should perhaps come at the problem from the opposite direction. Instead of trying to find some way in which literature generates an alternative perspective—such as that of the "judicious spectator"—we should recognize that when readers write and talk about literature they are, in some sense at least, talking about themselves and their own reactions, and rather than seeking to find some methodology that will *emancipate* them from this perspective, they should *embrace* it. Literature alone will not lift readers out of solipsism but conversations about literature might. Literature, on this alternative account, would offer a way out of the potential political solipsism of liberalism by offering citizens an opportunity to talk about their fears, concerns, hopes, and desires. They would be able to do so, furthermore, at a level of potential abstraction that arises from being seen to talk about literary events and characters rather than directly about themselves. It is a model in which literature can serve as the ostensible subject matter of a conversation about politics. It is also one that has a clear historical pedigree, empirical support from recent work on reading groups, and a connection to some of the more plausible aspects of the most recent attempts to theorize the relationship between literature and liberal democracy.

SPEAKING OF BOOKS

In *The Structural Transformation of the Public Sphere*, Jürgen Habermas argues that in the seventeenth and eighteenth centuries, public discussion of literary works was a crucial factor in the development of bourgeois civil society. Reading and discussing books in literary salons, he writes, "provided a training ground for a critical public reflection still preoccupied with itself—a process of self-clarification of private people focusing on the genuine experiences of their novel privateness."[4] Habermas's argument is, of course, predicated upon his broader theory of communicative action, that which suggests that the end point of human interaction is some notion of "understanding." One does not, however, have to buy into this argument in its entirety in order to make the claim that is being made here: that literary *discussion* rather than literature per se is the more likely origin of any moral and political improvement that we see arising from the approach outlined by Nussbaum and Rorty. Replacing Habermas's "agreement" model of discussion with a weaker "recognition" standard, one that suggests that there is potential benefit to be derived from the *process* of discussion—that which arises from finding a fellow reader or a fellow enthusiast of a particular genre or author or novel, the sort of thing that Richard Rorty calls "solidarity"—might allow us to see the ways in which such literary discussion can potentially enhance the practice of liberal democracy, without necessarily producing the clear agreements that Habermas's theory seems to require. Indeed, recent work on the increasingly popular phenomenon of book clubs and other reading groups suggests that there is at least some anecdotal evidence to support these claims.

In her best-selling work, *Reading Lolita in Tehran*, Azar Nafisi—a professor of literature at Johns Hopkins University—describes a reading group she conducted in Iran with a diverse group of Muslim women. She notes the ways in which the books that the group read "led us finally to question and prod our own realities, about which we felt so hopelessly speechless," provoking a shared sense of community—one that was by no means without tension and controversy—around a set of shared questions.[5] That Nafisi had this experience under a totalitarian regime suggests that democracy—where such discussion is actually encouraged rather than repressed—might be even more successful in generating such critical and constructive dialogue. Indeed, discussing the now-defunct Great Books course at Stanford University in the late 1980s, John Seery asserts that a course whose aim was "simply to read and try to make sense of" the Western canon, "somehow created a community of readers, of questioners, of Socratic seekers. Students drew together in this common project and discovered that it was enjoyable to think together. These texts . . . fostered reading communities." Seery declares, furthermore, that "these little classes were the closet thing I have seen to successful liberal communities in practice—little educational utopias."[6] Nor, it seems, do such reading groups have to be conducted by college professors in order to generate such community-building effects. As anybody with any experience of reading groups can attest, the discussion in such meetings is seldom, if ever, confined to the text at hand. Elizabeth Long notes that "reading groups often form because of a subtext of shared values, and the text itself is often a pretext (though an invaluable one) for the conversation through which members engage not only with the 'authorial' other but with each other as well."[7] Similarly, although her reading project was famously dismissed as "the carpet bombing of the American mind" by the late Alfred Kazin,[8] Oprah Winfrey's "Oprah's Book Club" provides compelling evidence of literature's ability to generate moral and political discussion that is of potential benefit to the practice of liberal democracy, even among those without the apparent subtext of shared values identified by Long.[9] Indeed, Cecilia Konchar Farr makes a compelling case for connecting Winfrey's Book Club to a long tradition of women's book clubs, noting the ways in which the discussion of the book is often a pretext for discussing personal values and moral and political issues that might not normally be raised in a public forum.[10]

This suggestion—that literature might generate moral and political values that will enhance the practice of liberal democracy by serving as the ostensible subject matter for an ongoing dialogue between citizens—is also connected to the previous work in this area. Although both Nussbaum and Rorty seem to suggest that text alone will do the work that is required of it in liberal democracy, both identify dialogic elements in their approach. Richard Rorty conceives of liberalism as an ongoing, ungroundable conversation into which he seeks to draw various different groups through storytelling. Similarly, Martha Nussbaum—borrowing from Wayne Booth—offers a theory of critical literary discussion that she calls "coduction." The aim of this process on Nussbaum's account is to come to a "proper understanding" of the text—which, as we have seen, essentially means that which corresponds to her own reading—so that we might use this understanding to inform liberal practitioners about the situated agents behind the labels inevitably imposed by liberal reasoning (the sort of labels to which Butler also raises significant objections in her work). Like Habermas, however, Nussbaum's approach seems to be predicated upon the assumption that such discussion needs to reach some kind of agreement, in this instance, upon the "proper" reading of a text. In this it seems to work against the element of contingency that she and others wish to transplant from literature to politics, simply seeming to replace one rigid category with another. In the model that is being sketched here, such agreement is unnecessary, for often—but obviously not *always*—the very discussion can itself be useful.

"CONTEXTUALIZED ABSTRACTION"

Literature, it is being suggested, might be thought to enhance the practice of liberal democracy—or at least have the potential to do so—by providing the ostensible subject matter for public discussions about moral and political issues. Such a theory draws on the dual notions that public discussion of literature provides a way for a citizenry to discuss politics in a manner that actually facilitates rather than truncates discussion, and that such discussion is indeed beneficial to the practice of liberal democracy. The potential benefits of this model of literature in liberal-democratic politics are twofold.

In the first instance, by talking about literary characters and events, individuals might be able to reap the benefits of *abstraction*. Although their concerns may be personal, participants in the discussion might be able to talk about such concerns in a way that detaches them somewhat from their innermost selves. The double mechanism here might be to allow them to talk about issues they would not normally bring to a public forum—because they would be seen to be dealing with fictional rather than actual examples—and secondly to talk about these matters in a way that allows for a more considered approach to such matters than might emerge if they were seen to be talking *directly* about themselves. This account of literature in politics offers some middle ground between complete embeddedness and total abstraction, for the second potential benefit of this approach is, somewhat paradoxically perhaps, given that the first is abstraction, *context*.

Traditionally, liberal theories of politics and society have relied upon thought experiments such as John Locke's "State of Nature" or John Rawls's "Original Position" to generate critical discussion on matters political. The problem with such Lockean or Rawlsian models is that in addition to generating often unhelpful and misleading debates about the ontological status of such devices, they also promote a sort of "how would you think about this issue if you were somebody else?" approach to politics. It is precisely this that draws the ire of communitarian and feminist critics of liberalism. Such models, they argue, do not fully capture the complexities of a situated agent's existence. It is precisely for this reason that Nussbaum and others have turned to literature to augment such models. "Contextualized abstraction" as a model of literature in liberal-democratic politics may go some way toward opening up the possibility of a dialogue between readers informed by a perspective that is both *removed* from the participants and informed by their interpretations of the literary context.

Contextualized abstraction offers the two values—contingency and solidarity—for which both Rorty and Nussbaum turn to literature in the first place. In it, literature functions as the ostensible subject matter in an ongoing, potentially transfiguring dialogue about politics in which the contingency arises from the recognition that differently situated people may interpret the same text in different ways. Recognizing that another's reading may emerge from a different life experience might well be a step toward reaching some kind of recognition as another's status as "fellow human being," "fellow citizen," or even "fellow reader," something that might serve to temper potentially hostile and potentially incommensurable debates by breaking down the moral distance between persons that makes cruelty—of all kinds—possible. This would certainly seem to be the implication of David Miller's work on deliberative democracy, where he notes that in modeling political dialogue, those people allowed a few minutes of conversation with their fellow game participants are more likely to be generous in their allocation of resources than those who are not. "Broadly speaking," writes Miller, "discussion has the effect of turning a collection of separate individuals into a group who see one another as co-operators."[11] It is this "fellow feeling" that Adam Smith believed was essential to the proper functioning of liberal-democratic societies, and that which Nussbaum and Rorty (in the guise of "solidarity") also seek to derive from literature. In this instance, however, it is the *discussion of* literature that is at the root of the potential improvement, not the texts in and of themselves.

In order, however, to avoid the suspicion that this theory is simply a re-hashing of Mill's discussion of the value of discourse in *On Liberty* or the rather trite and banal suggestion that "it's good to talk," it is perhaps necessary to say something about what literature per se might bring to such a discussion. Not unconnected to this aspect of the claim, it is also necessary to say something about the theory of reading that underpins the approach, not least because many of the previous accounts seemed to rest upon implausible claims about the impacts of texts upon their readers.

WHY LITERATURE?

In her discussion of the role of literature in liberal democracy, Martha Nussbaum prevaricates about whether there may be other media that can have the same effect. Initially she suggests that film and music are simply too "dreamlike" to have the effects that she desires, but eventually she expands her list of potentially useful media to include movies such as *Schindler's List*.[12] For Richard Rorty, on the other hand, literature is but one of many possible sources of moral improvement: his list includes comic books, documentaries, movies, television shows, and plays. As far as the theory of contextualized abstraction is concerned, it may be that Rorty is right to suggest that there are multiple possible forms of media that can generate the desired outcome, not least because it is the conversation rather than the media that is doing most of the work in this theory. It may well be, however, that literature has certain qualities that make it *particularly* useful for these purposes, not least among which is the effort that is required from reading that does not always emerge from, say, songs or movies.

Reading is often a much more conscious and deliberate act than listening to a song or watching a movie, and as such it may be more conducive to the sort of self-reflection that this process of reading and discussion requires. Indeed, it will further be suggested that literature may offer readers the opportunity to move between worlds—*written* and *unwritten*—as a source of insight into the political, itself a recreation of a much older trope in political thought. Nevertheless, as this study has hopefully shown, the *way* in which we read such texts is a crucial part of the success of any such project aimed at enhancing the practice of liberal democracy through literature. The very ubiquitousness of what Rorty calls "methodological reading" in both literary-political criticism and political-literary criticism—that which simply beats the text into a shape that serves the critic's purpose or corresponds to her ideological preconceptions— suggests that, as it currently stands, this theory of contextualized abstraction is overly optimistic. For this reason, this account of literature in liberal-democratic politics demands a theory of reading, one that identifies a way to overcome the methodological reading that is the antithesis of this approach.

How to Read a Novel in a Democracy

Writing at the turn of the fifth century A.D., St. Augustine of Hippo, a figure profoundly concerned with the relationship between the text and the world, expressed concern that human beings were being "hurled into an abyss of their own theories."[13] The explosion of "Theory" as a subfield in literature departments in the late twentieth century suggests that Augustine's fear had come true, especially when people such as Terry Eagleton refused to connect Theory to any specific literary or cultural artifacts, arguing that it was a source of insight in and of itself, separate from any text or event. Amidst all of this Theory and the inevitable quest for the "next big idea," the idea of reading as an *art*—something to be practiced and cultivated—seemed to be lost. Indeed, Jean-Michel Rabaté—himself not immune to the allure of Theory—suggested that it had become something of a "power tool" for critics to attack texts and the world beyond it. Such an approach, he suggested, killed the creativity of reading. "Boredom," he wrote, "was massively institutionalized in American universities when Theory gave birth to endless copycat readings killing any sense of the 'new' in texts; quite often, this hardnosed insistence of fundamental issues . . . was totally blind to the singularity of a text."[14] Reading had become methodological, and the hope for transfiguring dialectic of the sort identified by Rorty seemed all but lost. Critics—for reasons that will be discussed in the next chapter—often simply read into texts that which they wanted to see, and used it as evidence for their position. In these circumstances, literature, to borrow from Marx, became another arena in which men, women, and the transgendered became conscious of their conflicts and fought them out. Political debates were often simply repeated at the level of literature, and with the texts refusing to adjudicate between competing positions in the way that many of these theorists thought that they should, the debates often proved incommensurable, shrill, and destructive.

In these circumstances, perhaps, it may seem somewhat naïve or misguided to try to revive a role for literature in moral and political debate. With the dominant trend in the Academy seemingly toward methodological reading and shrill political discussion, literature seems to have lost its capacity for transfiguration and with it any hope of enhancing liberal-democratic practice. Nevertheless, in addition to the sort of headline-grabbing conflicts that make up the stuff of academic folklore and fiction, there is a large corpus of perfectly civil interactions that constitutes the main body of critical literary discussion but does not draw as much attention as a good literary feud. Furthermore, there is clearly a difference between the way professional literary critics and what we might call "lay" readers approach, read, and talk about texts.

In his novel *Flaubert's Parrot*, Julian Barnes's fictional Geoffrey Braithwaite asserts: "I can't prove that lay readers enjoy books more than professional critics, but I can tell you one advantage that we have over them. We can forget." Professional critics, he continues, "are cursed with memory: the books they write about can never fade from their brains. They become family. Perhaps this is why some critics develop a faintly patronizing tone towards their subjects."[15] Although itself obviously not evidence of the veracity of this claim, Barnes's fictional example nevertheless captures an apparent difference between the way in which lay and professional readers approach the same texts. As work on literary book clubs has suggested, lay readers are less likely to construct the text and its author and more likely to personalize their readings, replacing the sort of objective voice—"the text says," the novel claims," and so forth—that, as we have seen, is endemic to much professional literary criticism—with a more subjective voice: "I think," or "It seems to me."[16] Having less invested in them—personally and professionally—lay readers might be more capable of using literary texts constructively in the sort of practical political discussion being outlined here. They are less likely to be practitioners of methodological reading, something that must be avoided if a transformative conversation about politics through literature is to occur. As Richard Rorty notes, "You cannot . . . find inspirational value in a text at the same time you are viewing it as a product of a mechanism of cultural production."[17] Nevertheless, the theory of contextualized abstraction relies upon the assumption that such readers will still read themselves into the text in important ways while simultaneously maintaining a certain humility before it. It may well be that this is indeed the position of most lay readers—both knowing and unknowing—but it may also be that literary critics have an essential role to play in cultivating this perspective among their students.

In *Reading After Theory*, a book in which he seeks to defend the study of literature from the study or practice of politics, Valentine Cunningham notes that a certain amount of theory is necessary to any kind of reading. "Reading," he writes, "always comes after theory. We all, as readers, trail behind theory, theory of some kind or another."[18] In so doing he identifies the sort of "stage-setting" information that Ludwig Wittgenstein regards as being essential to philosophy. For this reason, Cunningham finds the story of Augustine's conversion in his *Confessions* deeply problematic. For Cunningham it seems to promulgate what he calls the Western myth of the "Open Book and the Free Individual." Cunningham is not opposed to this idea of literary transfiguration, nor indeed to Theory per se, but simply to the suggestion that the text alone will do the work that is required of it, with no input or effort on the part of the reader. This notion that the reader has a significant role to play in her own experience was, however, something of which Augustine himself was acutely aware. In his own texts he was deeply concerned to draw the reader through a transformative process that brought the reader closer to God. "Let the reader," he wrote, "where we are equally confident stride on with me; where we are equally puzzled, pause to investigate with me; where he find me erring, call me to his side. So we may keep to the path, in love, as we fare on toward Him 'whose face is ever to be sought.'"[19] For Augustine, reading was a process of *lectio divina*, a way of listening to the text, as historically of course reading was literally listening for most people in this period. This process involved reading, meditating on what was read, and listening for the voice of God. Cunningham offers us a secular parallel when he suggests that although we are indeed guided by theory in our reading, we should also seek to listen to what we read by "letting literary texts speak in their own voice."[20] The question remains, of course, about how one might seek to achieve this goal. It may be that Vladimir Nabokov, a writer who (despite his best efforts to the contrary) has found himself at the center of many of the recent discussions about literature and politics, has something to offer us in this regard.

As a professor of literature at Cornell in the 1950s, Nabokov was known for setting examination questions such as "List the contents of Anna's handbag," or "Describe the wallpaper in the Kareninas' bedroom." Although few students were ever able to identify such details—Nabokov is said to have awarded bonus marks to the student who suggested that the wallpaper pattern might be "little trains"[21]—they were, nevertheless, forced to pay close attention to the details of the text and, in Nabokov's words, to "enter the world of the novel." While there are many who would dismiss Nabokov's attention to detail as fetishistic fastidiousness, his approach to literary criticism may provide a model for an approach to literature that will enhance the practice of liberal democracy while remaining consistent with its principles. In asking his students to pick out such details, Nabokov was in effect asking them to break out of whatever "methodological reading" habits they had developed and to see the world of the novel as an alternate reality:

> Nothing is more boring or more unfair to the author than starting to read, say *Madame Bovary*, with the preconceived notion that it is a denunciation of the bourgeoisie. We should always remember that the work of art is invariably the creation of a new world, so that the first thing we should do is to study that new world as closely as possible, approaching it as something brand new having no obvious connection with the worlds we already know. When this new world has been closely studied, then and only then let us examine its links with other worlds, other branches of knowledge.[22]

Although Nabokov himself appeared to be something of a tyrant when it came to textual reading—the assuredness of his readings makes even Martha Nussbaum's readings look like fumbling, apologetic assertions—his approach suggests a way in which literature might be read so as to capture its transformative potential for individuals to think about the texts for themselves, as a precursor to entering into dialogue with others. It is a two-stage process. Positing the text—the *written* world—as another world to be explored independently of the world in which we live—the *unwritten* world—seeks to break the reader of her "methodological" habits. Then, and only then, putting that world in dialogue— or "reflective equilibrium"—with the *unwritten* world creates the possibility of a dialectical space for critical reflection, one that is informed both by literature's transformative potential and by the reader's own experience of the *written* and the *unwritten* worlds. This is perhaps what Nussbaum means to suggest when, in her book on liberal-democratic education, she cites Seneca's assertion: "Let there be a space between you and the book."[23]

This approach to literary interpretation is one in which the reader learns to listen for the voice of the text—something that may also help her listen to non-literary persons in the unwritten world—by paying attention to the details of the text before bringing her own life experience of theory to bear upon it. Such a theory does not rely, however, on some metaphysical notion of intrinsic textual meaning, or a belief in impartial observation; it simply suggests that readers can seek to overcome their own tendencies to impose meaning onto texts by reading a text in a particular way, one that is somewhat akin to the listening identified by Augustine. In order for this approach to have an impact upon the reader, the "voice of the text" does not actually have to exist; it can simply serve as an ideal toward which the reader aspires, a destination that it is never reached in a potentially transfiguring journey, the sort of thing Walt Whitman suggests about his ideal America in "Democratic Vistas." Such an approach requires what novelist and critic Jeanette Winterson memorably called "the paradox of active surrender" to the text.[24] It is, however, an approach that is likely to draw the—possibly misplaced—ire of many contemporary political literary critics, in that it seems to advocate for a return to what they consider a deeply problematic "aesthetic" approach to literature.

The Politics of
Contextualized Abstraction

In making the claim that in order to enhance the practice of liberal democracy through reading it might be necessary to return to an older "aesthetic" tradition of literary criticism, one immediately runs the risk of appearing to be a social or political conservative, possibly gaining unlikely supporters and alienating those with whom one might be expected to have a political affinity. Given the ways in which the political reading of literature often seems to prop up what might be considered worthy positions with bad arguments—a problem that will be discussed in much greater detail in the next chapter—it would not be surprising that making such a claim would generate the shrill responses and high-pitched exchanges of opinion with which literary studies have become synonymous in recent years. As John Seery's account of his experience as an instructor in the Great Books program at Stanford in the 1980s suggests—a program that was derailed by what he argues were deeply problematic claims about "dead white male hegemony"—there is often no necessary correspondence between the social or political worth of a particular position and the validity of the arguments used to support it.

What this brief digression is meant to suggest is that the argument for a return to a particular way of reading does not itself correspond to any particular political position beyond that suggested by a desire to enhance the practice of liberal democracy. It is not a suggestion that politically motivated literary critics should abandon their quest for social justice nor stop doing so through the medium of literature, even though—as the next chapter makes clear—there are significant methodological problems with such approaches that makes them ill suited for the rigorous self-critique that a tough-minded political thought and action probably requires. This is, rather, simply a suggestion about reading in a *specific* context for a *specific* purpose. If we do indeed seek to enhance the practice of liberal democracy through the reading and discussion of literature, then the best way to operationalize this claim is to promote a particular way of reading: a pedagogy of indirection that encourages Winterson's "paradox of active surrender" to a literary text by leading readers to see it as another world, separate from but nevertheless related to the world in which they live, work, and read. Furthermore, it may be that such an approach is itself not only not inconsistent with such self-consciously ethico-political readings, but it may actually serve to enhance them.

Regarding the *written* world of literature as—initially at least—separate from the *unwritten* world in which it is written, instead of a simple manifestation of the latter's politics, tensions and problems may serve to enhance the sort of political-literary criticism of Eagleton and others by offering the possibility of genuine critical reflection, as opposed to simple methodological reading. Coming to the text with a preconceived notion of its content, one is—for reasons that will be discussed in more detail in the next chapter—unlikely to find little else in it. Coming to it as another world to be explored and then contrasted with our own is perhaps more likely to be a fecund source of critical insight, not least because so doing offers the possibility of what Sheldon Wolin calls the "Theoretical Journey" between worlds that has been a hallmark of political theory since the very beginning.[25]

The idea of journey and return as a source of insight is a prevalent theme in political thought—from Homer's Odysseus, to Plato's cave dweller, to Thomas More's Raphael Hythloday, to Wolin's Tocqueville—and is itself implicit in the Greek noun *theoros*—the origin of the modern word "theory"—which has the connotation of both spectator and ambassador sent to another city to report on activities.[26] Philip Roth is a writer who has made much of this distinction between *written* and *unwritten* worlds and the critical perspective the journey between them seeks to engender in the reader. Indeed, his playfulness about the distinction is itself part of this method. As, for example, we hold in our hands texts called *I Married a Communist* and *The Human Stain*, texts written by Philip Roth, and read about other texts of the same name *within* these texts that are not the texts that we are reading, we should perhaps be reminded that artifacts in the *written* world—though similar in many respects— are not the same as artifacts in the *unwritten* world, and that as such we should be suspicious of treating them as such. The temptation to do so, and then the reminder that we should not, creates perhaps that space of discomfort in which thinking occurs, and it is in this moment of uncertainty that is generated by this distinction that the possibility of transfiguration and dialectic occurs. It is a moment that is unlikely to occur in the sort of methodological reading that marks much political-literary discussion but one that is by no means incompatible with it.[27] Seeing the world of the text as an alternative reality to our own offers the possibility of a genuine reflective equilibrium, one in which the "lessons of the text" and the background theory that underpins these lessons are *both* subject to critical consideration.

CONCLUSIONS

"Schools and universities," wrote Italo Calvino, "ought to help us understand that no book that talks *about* a book says more than the book in question."[28] If we are indeed to capture the transformative power of literature for the purposes of generating values conducive to the practice of liberal democracy, then we would do well to remember Calvino's advice. Theories of literature in democratic politics that rely on the theorist's reading of the text to tell us how to react are literally preposterous in that the end comes before the beginning. If we are to use literature to enhance democratic practice, then we need to find an approach that generates contingency and solidarity out of the multiplicity of possible textual readings, one in which the reader-citizen is ultimately treated as an *end* and not a *means*. To achieve this contextualized abstraction as a theory of literature in liberal politics suggests, we may need a pedagogy of indirection, one that teaches us to read first and to think and talk about politics second. The paradox here may well be that reading and literature can indeed enhance democratic practice, but only when it does not *directly* seek to do so. As the next chapter suggests, once it seeks to do this directly, political-literary criticism seems to run into a number of methodological problems that render its claims highly suspicious.

Chapter 7

Beyond the Dolorous Haze
Literature in Political Thought and Analysis

> Then it shows great folly . . . to suppose that one can transmit knowledge of
> an art through the medium of writing, or that written words can do more
> than remind the reader of what he already knows on a given subject.
> —Plato, *Phaedrus*[1]

In *Contingency, Irony, and Solidarity*, Richard Rorty argues that there is a
"numinous haze" that surrounds "writers who are not associated with any particular discipline, and are therefore not expected to play by any antecedently
known rules." It is a haze that, he suggests, means they are "let off a lot of bad
questions."[2] One of the broad aims of this work has been to cut through that
haze by asking a number of these "bad questions," examining carefully the veracity of the claims made on behalf of these approaches and the validity of the
philosophical arguments underpinning them. Having addressed the *epistemological and ontological* question at the outset and made some suggestions about
how we might resolve some of the more problematic issues raised by it (and
done the same for the *moral and political* question in the previous chapter), what
follows is an attempt to offer a number of suggestions about how we might
resolve some of the difficulties posed by the *methodological* question.

So far it has been suggested that the *privileged observer* and the *portability*
claims have been undermined by two key problems: the failure to establish an
account of the relationship between the *written* and *unwritten* worlds that permits the critic to use evidence from the former to support claims about the
latter, and the confusion over the relative strengths of the standards of justification that pertain in the study of these worlds. The analysis has, however, been
largely predicated upon a discussion of the work of Terry Eagleton, a Marxist

literary critic. A standard response from those whose political-literary readings are challenged in this way is to suggest that there are indeed problems with certain approaches to literary texts, but that there is something about their own method—be it poststructuralist, feminist, liberal, or queer—which secures the veracity of their insights in a way that distinguishes it from rival approaches. For Eagleton, it is his understanding of Marxist theory; for Martha Nussbaum, the self-evidence of her own interpretations; and for the New Historicists, their sensitivity to historical issues. It will, therefore, be useful to give an account of another approach diametrically opposed to Eagleton's—the "classical perspective"—whose readings suffer from similar methodological concerns. While the Marxist and the classical perspectives constitute only a very small sample of the textual approaches subsumed under the label "Literary Theory," their very opposition makes this a useful comparison. That their readings suffer from similar confusions suggests that these problems may be endemic to political-literary analysis, as it is currently formulated, regardless of its underpinning methodological assumptions or ideological perspective. Having established this claim, the chapter will conclude by identifying a number of ways in which some of these confusions might nevertheless be mitigated or overcome in a more tough-minded approach to the literary in political thought and analysis.

The Classical Perspective

Drawing on the work of Leo Strauss, the classical perspective is a long-standing and an influential approach to literature within the American Political Science Association. In a 2001 article in the Association's premier journal, the *American Political Science Review*, concerning the political insights offered by Robert Penn Warren's *All the King's Men*—the last time, as of writing, the journal published a political interpretation of a literary work—Joseph H. Lane Jr. summarized the outlook of the classical perspective thusly: "The classical political thinkers insisted that some people could free themselves from the prejudices of the political society around them and write self-consciously about both its good and bad features."[3] The argument holds that some people—simply as a consequence of who they are—have an inherent privileged observer status, and that, furthermore, their insights are as valid as those of social science. It is an argument that seems to correspond to some of our unexamined intuitions about great writers such as Shakespeare or Tolstoy: authoritative literary giants from whom a well-placed quotation can seemingly end any kind of dispute. It is also an approach that stands in direct contrast to the materialism of Eagleton and the New Historicists. Whereas historicism starts, according to literary critic Paul A. Cantor, "with a somewhat vaguely, but comprehensively defined historical moment, and uses that to explain a whole series of phenomena, including cultural or political forms," the classical perspective "begins from the fact of a consciously chosen form of government and uses that to explain the form that a host of related phenomena in the community take, including the fine arts."[4] It is an approach that stresses the power of human agency, not social forces, in the construction of the human world.

Using this classical perspective, Joseph Lane makes a number of claims about Robert Penn Warren's *All the King's Men*. He suggests that "it is not a very hopeful novel,"[5] and he asserts that "Warren reveals what appears to be a necessary connection between passionate oratory, political Machiavellianism, and a concern for the common good that may be endemic to certain types of democracies."[6] Indeed, much of Lane's article is turned over to showing how the American system of government tends to promote political nihilism among society's "more thoughtful members."[7] That such views correspond to the rather pessimistic Straussian perspective on democracy suggests that Lane might simply be reading into the text that which he already believes to be the case: what—following Socrates' identification of this tendency in Plato's dialogue of the same name—we might call the *Phaedrus* problem. As Richard Posner would surely point out, however, such a claim could be an example of the "genetic fallacy": it is perfectly possible that Lane and Penn Warren hold similar views on the problems of democracy, and that this is a case of coincidence, not causality.[8] Once again, however, the onus seems to be on Lane, not the critic, to explain why this is not simply an example of methodological reading, not least because the classical perspective itself seems to be particularly susceptible to charges of methodological circularity.

CIRCULARITY AND THE CLASSICAL PERSPECTIVE

The classical perspective is predicated upon the suggestion that literary texts—the *written* world—can give us insight into the world in which we readers live, work, and engage in politics—the *unwritten* world. Lane, for example, argues that *All the King's Men* shows us that democracies are rife with corruption, and that "this corruption has an especially corrosive effect on society's most thoughtful members, who are apt to see in the realities of modern, materialist, democratic politics the sources of nihilism."[9] The *depiction* of this state of affairs within the *written* world of the novel, the argument seems to go, tells us that such a state of affairs exists in the *unwritten* world. Methodologically, this is obviously a somewhat problematic assertion, for while it is always possible that what Lane says about contemporary democratic politics in the American context is true, we simply cannot conclude this on the basis of an account of

Robert Penn Warren's work. It is an empirical claim about the *unwritten* world, not a literary claim about the *written* one. It is a claim that has to be established independently of the simple depiction of such a state of affairs by an author. Indeed, the lower standards of justification required for analysis of the *written* world, along with the ability of a Rorty, an Eagleton, or, indeed, a Lane, to make the text speak with his own voice, means that we should be suspicious of claims about what the *written* world "shows" us about the *unwritten* world, not least because—as is argued later—there are at least two senses of the word "show" that are often confused in the political analysis of literary texts. The classical perspective holds that the veracity of such insights is nevertheless secured by the "special genius" of the author.

The classical perspective holds that certain individuals are capable of unique insight into the political. It is nevertheless a theory that appears to mistake its own assumptions for evidence. On the classical perspective, one might believe that a writer, *W*, is the sort of person—a "special genius"—who is capable of rising above her age and reflecting upon her epoch. Reading *W*'s fictional work—her creation of a *written* world—one might deduce what one believes to be her insights, *I*, into the politics of the *unwritten* world in which she writes. The problem here, of course, is that *W*'s status as a special genius is simply asserted, and yet this is the basis for the claim that her insights, *I*, are to be valued. For this argument to avoid circularity, there needs to be some way of verifying—beyond the simple assertion of it—that *W* is indeed a special genius. To know this, we need to know that her insights (*I*) in the *written* world of the text are valid in the *unwritten* world. We need some independent verification of the value of *I* before we can say that *W* is a special genius. Even if we *did* have some such verification of *W*'s special genius, it is, however, still not clear that we have enough evidence to take *all* of *W*'s insights at face value: one might, for example, think that T. S. Eliot captures something valuable about the conditions of modernity, but we might still balk at the anti-Semitic aspects of his work. Even if a writer could be shown to be a special genius, we would still need some way to distinguish between an author's valid and invalid insights.

In the piece by Lane there is no attempt to explain why Robert Penn Warren is such a special genius, nor perhaps could there be. It is not clear what such an explanation would look like. The special genius status is secured by the author's insights, and the author's insights by his status as a special genius. In the face of such circularity, it seems that the special genius status is simply assumed. This assumption nevertheless forms the basis of the claim that Penn Warren has something unique to tell us about the political. In the absence of some such discussion to the contrary, it is hard not to conclude that Lane regards Penn Warren as a special genius because his insight, *I*, corresponds to something that Lane already believes to be true about American politics: that *I* validates and is validated by Lane's own preexisting beliefs. In effect, Penn Warren achieves his status as special genius because he appears to agree with Lane's view of American politics. It is a conclusion that is potentially flattering to both parties. It is a conclusion that is also doubly susceptible to the *Phaedrus* problem in that both it and the method by which it is reached are underpinned by the critic's own reading of the text.

In its apparent circularity and methodological confusions, the classical perspective seems then to be no different from many of the other approaches that we have seen to the political analysis of literary texts. Indeed, such work often seems to be part of an attempt by politically motivated readers of literature to marshal the works of—preferably dead—authors behind their own political perspective in order to enhance the position in the eyes of others. It may be that such political work on literature has less to do with analysis than with advocacy, and with the invocation of authority. For reasons that probably have much to do with the valorization of authors in our culture, "showing" that a Shakespeare, a Tolstoy, or a Morrison held a particular political view becomes, somewhat surprisingly, an argument in its favor. It is a deeply flawed rhetorical device that should never be allowed to gain much leverage in political thought and analysis. It is perhaps a measure of the conceptual problems at the heart of the classical perspective that Paul Cantor uses such a claim to justify his method. "Virtually everyone who has thought about the issue," he writes, "including Plato and Aristotle, would acknowledge that people are influenced by their historical circumstances, but only historicism argues that those circumstances fully determine what the authors think."[10] In the manner of an Eagleton or a Rorty, Cantor simply caricatures the position of his opponents and offers his own as an alternative, clearly ignoring the nuances of the Marxist position underpinning historicism.[11] His approach is perhaps an illustration of the distinction between the lower standards of justification demanded by the *reading* of a literary critic and those demanded by the *argument* of a social scientist or philosopher.

It may be, however, that such advocacy disguised as analysis is less deliberate than this account suggests, and that there is a more charitable account of this confusion, for the haze that surrounds political work on literature may obscure a number of important conceptual distinctions, even to the advocates of the approach, which may lead them to make genuine methodological errors rather than deliberate political gambits. Foremost among these confusions is, perhaps, that between two different senses of the verb "to show."

DISPLAYING AND PROVING: TWO SENSES OF "TO SHOW"

The verb "to show" has many meanings in the English language, and each clearly depends on the context in which it is used: we might think about the difference between "to show" in an art gallery and "to show" in a horse race. In much of the work we have seen on literature and politics, there appear, however, to be two key senses of the verb "to show" that seem to be commonly and crucially confused. In the first instance we might think of the sense of the verb that implies "to display." In this, what we might call the *weaker* sense of the verb, as it is used in the work on politics and literature, we should think of the way in which a realtor or car dealer might "show" us other options, thereby raising a possibility or a potential. The effect here is perhaps to lead us to reconsider or reconfirm our first choice: if not necessarily to abandon it, then at least to think about it in a new way. Such a device is, of course, a recurrent one in political thought—from the Ideal City in Plato's *Republic* to John Rawls's "Original Position"—where the creation of an alternative perspective can be used to generate critical leverage on various phenomena, including our political community or our conception of justice. This sense of the verb offers—as a source of insight—the same potential movement between worlds that was discussed in the previous chapter.

The second, *stronger* sense of the verb "to show" implies "to demonstrate" or "to prove." This does not necessarily imply some sort of logically valid argument, or a truth claim based upon a representationalist epistemology, but simply a claim that is valid within the prevailing standards of justification for a particular analytical approach. It could mean a math proof, the sort of evidence we utilize in science, or even the sort of evidence we utilize in the courtroom, where the prevailing standard of justification is usually "beyond a reasonable doubt." All of the thinkers in this study use both of these senses of the verb "to show" in their work, but it may well be that—as far as claims predicated upon literary readings alone are concerned—only the weaker sense is legitimate in social science and political thought.

When Rorty argues that literature "shows" us the kinds of cruelty of which we ourselves are capable, he is using the *weaker* sense of the verb. Literature, he is suggesting, holds up a mirror—albeit of the distorted funhouse variety—to our innermost selves and potentially forces us to think differently about our capacity for cruelty. Much the same might be said for Nussbaum's claims about what literature "shows" us about ourselves and Butler's attempts to use literature to transfigure our conceptions of gender or sexuality. It also may be the sort of thing that Joseph Lane has in mind when he argues that Robert Penn Warren "shows us the crisis of our age by revealing its specific features in our nation and our political culture."[12] In this instance, he is suggesting that Warren holds up a mirror to our society, perhaps making us see things in a way that we had never seen them before. For somebody like Eagleton, however, who largely rejects the notion of a transfiguring text—he is the most "knowing" of readers—such a claim is, of course, a fiction. He is much more of a believer in the rather more problematic argument that literature can "show" us something about the *unwritten* world in the stronger sense of the word.

Eagleton believes that his reading of the *written* world shows us something—in the sense of evidentiary proof—about the political and social formations in the *unwritten* world in which such literature was created. Similarly, when Martha Nussbaum moves from suggesting that literature alerts us to something about ourselves to her claim that she can compensate for the dearth of black students in her classes by "reading and imagining," the confidence with which she assumes that such data allow her to prescribe for African Americans suggests that she too moves away from the weaker sense of the verb "show" to the stronger. It is a shift that we also see in the work emerging from the classical perspective, such as when Joseph Lane moves away from the weaker sense of the word to the claim that *All the King's Men* "shows" us that political corruption has a corrosive effect on society's "most thoughtful members." Simply because Penn Warren chooses to depict such events in the *written* world does not make such a claim valid in the *unwritten* one. In both of these instances, the thinkers seem to have conflated two senses of the verb "to show," mistaking the weak for the strong claim. As with the strong and weak theses about language set out in chapter 1, almost all of these thinkers identify the weaker sense of "show" as being relevant, but then act as though the stronger sense is operative.

CONFLATING WORLDS, CONFLATING MEANINGS

As the examples of Emma Bovary and Don Quixote suggest, in the *written* world, the confusion or conflation of the world of the text and the world in which such texts are written often has disastrous consequences for literary characters. As the argument being made here has suggested however, that the conflation of the *written* and *unwritten* worlds was a problem for such literary figures, does not mean, of course, that it will always be a problem for those of us engaged in political thought and analysis in the *unwritten* world. Such a claim is merely a hypothesis, one that has to be proven by the standards appropriate to the *unwritten* world. As such, we might say that Philip Roth's homily about a father calling out a warning to his winter-sports-pursuing son is also merely *suggestive* of the possible consequences of such a confusion:

"Oh watch it sonny!"—the father calls after him—"you're skating on thin ice!" Whereupon the rebellious and adventurous son in hot pursuit of the desirable exotic calls back, "Oh, you dope, Daddy, that's only an expression," already, you see, a major in English. "It's only an expression"—even as the ice begins to groan and give beneath his eighty-odd pounds.[13]

Roth's homily raises the possibility that we too might be skating on methodological thin ice if we fail to recognize that the *written* and *unwritten* worlds are worlds of different consequences and different justifications, and that conflating or confusing them might have equally disastrous consequences for us. To see whether this is actually the case in the *unwritten* world requires a careful study, one employing the standards of justification appropriate to that world: the sort of thing that has, for better or for worse, been attempted here.

The most obvious potential consequence of conflating the two different senses of the word "show," and the two different sets of standards of justification appropriate to analysis of the *written* and *unwritten* worlds, is that we permit arguments justified by the weaker standard of justification—arguments about the *written* world—to gain undue critical purchase and political leverage in the *unwritten* world. Simply because a text "shows" us something about the *unwritten* world in the weaker sense of the term does not, obviously, mean that it "shows" us about the *unwritten* world in the stronger sense of the word. Nevertheless, amidst the confusion identified by Rorty, this distinction often seems to be lost, not least because of the *Phaedrus* problem in which correspondence is mistaken for evidence. It is a problem that is possibly exacerbated by the self-selecting nature of the audiences for political readings. Political literary critics and literary-minded political theorists often use such examples to illustrate claims with which the audience for their work can be expected to have broad sympathy: few social conservatives are, for example, going to bother to take the time to read carefully through the densely layered, politically radical works of Judith Butler, just as few radicals are likely to agree with Richard Rorty's reading of Nabokov. As such, the audience for their work is likely to find her literary approach particularly resonant, possibly mistaking the experience of "I hadn't thought of the problem quite like that before," for "That's how it is," mistaking *dialectic* for *revelation* (a distinction about which more will be said in the final chapter). Alternatively, they might make what appears to be the classical perspective mistake of believing that just because an author appears to agree with their worldview, that such an agreement between author and reader is some kind of evidence for the plausibility of their initial belief. In the final chapter, it will also be suggested that such confusions—though seemingly innocuous—have potentially serious *political* consequences. For now, the focus is on the implications of this potential confusion for literary-inspired political analysis: something about which Plato —identifier of the *Phaedrus* problem—may have much to tell us.

GYGES AND THE CAVE:
PLATO ON TWO KINDS OF LITERARY EXAMPLE

Despite Socrates' apparent prevarication over the proper role of the poets in his Ideal City, Plato's *Republic* is a text that is itself replete with poetic imagery and literary examples: the Ship, the Sun, the Line, the Myth of Er, and indeed the Ideal City itself. However, in two other literary examples—the Ring of Gyges and the allegory of the Cave—Plato may tell us most about the proper role of literature in political thought and analysis. The story of Gyges is told by Glaucon in Book II in order to support his claim that people are only just because they fear the consequences of not being so. Removing the consequences, he suggests, removes the justness. Glaucon recounts the noticeably poetic tale of Gyges, who finds a ring that makes him invisible. If there were two such rings, says Glaucon—weaving yet more fictionality into his example—and they were given to two different men, one just and one unjust, then the two men would both act unjustly because the fear of sanction had been removed. "And yet someone could say," concludes Glaucon, "that this is a great proof that no one is willingly just but only when compelled to be so."[14] Warming to his theme, and indeed his fictional method, Glaucon then goes on to describe two men, one just, one unjust, who appear to be the opposite, suggesting that the unjust man who merely *appears* to be just will be happier than his just but apparently unjust counterpart.[15]

In making this argument, Glaucon—who is, of course, a *written* world recreation of Plato's *unwritten* world brother—employs a then-well-known fictional example, the story of Gyges and his ring, to "show" that justice is simply the consequence of a fear of sanction. He then offers another fictional example—this time of his own construction—to "show" that the unjust man who appears just is better off than his opposite. It might be noted, of course, that Glaucon—who has agreed to make the counterargument against Socrates, even though he does not believe the position he is defending is the correct one, thereby engaging in an even greater degree of fictionality—also hedges his claims about the status of the Ring of Gyges example with the caveat "someone could say," all of which suggests perhaps that Plato the author is aware of the problems of using fiction as evidence for claims about the nonfictional world. It is a suggestion that seems to be confirmed by Socrates' response to Glaucon's two stories. "[M]y dear Glaucon," he notes, "how vigorously you polish up each of the two men—just like a statue—for their judgement."[16] Placing this comment in the mouth of Socrates suggests that Plato is aware of the problematic nature of this kind of claim: that just because a state of affairs is depicted in a particular way in fiction does not make it so in fact. It is perhaps a comment that should make us think differently about Socrates' own use of fictional examples, most obviously his "city in speech," and about whether Plato thinks that such examples can show us something about the political in the stronger sense of the term set out earlier. The allegory of the Cave suggests that he is more comfortable with the weaker sense of the verb.

The allegory of the Cave is a fictional tale told by Socrates. His aim in telling it is perhaps somewhat different from that of Glaucon, whose example is meant to show us something in the sense of being empirical proof for a claim.

Having told the tale of the Cave—of the man who goes up to the light and then returns to tell his fellow Cave dwellers what he has seen—Socrates remarks that if such a man "were intelligent," he would undoubtedly be changed by his experience. Faced with one who seemed confused, such a man would not dismiss the confused man with laughter, but rather ask himself whether this confusion emerged from a greater ignorance or a greater brilliance: he would consider the confused man's perspective, not simply dismiss it.[17] In this sense, the literary example "shows" us something in the sense of depicting an alternative. It also "shows" us—the weaker sense—the effect that such a depiction can have on the soul of an individual: it can make him or her more open to alternative perspectives, in precisely the same way that is suggested by both Nussbaum and Rorty. In modernity, post- or otherwise, some of us might balk at using the word "soul," replacing it, perhaps, with "attitude" or "worldview"; nevertheless, Plato shows us—in the weaker sense of the term—that literary examples *can* have such an effect. That Socrates' comments are not here followed by the sort of caveat that followed Glaucon's use of fictional examples illustrates perhaps that Plato considers such a use much less problematic than in Glaucon's case.

That it is *Plato* who shows us this is, of course, no greater evidence for its validity than if we had just come to it on our own, or merely read it on a fortune cookie: to suggest otherwise would be to fall into some of the fallacies of the classical perspective. It nevertheless shows us that—as the classical perspective indeed suggests—great writers can raise interesting possibilities. Furthermore, it may be that Plato offers us a useful distinction between the problematic use of literature as empirical evidence—the Gyges example—and the more acceptable account of literature as a source of dialectic—the Cave example—one that we ourselves can employ when we use literary examples in political thought and analysis.

METHODOLOGICAL SUGGESTIONS

It has been argued here that the haze of interdisciplinarity that surrounds the current attempts to use literature in political thought and social science permits all kinds of problematic claims. Most obviously, there is the issue of claims about the *unwritten* world being justified by the standards of justification appropriate to the *written* world. In the confusion that emerges from the possibly deliberate attempt to blur this distinction, claims about what literature can "show" us—in the sense of depicting or displaying—become claims about what literature can "show" us in the sense of proving or providing evidence. As was stated at the outset, however, the aim of this analysis has not been to *dismiss* the suggestion that literature can be of value to political thought and analysis but to *place* it. Whereas politically minded literary critics have often sought to embrace political concerns and issues with more enthusiasm than analytical rigor, it is here being suggested that political theorists, philosophers, and social scientists should approach literary texts with considerably more caution. The study outlined here suggests a number of recommendations:

First, we should keep in mind the—albeit by no means clear-cut—distinction between the *written* and *unwritten* worlds. If we seek to use evidence from the *written* world of fiction to support claims about the *unwritten* world, then we must provide a clear and compelling, and above all plausible, account of the way in which we conceive of the relationship between the two worlds. Furthermore, we must explain why and how this relationship allows us to use evidence from one to support claims about the other. It may be, however, that the problems involved in offering such an account will indicate that—for the most part, at least—we simply cannot use literature to "show" us anything about the *unwritten* world in the stronger sense of the term outlined earlier.

The caveat "for the most part" is included here because it may be that we could do empirical work that suggested that, for example, images of social class were more prevalent in nineteenth-century literature than in similar literature of the twentieth century. Such an analysis would simply be using literary texts as an artifact of the *unwritten* world, and as such, it should be driven by the standards of justification appropriate to it. It is the sort of work we see in Jonathan Rose's study, *The Intellectual Life of the British Working Classes*. Rose offers an analysis of the reading habits of British working classes and seeks to find ways in which these people actually used such texts in their political lives: his work does not simply rely upon alleged depictions of class politics in the *written* world to tell us how such texts were used, but rather upon an empirical analysis of the lives of the readers themselves. It is the difference between asserting that workers used literary texts to make sense of the world because a literary character does so in the *written* world of a novel, and showing that workers did so by providing evidence of their reading habits and public speeches in the *unwritten* world. It is work in which the depictions of class politics in literature become part of his analysis, but in which Rose maintains the important conceptual distinctions that are absent from much of the work that we have seen discussed in this study. He does so most notably by employing the standards of justification appropriate to his analysis of each world.[18]

The second methodological suggestion we should take from the preceding analysis is that we should always bear in mind Plato's distinction between the literary examples of Gyges and the Cave. We should recognize that although political and philosophical claims can often be made more clearly and more effectively by employing literary examples to illustrate our claims, we should not mistake the *illustration of* the claim—as Glaucon does with the Ring of Gyges example—for *evidence for* the claim. Nevertheless, we also should recognize that simply because literature cannot—for the most part—show us anything about the politics of the *unwritten* world in the stronger sense of the term does not mean that it cannot show us anything in the weaker sense of the term.

That literature can and does show us the contingency of our knowledge—though obviously not *necessarily* so, as this effect relies crucially on the way in which it is read—or can lead us to think about the *unwritten* world in new ways simply cannot be denied. We should, however, see this simply as the *beginning* not the *end* of the process of political analysis. That literature can show us something—in the weaker sense—about how crime might be the product of poverty or that terrorism might be bred out of a particular type of education might mean that we should adjust our empirical study of the *unwritten* world in ways that might help us test these theories as hypotheses. In this, literature, like Plato's allegory of the Cave, may show us how little we truly know, cultivating an attitude—or a state of the soul—of humility toward the world that is appropriate to social science and political theorizing. It is by showing us how contingent our knowledge actually is that the *written* world of literature can lead us to make better arguments and stronger empirical claims in the *unwritten* world. In this, of course, literature can itself surmount the *Phaedrus* problem in an interesting and unexpected way: if we read it with appropriate humility, accepting its limitations as a source of information about the *unwritten* world, then it can serve as a philosophical reminder of the imperfection of our knowledge rather than merely as a prop to overly bold claims.

It might legitimately be asked, however, how the claims being made here differ from Nussbaum's dual suggestions—with which we began this analysis—that literature can show us the contingency of our own perspective and lead us to look beyond narrow analytical frameworks. The answer to such a question is that it does not, except insofar as—and this is *crucial*—this account recognizes its own contingency. It does so most obviously by highlighting—in contradistinction to Nussbaum—that such insight depends on *the way in which texts are read* and, furthermore, that such insight "shows" us something in the weaker, not the stronger, sense of the term outlined earlier. It is an approach that encourages us to keep in mind the Gyges/Cave distinction and, as such, always to ask ourselves what *type* of claim we are making about our literary examples. In this, of course, it finds its literary parallel in the recent works of writers such as Ian McEwan and Jonathan Coe, writers who have incorporated into their novels an awareness of the constructedness and ultimate incompleteness of literary narratives.

Literature can often show us then—in the weaker sense of the term—much more than simple statistics or formal modeling. It can show us how little we know and, indeed, how little we know about *how* we know. It can even call its own perspective into question in a way that the more formal methods of social science cannot. It is itself, however, always an incomplete picture. Any political reading of a literary text is necessarily a subjective account of an already subjective account of the world. Forgetting this, we forget—in the manner of Martha Nussbaum—the contingency for which we turned to literature in the first place, and we run the risk of a return to the overly bold causal and empirical claims for which the turn to literature was supposed to be a corrective. There can be little doubt, for example, that as the classical perspective suggests, there are some literary figures whose insights into the political are worth taking seriously. The methodological suggestions offered here are simply meant to guard against the ease with which those insights, or worse still a critic's subjective account of those insights, slip into oracular observations about the political, observations that are secured only by the author's canonical reputation or the critic's reliance on the author. Just as Nussbaum observes that people can be mistaken about what is happening to them in all kinds of ways to justify the turn to literature, we might note that authors too can be wrong about what is happening in and to society, not least because expertise in one area—such as literature—does not necessarily travel well to another.

CONCLUSIONS

The *methodological claim* suggests that literature can show us things that the more traditional forms of social science cannot. It is a claim that is partially true and partially false. It can "show" us in the weaker sense, but not the stronger. Most obviously, literature cannot—as a general rule—serve as empirical evidence for claims about the *unwritten* world, because the standards of justification demanded by literary analysis are lower than those required for analysis of the *written* world. At best, such claims can serve as hypotheses to be tested and considered by the appropriate standards for *unwritten* world analysis. Indeed, returning to the sort of two-stage reading process advocated in the previous chapter—a two-stage process that was a feature of textual reading in the ancient world[19]—we might move back and forth between worlds in a kind of reflective equilibrium to see if we are indeed capturing some political phenomenon identified by an author, or whether that author's insights are misplaced. It may be that somebody tells a powerful story about the ways in which criminality emerges from social conditions, but that a closer inspection of the empirical data might contradict or mitigate such claims in interesting ways. Such a conclusion would certainly not validate or invalidate an author's literary worth— we judge and *should* judge such claims by different standards—but it may lead us to appreciate that author's work less for its political insights and more for its aesthetic or other values. Alternatively, it might be that the depiction of a particular state of affairs—the hopelessness of poverty, for example—might lead us to pay attention to it as a potential causal factor in criminal analysis, thereby causing us to correct for something we had overlooked. Such an analysis would, however, have to be focused on the *unwritten* world and justified by the standards appropriate to it.

Where literature can generate most insight for political theorists and social scientists is alerting us to the inadequacy of our models. Showing us—in the weaker sense of the term—that we might have overlooked certain factors should not lead us to believe that we now have a complete picture in the manner of a Nussbaum, but should rather, in the manner of Plato's Cave allegory, alert us to our capacity to be mistaken, and thereby to inculcate a productive attitude of humility in us as readers, thinkers, and social scientists. Literature can, that is to say, lead us to consider alternative possibilities, but it is not—for the most part—itself evidence for the existence of these possibilities. As it stands now, however, the sort of work advocated by Nussbaum, and engaged in by Butler, Rorty, and Eagleton, does not necessarily promote such values of openness and contingency, because almost all of them promote a knowing or revelatory approach to the text: confusing two senses of the word "show." It is this that suggests that the import of this analysis may have significance beyond the classrooms and faculty lounges of academia by cultivating a problematic and potentially destructive form of political discourse within it.

Chapter 8

Conclusion
The Literary Turn and Contemporary Political Discourse

"'Because if we look in the dictionary, what do we find as the first meaning of 'spook'? The primary meaning. '1. *Informal.* a ghost; specter." 'But Dean Silk, that is not the way it was taken. Let me read to you the *second* dictionary meaning. '2. *Disparaging.* A Negro.' That's the way it was taken."
—Philip Roth, *The Human Stain*[1]

In Philip Roth's novel *The Human Stain*, Coleman Silk, an African American who has passed for white his entire adult life, is forced to resign from his job as a college literature professor when a number of African American students take offense at his use of the word "spooks" to describe people absent from his class. Silk reminds his accusers that the primary meaning of the word is that of ghost or specter. They in turn remind him of the second, more disparaging meaning of the word. In this literary example—in which the text is crucially being used for *illumination* of an already established *unwritten* world claim rather than as *evidence* for that claim—the whole tragic novel turns on the *reading* of a single word. It is one in which the standards of justification appropriate to the *written* world—in which a reading may be considered valid because it *can be* read in a certain way—are misapplied to the *unwritten* world, where context and intent matter. It is a confusion that this study has suggested is at the heart of both the political turn in literary analysis and the literary turn in political thought and analysis. It is also a confusion that may be spreading to the world beyond academia. In January 1999, David Howard, a white aide to Anthony A. Williams, the African American mayor of Washington, D.C., was forced to resign from his job for using the word "niggardly" to describe his management of a tight budget. The similarity between this word—meaning "miserly" or "stingy"—and an offensive racial epithet was enough for Howard to lose his job, at least temporarily, when a number of the District's employees complained.[2]

Although it is obviously implausible to draw a direct causal arrow between the decline of *argument* and the rise of *reading* as critical modes in the Academy and the undoubted shrillness of much of our contemporary political discourse, there can be no doubt that teaching an entire generation of students that *reading* is a legitimate critical mode in the *unwritten* world is doing little to cultivate the sort of critical self-reflection that constructive political dialogue requires. Part of the aim of this study is, therefore, the possibly quixotic one of restoring some degree of rigor and civility to political discourse by pointing out the negative consequences of the literary turn for political dialogue within the Academy in the hope that this will also filter into the broader political discourse. This is not, of course, to overestimate the significance of this—or indeed *any*—academic work for the world beyond the college walls. Nevertheless, it may be that—as John Seery has convincingly argued in his study *America Goes to College*—how we think and talk about politics in the classroom will affect how our students think and talk about politics outside of it.[3] In this, perhaps, this work is also a piece of political theory in Hanna Pitkin's definition of the term, concerned as it is with those things that might be different if we chose to change them.[4]

In the absence of a detailed empirical study, the following claims are obviously somewhat speculative: suggestions perhaps for further investigation by those more qualified than this author for engaging in the kind of work that such an analysis requires; nor are they meant to suggest that the literary turn can have no positive impact upon our contemporary political discourse—indeed, such a claim would stand in direct contradiction to the model of literature in democratic discourse, advocated in chapter 6. They are merely meant to suggest the ways in which—as they currently manifest themselves—some of the assumptions of the literary and political turns might play themselves out in academic discourse and then, through the mechanism of the students being churned out of our colleges and universities, in our broader political culture.

One of the primary justifications offered for the turn to literature in political thought and analysis is that it offers some element of contingency: the recognition that social science modeling or philosophical models could not incorporate every aspect of human existence, and that we should look beyond such models in our social and political analysis. As we have seen, however, although there is much of value in this claim, it has become something of a platitude: endlessly repeated as the justification for all kinds of political-literary analysis or literary-political analysis, regardless of whether or not that particular mode of analysis generates the insight or contingency that we are said to seek in literature. Indeed, it has become apparent that this platitude has often generated a certain "knowingness" that is the antithesis of contingency. Very seldom, it seems, do political-literary critics and literary-political analysts find in a text something that they did not expect to see there. Such work has become the process of using ever-more-complicated theoretical apparatus to reduce texts to simple political categories or lessons. Motivated by a belief that they are doing "political work," such readers set about showing us how even the most playful, original, and allusive literary text is far from original and is—to adopt the language of such readings—always already an example of some other phenomenon, genre, or trend. In the political interpretation of literature, Nietzschean *resentiment* seems to rule the day. The platitudes upon which such work has rested— "reading is good for you," "literature gives us insight into other ways of being," "the literary is political"—have been worn smooth with overuse, and the methodological caveats that mitigate the more egregious forms of reductive political reading are lost amidst the rush to show the ways in which the apparently unique—the literary text—is, in reality, all-too-predictably political. This is not to suggest, of course, that this is what *all* literary critics are doing. Multiple textual approaches to literary analysis are unconcerned with, and do not encroach upon, the political. The concern of this study is simply those that make their literary analyses with a view to offering political insight. These approaches, it is being argued, contribute to the shrillness of our contemporary culture.

How, then, might such approaches play themselves out in the lives of our students and in our broader political culture? Precisely by encouraging us—in the words of a classic of the self-help genre—to "read people like a book." If we are used to approaching texts with sensitivity and humility, exploring them as another world, different than our own, accepting the possibility that they might show us something unexpected, new, or surprising, then such an endeavor might well produce a civil and constructive engagement, one that is possibly beneficial to both parties as well as the broader democratic polity. If, however, as we have seen happen with the institutionalization of methodological reading and the ascendance of Theory in the Academy, we learn to reduce texts to previously existing categories, to make them examples of other trends, or to beat them into shapes that serve our own political purposes, then "reading people like a book" becomes a deeply problematic political exercise. It leads to treating people as means and not as ends, in the manner of a Richard Rorty: a figure for whom the differences between people and fictional people appear to be relatively minor. It produces the sort of inability to listen to others that marks both Spivak's and Nussbaum's work on Third World women, an inability that makes—in Rorty's language—all kinds of cruelty possible. Indeed, if this approach can corrupt Martha Nussbaum, a careful, reasoned, and insightful thinker, then it has the potential to make Mary Daltons of us all: well-meaning but ultimately misguided do-gooders with little or no capacity for critical self-reflection.

This potential for making Mary Daltons out of ourselves and others is exacerbated by the malleability of literary texts and the kinds of debate they can generate. Given that literary texts often refuse to answer back and can easily be beaten into shapes conducive to our political perspectives, the cultivation of political *readings* rather than political *arguments* has the potential to produce a generation of students that is simply unfamiliar with the process of making and considering possible counterarguments to its own positions. Such students only receive training in justifying their own positions by marshalling *written* world evidence for a position, evidence that is, because of the *Phaedrus* problem, inevitably found. The sort of shrillness described by MacIntyre emerges because these texts simply refuse to adjudicate between competing readings in a way that would resolve political disagreements between the readers.[5] In such a dispute, readers with competing political interpretations can point to textual "evidence" that supports their own particular reading. Failing to see the ways in which texts can support multiple possible readings, and thereby receiving only confirmation of their own position, such readers not only receive confirmation of what they already believe to be true but also evidence of the wrongheadedness or stubbornness of their fellow reader, one who simply refuses to see the "evidence" right before his or her eyes. Such students are, perhaps, never taught the difference between an *argument* and a *reading* and, indeed, the appropriate time to employ one rather than the other, for *readings* only suggest possibilities about the *unwritten* world; *arguments* in, and evidence from, the *unwritten* world decide between such possibilities, a distinction that is perhaps obscured by the overreliance on dialectic as a political method.

DIALECTIC AND REVELATION

As Plato's example of the Cave suggests, literature can lead us to think differently about the world and the way that we live. This is indeed one of its strengths as a tool of social thought and political analysis. It can show us the contingency of our knowledge and lead us to a state of the soul or an attitude of the mind appropriate to searching philosophical reflection and nuanced political analysis. Nevertheless, the rather robust accounts of the dialectical experience of literature that make up the literary turn misleadingly prioritize a single textual response. There are at least two others. The first possible reader reaction is simple indifference: those left cold by the supposedly transfiguring text. The second is the transfiguring change itself: the person pushed into a rigorous scrutiny of everything he or she believes in and lives by, what we are here calling *dialectic*. The third is what we might call *revelation*: the nontransfiguring change.

Dialectic is a matter of coming to see the world differently, of understanding it in a different way. As with Thucydides' juxtaposing of his accounts of Pericles' Funeral Oration and the Plague of Athens, it gives us two perspectives and forces us to synthesize them into a third: to see that neither view of Athens is fully reliable, and that we must become the sort of person who considers such extreme views distorting. *Revelation*, in contrast, changes our view of the world but does not change who we are as people: it simply replaces one story with another in a way that has no impact upon the self or the way in which such views are held. In the given instance it would, for example, lead one to replace one's belief in Pericles' account of the perfect Athens with the second account in which every virtue identified by the speaker is undercut by its opposite. One might come to see the Athens of the Plague as the *true* Athens and to scorn Pericles' idealization of the city. In the case of *revelation*, one would hold the new position with precisely the same degree of conviction that one held the previous position. One would not change as a person—even if it felt this way— one would simply change one's views about the world, but not the way in which they were held. *Dialectic*, in contrast, demands both journey and return. Had Plato's Cave dweller simply replaced one conception of reality with another— the Cave wall for the light—we might say that he had experienced only *revelation*. It is the second stage of the process, the return and consideration of the alternative in conjunction with the original view, that makes a change potentially dialectical. *Revelation* suggests only half of this process: seeing the world differently, but without the reflective and potentially transfiguring aspect of dialectic. The religious overtones of this word are not, of course, meant to suggest that a religious experience could never be dialectical; indeed, an Augustinian religious experience would almost certainly be dialectical in the sense that it would show us how little we knew of the Christian God, and perhaps inspire in us the desire to seek Him out. "Revelation" is chosen only because of the sense of a "revealed truth" being made plain that accompanies this experience.

The significance of this distinction between dialectic and revelation for the academic and political discourse emerging from the literary turn is clear. Gaining a theoretical apparatus with which to regard the world or the text, one begins to see in it elements that one had previously overlooked. If, however, one fails to recognize that these new elements are a product of one's new way of seeing, then one might, as was previously noted, mistake the experience of "I had not seen that before," for "That's how it is." As a result, attempts at dialectic that produce only revelation are likely to cultivate a kind of fundamentalism in which the text is used as evidence to support one's position, making one intolerant of conflicting opinions. In this perhaps the literary turn can cultivate a kind of—albeit often highly secular—faith-based political argument. There often emerges a kind of in-group and out-group—the sort of thing we saw in response to Judith Butler's work—between the enlightened and the unenlightened, the belief being that if only the unenlightened could come to see the world in the way of the enlightened, then there would be political agreement.

THE LITERARY TURN AND POLITICAL DISCOURSE

As it stands then, far from producing values of benefit to liberal democracy, the literary turn in the contemporary Academy seems to produce their opposite: instead of contingency, certainty; instead of tolerance and respect for others, intolerance and arrogance; instead of civilized discourse, shrill and divisive encounters. In the absence of philosophical premises and argument, there is simply nowhere for such disagreements to retreat in order to adjudicate between positions. It is for this reason that they often devolve into the personal, with the failure to see the text and the reading in a prescribed way being seen as belligerence, defiance, or ignorance. In such circumstances, it is perhaps not too much of a stretch to see these problematic values being replicated in the broader political culture, contributing to, and certainly not easing, the shrillness of our contemporary political discourse.

In making such claims it is not, as has been repeatedly stressed, being suggested that the literary turn could never do the opposite: that it could never produce values and insights useful to analytic insight and political discussion. It is simply to point out that continuing to perpetuate the confusion between the *written* and *unwritten* worlds and their respective standards of justification, between *readings* and *arguments*, means continuing to perpetuate a lack of conceptual clarity and analytical rigor. In order to move beyond these problems, it is clear that we need a more tough-minded approach to literature in contemporary political thought and analysis, one that recognizes the problems created by the conceptual confusion identified in this study. Then, and only then perhaps, will we be able to access the benefits of the turn to literature in political thought and analysis in a useful and convincing fashion. Indeed, in addition to benefiting the practice of liberal democracy, we also may gain the respect of our more empirically minded colleagues, and with it the possibility that they will begin to take seriously this work on politics and literature. Until then, however, they will rightly perhaps continue to ignore our work and insights in favor of their own partial views of reality, and the more complete and nuanced picture of the political that we all—both empirical modelers and advocates of political literary analysis—claim to seek will remain frustratingly elusive.

Notes

INTRODUCTION

1. Italo Calvino, *The Uses of Literature* (New York: Harcourt & Brace Company, 1986), 93.

2. For a decidedly partisan discussion of the debate, see John M. Ellis, *Literature Lost: Social Agendas and the Corruption of the Humanities* (New Haven, CT: Yale University Press, 1997); Jeffrey Wallen, *Closed Encounters: Literary Politics and Public Culture* (Minneapolis: University of Minnesota Press, 1998).

3. Noting that many of the texts written "at the height of the Theory years are unreadable today," Jean-Michel Rabaté is among a number of contemporary literary theorists who have sought to strip away some of the excesses of the political turn to reveal what is of value in literary theory. See Jean-Michel Rabaté, *The Future of Theory* (Malden, MA: Blackwell, 2002), 92. See also Valentine Cunningham, *Reading After Theory* (Malden, MA: Blackwell, 2002); Gayatri Chakravorty Spivak, *Death of a Discipline* (New York: Columbia University Press, 2003). For a discussion of these arguments, see Simon Stow, "Theoretical Downsizing and the Lost Art of Listening," *Philosophy and Literature* 28 (2004): 192–201.

4. Alasdair MacIntyre, *After Virtue: A Study in Moral Theory*, 2nd ed. (Notre Dame, IN: University of Notre Dame Press, 1984), 8.

5. Ibid.

6. See, for example, Ann Coulter, *Slander: Liberal Lies about the American Right* (New York: Three Rivers Press, 2002); Al Franken, *Lies and the Lying Liars Who Tell Them: A Fair and Balanced Look at the Right* (New York: Dutton, 2003); Bill O'Reilly, *The No Spin Zone: Confrontations with the Powerful and Famous in America* (New York: Broadway Books, 2001).

7. See Stanley Fish, *There's No Such Thing as Free Speech . . . And It's a Good Thing Too* (New York: Oxford University Press, 1994).

8. See, for example, Catherine Zuckert, "On Reading Classic American Novelists as Political Thinkers," *The Journal of Politics* 43 (1981): 683–706; Zuckert, "Why Political Scientists Want to Study Literature," *PS: Political Science and Politics* 28 (1995):

189–180; Werner J. Dannhauser, "Poetry vs. Philosophy," *PS: Political Science and Politics* 28 (1995): 190–192; Joseph H. Lane Jr., "The Stark Regime and American Democracy: A Political Interpretation of Robert Penn Warren's *All the King's Men*," *American Political Science Review* 95 (2001): 811–828.

9. Paul A. Cantor, "Literature and Politics: Understanding the Regime," *PS: Political Science and Politics* 28 (1995): 195.

10. See Martha Nussbaum, "The Professor of Parody: The Hip Defeatism of Judith Butler," *The New Republic* 22 (1999): 37–45.

11. Martha Nussbaum, *Upheavals of Thought: The Intelligence of Emotions* (Cambridge: Cambridge University Press, 2001).

12. John Rawls, *A Theory of Justice* (Cambridge, MA: Harvard University Press, 1971).

13. See, for example, Michael Sandel, *Liberalism and the Limits of Justice* (Cambridge, MA: Harvard University Press, 1982); Charles Taylor, *Sources of the Self: The Making of the Modern Identity* (Cambridge, MA: Harvard University Press, 1989).

14. John Rawls, *Political Liberalism* (New York: Columbia University Press, 1993); Rawls, *Collected Papers* (Cambridge, MA: Harvard University Press, 1999); Rawls, *Justice as Fairness: A Restatement* (Cambridge, MA: Harvard University Press, 2001).

15. See, for example, Robert D. Putnam, *Making Democracy Work: Civic Traditions in Modern Italy* (Princeton, NJ: Princeton University Press, 1994); Putnam, *Bowling Alone: The Collapse and Revival of American Community* (New York: Simon & Schuster, 2000); *Democracies in Flux: The Evolution of Social Capital in Contemporary Society*, ed. Putnam (New York: Oxford University Press, 2002).

16. Given that Martha Nussbaum describes her political philosophy as "Aristotelian Social Democracy," her liberal pedigree might be open to question. She states, nevertheless, that her work is part of a liberal tradition that includes John Stuart Mill, John Rawls, and Adam Smith. See Martha Nussbaum, "Aristotelian Social Democracy," in *Liberalism and the Good*, ed. R. Bruce Douglass, Gerald M. Mara, and Henry S. Richardson (New York: Routledge, 1990), 203–252; Martha Nussbaum, *Poetic Justice: Literary Imagination and Public Life* (Boston: Beacon Press, 1995), 19.

17. See, for example, *Mapping the Ethical Turn: A Reader in Ethics, Culture, and Literary Theory*, ed. Todd F. Davis and Kenneth Womack (Charlottesville: University of Virginia Press, 2001); Spivak, *Death of a Discipline*.

18. Edward W. Said, *Culture and Imperialism* (New York: Vintage Books, 1994). For an interesting response to this argument, see Brian Southam, "The Silence of the Bertrams," *Times Literary Supplement* (February 17, 1995): 13.

19. Spivak, *Death of a Discipline*, 19, 50.

20. Elaine Scarry, "The Fall of TWA 800: The Possibility of Electromagnetic Interference," *New York Review of Books* 45 (1998): 6; Scarry, "Swissair 111, TWA 800, and Electromagnetic Interference," *New York Review of Books* 47 (2000): 14.

21. Quoted in Emily Eakin, "Professor Scarry Has a Theory," *New York Times Magazine* (November 19, 2000): 80.

22. Cunningham, *Reading After Theory*; Sigurd Burckhardt, "English Bards and *APSR* Reviewers," *American Political Science Review* 54 (1960): 158–166; Burckhardt, "On Reading Ordinary Prose: A Reply to Allan Bloom," *American Political Science Review* 54 (1960): 465–470; Allan Bloom, "Political Philosophy and Poetry," *American Political Science Review* 54 (1960): 457–464; Bloom, "Political Philosophy and Poetry: A Restatement," *American Political Science Review* 54 (1960): 471–473.

23. Paul Goodman, quoted in Philip Roth, *Reading Myself and Others* (New York: Vintage Books, 2001), xiii.

24. Somewhat post-hoc, Butler has offered some insights into her method. See "Can the 'Other' of Philosophy Speak?," in *Undoing Gender*, ed. Judith Butler (New York: Routledge, 2004), 232–250.

CHAPTER 1   *ARGUMENTS* AND *READINGS*

1. Thucydides, *History of the Peloponnesian War*, trans. Rex Warner (New York: Penguin Books, 1972), 242.

2. Ibid., 147.

3. Ibid. For wonderful discussions of this problem, see James Boyd White, *When Words Lose Their Meaning: Constitutions and Reconstitutions of Language, Character, and Community* (Chicago: University of Chicago Press, 1990); J. Peter Euben, *The Road Not Taken: The Tragedy of Political Theory* (Princeton, NJ: Princeton University Press, 1990).

4. Thucydides, *History*, 214.

5. Ibid., 221.

6. Ibid., 401.

7. See, John McWhorter, *Doing Our Own Thing: The Degradation of Language and Music and Why We Should, Like Care* (New York: Gotham, 2003).

8. John Rawls, *A Theory of Justice* (Cambridge, MA: Harvard University Press, 1971).

9. Ibid., 60.

10. See, for example, John Rawls, "Kantian Constructivism in Moral Theory," in *Collected Papers*, ed. Samuel Freeman (Cambridge, MA: Harvard University Press, 1999), 303–358.

11. See, for example, Michael Sandel, *Liberalism and the Limits of Justice* (Cambridge, MA: Harvard University Press, 1982); Charles Taylor, *Sources of the Self: The Making of the Modern Identity* (Cambridge, MA: Harvard University Press, 1989).

12. J. L. Mackie, *Ethics: Inventing Right and Wrong* (London: Penguin Books, 1977), 15.

13. Ibid., 28.

14. Ibid., 38.

15. Alasdair MacIntyre, *After Virtue: A Study in Moral Theory*, 2nd ed. (Notre Dame, IN: University of Notre Dame Press, 1984), 43–44.

16. John Rawls, "Justice as Fairness: Political not Metaphysical," *Collected Papers*, 394.

17. John Rawls, *Political Liberalism* (New York: Columbia University Press, 1993), 100.

18. Rawls, "Political not Metaphysical," 402–403.

19. See, for example, Brian Barry, "John Rawls and the Search for Stability," *Ethics* 105 (1995) 874–915: Norman Daniels, "Reflective Equilibrium and Justice as Political," in *The Idea of Political Liberalism: Essays on Rawls*, ed. Victoria Davion and Clark Wolf (Lanham, MD: Rowman & Littlefield, 1999), 127–154.

20. Ironically, in downgrading the Original Position and Veil of Ignorance to "devices of representation," Rawls seems to be adopting some of the more problematic methods of the literary turn. His choosers are now simply fictional. As their author, Rawls tells us what they are thinking. In this Rawls seems to be guilty of a methodological error that we see repeated in much of the work of the literary turn: he is using evidence from the fictional or *written* world to support claims about the nonfictional or *unwritten* world.

21. Rawls, *Political Liberalism*, 168.

22. Martha Nussbaum, *Upheavals of Thought: The Intelligence of Emotions* (New York: Cambridge University Press, 2001). See also Nussbaum, *Hiding from Humanity: Disgust, Shame, and the Law* (Princeton, NJ: Princeton University Press, 2004).

23. Martha Nussbaum, "Aristotelian Social Democracy," in *Liberalism and the Good*, ed. R. Bruce Douglas, Gerald M. Mara, and Henry S. Richardson (New York: Routledge, 1990), 203–252.

24. Richard Rorty, *Achieving Our Country: Leftist Thought in Twentieth-Century America* (Cambridge, MA: Harvard University Press, 1997); Rorty, *Philosophy and Social Hope* (London: Penguin Books, 1999).

25. Richard Rorty, *Contingency, Irony, and Solidarity* (Cambridge: Cambridge University Press, 1989), 21.

26. Ludwig Wittgenstein, *Tractatus Logicus-Philosophicus*, trans. D. F. Pears and B. F. McGuinness (London: Routledge, 1974).

27. Rorty, *Contingency*, 21.

28. Ibid., 9.

29. Butler asserts, for example, that she is well aware of "the limits of resignification as a strategy of opposition." See Judith Butler, *Excitable Speech: A Politics of the Performative* (New York: Routledge), 38.

30. Michel Foucault, *Language, Counter-Memory, Practice: Selected Essays and Interviews*, ed. Paul Rabinow (Ithaca, NY: Cornell University Press, 1990), 230.

31. Richard Rorty, *Consequences of Pragmatism* (Minneapolis: University of Minnesota Press, 1982), 93.

32. Sylvia Plath, *Collected Poems* (London: Faber and Faber, 1981), 142.

33. Ludwig Wittgenstein, *On Certainty*, trans. Denis Paul and G. E. M. Anscombe (New York: Harper & Row, 1972), 192.

34. John Sutherland, *Who Betrays Elizabeth Bennet?: Further Puzzles in Classic Fiction* (Oxford: Oxford University Press, 1999).

35. Ludwig Wittgenstein, *Philosophical Investigations*, trans. G. E. M. Anscombe (Englewood Cliffs, NJ: Prentice Hall, 1958), 5e.

36. Ibid., 20e.

37. See *Post-Analytic Philosophy*, ed. John Rajchman and Cornel West (New York: Columbia University Press, 1985).

38. Rorty is clearly aware that his *reading* of Wittgenstein is exactly that: a *reading*. In the spring of 2000, during Rorty's graduate seminar in the Department of Comparative Literature at Stanford University, I pointed out that Wittgenstein was more ambiguous on the relationship between language and the world than he suggested. Acknowledging my point, Rorty asserted, "When I said, 'Wittgenstein would say,' I meant, of course, 'What *my* idealized Wittgenstein would say,'" as if there were no difference between the two.

39. Foucault's friend (and sometime-colleague) Hans Sluga suggested that during his time at Berkeley, Foucault was familiar with Wittgenstein's work, though only in broad outline. Foucault also uses, in his *The Birth of the Clinic*, the very Wittgensteinian term *game* to refer to language, a word whose use he ascribed to certain unnamed "Anglo-American philosophers." See James Miller, *The Passion of Michael Foucault* (Cambridge, MA: Harvard University Press, 1993), 46, n.28.

40. Wittgenstein, *Philosophical Investigations*, 81e.

41. What Wittgenstein believes is, of course, less important than what is a plausible claim about the malleability of language.

42. Wittgenstein, *Philosophical Investigations*, 49e.

43. Richard Rorty, "Introduction," in Vladimir Nabokov, *Pale Fire* (New York: Alfred Knopf, 1992), v.

44. Wittgenstein, *Philosophical Investigations*, 8e.

45. Ibid., 15e.

46. Ibid., 92e.

47. Ibid., 113e, 137e.

48. Ibid., 5e, emphasis added.

49. Ibid., 45e.

50. Hanna Pitkin, *Wittgenstein and Justice*, 2nd ed. (Berkeley: University of California Press, 1993), 172.

51. Wittgenstein, *Philosophical Investigations*, 43e.

52. Wittgenstein, *On Certainty*, 283.

53. Wittgenstein, *Philosophical Investigations*, 31e.

CHAPTER 2   MARTHA NUSSBAUM

1. Harper Lee, *To Kill a Mockingbird* (New York: HarperCollins, 1995), 33.

2. Martha C. Nussbaum, *Poetic Justice: The Literary Imagination and Public Life* (Boston, MA: Beacon Press, 1995), 11. The nature of Nussbaum's project is captured here by her suggestion that there are to be more philosophically adequate foundations, but foundations nonetheless.

3. Ibid., 51.

4. Aristotle, *The Politics*, trans. Carnes Lord (Chicago: University of Chicago Press, 1985), 111.

5. Ibid.

6. Nussbaum, *Poetic Justice*, xiii.

7. Adam Smith, *The Theory of Moral Sentiments* [1853], quoted in Nussbaum, *Poetic Justice*, 73.

8. Smith, quoted in Nussbaum, *Poetic Justice*, 73–74.

9. Nussbaum, *Poetic Justice*, 75.

10. Stanley Fish, *Is There a Text in This Class?: The Authority of Interpretive Communities* (Cambridge, MA: Harvard University Press, 1980), 297.

11. Wayne C. Booth, *The Company We Keep: An Ethics of Fiction* (Berkeley: University of California Press, 1988).

12. Nussbaum, *Poetic Justice*, 10.

13. Ibid., 11, 33, 71.

14. Ibid., 90.

15. Music is, she says, insufficient, because its "contribution is in its very nature dreamlike and indeterminate in a way that limits its role in public deliberation;" although film is potentially more useful. "I am not," she says, "reluctant to admit that films may also make contributions to public life in related ways." See Nussbaum, *Poetic Justice*, 6. See also, Nussbaum, *Upheavals of Thought: The Intelligence of Emotions* (New York: Cambridge University Press, 2001).

16. Nussbaum, *Poetic Justice*, 6.

17. Ibid. 11.

18. Ibid. 33. This is probably something of a null set. I am grateful to Eric Naiman for this point.

19. Ibid. xiv. This fence is actually a recurrent trope in Nussbaum's work. See also Nussbaum, *Cultivating Humanity: A Defense of Reform in Liberal Education* (Cambridge, MA: Harvard University Press, 1997), 5.

20. Nussbaum, *Poetic Justice*, 99.

21. Ibid., 66.

22. Ibid., 3.

23. Ibid., 66.

24. Martha Nussbaum, "Exactly and Responsibly: A Defense of Ethical Criticism," *Philosophy and Literature* 22:2 (1998): 350.

25. Martha Nussbaum, "Aristotelian Social Democracy," in *Liberalism and the Good*, ed. R. Bruce Douglass, Gerald M. Mara, and Henry S. Richardson (New York: Routledge, 1990), 203–252.

26. Ibid., 225.

27. Nussbaum, *Poetic Justice*, 19.

28. Nussbaum, *Cultivating Humanity*, 14.

29. Hannah Arendt, *Eichmann in Jerusalem: A Report on the Banality of Evil* (New York: Penguin Books, 1994), 49.

30. Jonathan Glover, *Humanity: A Moral History of the Twentieth Century* (London: Jonathan Cape, 1999), 368.

31. Jeremiah Conway, "Compassion and Moral Condemnation: An Analysis of *The Reader*," *Philosophy and Literature* 23 (1999): 289.

32. Alexander Nehamas, "What Should We Expect from Reading? (There Are Only Aesthetic Values)," *Salmagundi* 111 (1996): 45.

33. Nussbaum, "Exactly and Responsibly," 352.

34. Ibid.

35. K. K. Ruthven, *Critical Assumptions* (New York: Cambridge University Press, 1979), 184.

36. Nussbaum, *Cultivating Humanity*, 34.

37. For Nussbaum on the "Stairmaster," see Nussbaum, *Cultivating Humanity*, 5.

38. Nussbaum, "Exactly and Responsibly," 353.

39. Ibid., 351.

40. Nussbaum, *Poetic Justice*, 77.

41. Adam Smith, quoted in Nussbaum, *Poetic Justice*, 73.

42. See, for example, Elaine Scarry, "The Difficulty of Imagining Other People," in Martha C. Nussbaum, *For the Love of Country?*, ed. Joshua Cohen (Boston: Beacon Press, 2002), 98–110.

43. Nussbaum, *Poetic Justice*, 2.

44. Ibid., xiv.

45. Ibid., 7.

46. Ibid., 19.

47. Nussbaum, *Cultivating Humanity*, 86–89.

48. Martha Nussbaum, *Love's Knowledge: Essays on Philosophy and Literature* (New York: Oxford University Press, 1990), 9.

49. Nussbaum, *Poetic Justice*, 9.

50. Ibid., 35.

51. Ibid., 28.

52. Jonathan Rose, *The Intellectual Life of the British Working Classes* (New Haven, CT: Yale University Press, 2001), 4.

53. Italo Calvino, *The Uses of Literature* (New York: Harcourt & Brace, 1986), 87.

54. Nussbaum, *Poetic Justice*, 8.

55. Briefly, that which suggests that texts are *made* and not *found*. See Stanley Fish, *Is There a Text in This Class?*

56. Nussbaum, *Poetic Justice*, 8–9.

57. Wayne Booth, *The Company We Keep*.

58. Nussbaum, "Exactly and Responsibly," 353.

59. Nussbaum, *Cultivating Humanity*, 156.

60. Ibid., 32.

61. Ibid., 42.

62. Plato, *Gorgias*, trans. Robin Waterfield (Oxford: Oxford University Press, 1994), 521a.

63. Franz Kafka, quoted in Philip Roth, *The Anatomy Lesson* (New York: Vintage Books, 1995), 200.

64. Stanley Fish, *Self-Consuming Artifacts: The Experience of Seventeenth-Century Literature* (Berkeley: University of California Press, 1972), 1.

65. Wayne C. Booth, "Why Banning Ethical Criticism Is a Serious Mistake," *Philosophy and Literature* 22 (1998): 368.

66. Simon Stow, "Unbecoming Virulence: The Politics of the Ethical Criticism Debate," *Philosophy and Literature* 24:1 (2000): 185–196.

67. Vladimir Nabokov, *Strong Opinions* (New York: Vintage Books, 1990), 66.

68. Nussbaum, *Poetic Justice*, 26.

69. As a consequence of this sort of argument, we see Jeremiah Conway using Bernard Schlink's novel *The Reader* as an empirical case study in his critique of Martha Nussbaum's theory of compassion. See Jeremiah Conway, "Compassion and Moral Condemnation: An Analysis of *The Reader*," *Philosophy and Literature* 23 (1999): 284–301.

70. Nussbaum, "Exactly and Responsibly," 345.

71. Nussbaum, *Cultivating Humanity*, 108.

72. Nussbaum, *Poetic Justice*, 47.

73. Nussbaum, *Cultivating Humanity*, 152.

74. There are a number of other, far more interesting readings of *Hard Times*. My own preference is David Lodge, "How Successful Is *Hard Times*?," in *Hard Times, Norton Critical Edition*, ed. George Ford and Sylvere Monod (New York: W. W. Norton & Company, 1990), 381–389.

75. Martha C. Nussbaum, "The Professor of Parody: The Hip Defeatism of Judith Butler," *The New Republic* (February 22, 1999).

CHAPTER 3   RICHARD RORTY

1. David Lodge, *Small World* (London: Penguin, 1995), 24.

2. Richard Rorty, *Contingency, Irony, and Solidarity* (Cambridge: Cambridge University Press, 1989), 8–9.

3. Rorty, *Contingency*, 80.

4. Richard Posner, *Public Intellectuals: A Study of Decline* (Cambridge, MA: Harvard University Press, 2001), 340. See also Chantal Mouffe, "Deconstruction, Pragmatism, and the Politics of Democracy," in *Deconstruction and Pragmatism*, ed. Chantal Mouffe (London: Routledge, 1996), 10.

5. Susan Haack, "Vulgar Pragmatism: An Unedifying Prospect," in *Rorty and Pragmatism: The Philosopher Responds to His Critics*, ed. Herman J. Saatkamp (Nashville, TN: Vanderbilt University Press, 1995), 139.

6. Richard Rorty, in *Against Bosses, Against Oligarchies: A Conversation with Richard Rorty*, ed. Derek Nystrom and Kent Puckett (Charlottesville, VA: Prickly Pear Pamphlets, 1998), 57.

7. Richard Rorty, *Truth and Progress: Philosophical Papers*, vol. 3 (Cambridge: Cambridge University Press, 1998), 12.

8. Vladimir Nabokov, *The Gift* (New York: Vintage, 1991).

9. Richard Rorty, *Objectivity, Relativism, and Truth: Philosophical Papers*, vol. 1 (Cambridge: Cambridge University Press, 1991), 1.

10. Rorty, *Contingency*, 194.

11. Judith Shklar, quoted in Rorty, *Contingency*, xv.

12. Joseph Schumpeter, quoted in Rorty, *Contingency*, 46.

13. Rorty, *Contingency*, xvi.

14. Ibid., xvi.

15. Ibid., 174.

16. Ibid., 78.

17. Stanley Fish, *Self-Consuming Artifacts: The Experience of Seventeenth-Century Literature* (Berkeley: University of California Press, 1972), 1.

18. Philip Roth, *American Pastoral* (New York: Vintage Books, 1997), 9.

19. John Stuart Mill, *Autobiography* (London: Penguin Books, 1989), 120.

20. Vladimir Nabokov, *Strong Opinions* (New York: Vintage Books, 1990), 34–35.

21. Ibid., 19.

22. Ibid., 96.

23. Ibid., 33.

24. Ibid., 156.

25. Richard Rorty, *Achieving Our Country: Leftist Thought in Twentieth-Century America* (Cambridge, MA: Harvard University Press, 1997).

26. Nabokov, *Strong Opinions*, 98.

27. Ibid., 94.

28. Vladimir Nabokov, *The Defense* (New York: Vintage, 1990), 140.

29. Thomas Kuhn, *The Structure of Scientific Revolutions*, 3rd ed. (Chicago: University of Chicago Press, 1996).

30. Vladimir Nabokov, *Bend Sinister* (New York: Vintage, 1990), 56.

31. Vladimir Nabokov, *Look at the Harlequins!* (New York: Vintage, 1990), 9.

32. Richard Rorty, "Introduction," in Vladimir Nabokov, *Pale Fire* (New York: Alfred Knopf, 1992), viii.

33. Ibid., xiii.

34. Rorty, *Contingency*, 163–164. It is interesting to note that while most of Rorty's agents are female, the incurious are almost always male.

35. Rorty, "Introduction," v.

36. See, for example, Stanley Fish, *Is There a Text in This Class?: The Authority of Interpretive Communities* (Cambridge, MA: Harvard University Press, 1980).

37. Richard Rorty, "The Pragmatist's Progress," in *Interpretation and Overinterpretation*, ed. Stefan Collini (Cambridge: Cambridge University Press, 1992), 97.

38. Rorty, *Contingency*, 127.

39. Richard Rorty, "The Inspirational Value of Great Works of Literature," *Raritan* 1 (1996): 15.

40. Richard Rorty, *Consequences of Pragmatism* (Minneapolis: University of Minnesota Press, 1982), 151.

41. See Simon Stow, "The Return of Charles Kinbote: Nabokov on Rorty," *Philosophy and Literature* 23 (1999): 65–77.

42. Rorty, *Contingency*, 100.

43. Ibid., 87.

44. John Stuart Mill, *On Liberty and Other Essays* (Oxford: Oxford University Press, 1991).

45. John Rawls, *A Theory of Justice* (Cambridge, MA: Harvard University Press, 1971).

46. Nabokov, of course, once described himself as "a stand-in for Hitchcock." See Nabokov, *Lolita: A Screenplay* (New York: Vintage, 1997), xii.

47. Rorty, *Contingency*, 133.

48. Terry Eagleton, *The Ideology of the Aesthetic* (Oxford: Basil Blackwell, 1990), 383.

49. Rorty, *Contingency*, 133.

50. Ibid., 13.

51. Ibid., 12.

52. David L. Hall, *Richard Rorty: Prophet and Poet of the New Pragmatism* (Albany: State University of New York Press, 1994), 9, 228.

53. "'When *I* use a word,' Humpty Dumpty said, in a rather scornful tone, "it means just what I choose it to mean—neither more nor less." See Lewis Carroll, *Alice's Adventures in Wonderland and through the Looking Glass* (London: Penguin, 1998), 186.

54. The first name is Hazel.

55. For, as Leona Toker points out, Rorty is an excellent reader of the texts he uses in his work. See Toker, "Liberal Ironists and the 'Gaudily Painted Savage': on Richard Rorty's Reading of Vladimir Nabokov," *Nabokov Studies* 1 (1994).

56. Richard Rorty, "A Tale of Two Disciplines," *Callaloo* 94 (1994): 581.

57. Rorty, *Contingency*, 145. It is an assertion that once again throws his comments about Nabokov's intent into sharp relief.

58. Rorty, "The Pragmatist's Progress," 106–107.

59. "What is the reading of a text, in fact, except the recording of certain thematic recurrences, certain insistences of forms and meanings? An electronic reading supplies me with a list of the frequencies, which I have only to glance at to form an idea of the problems the book suggests to my critical study." See Italo Calvino, *If on a Winter's Night*

a Traveler, trans. William Weaver (New York: Everyman, 1993), 182. See also Ludwig Wittgenstein, *Philosophical Investigations*, trans. G. E. M. Anscombe (Englewood Cliffs, NJ: Prentice Hall, 1958), 63e.

60. Harold Bloom, *The Anxiety of Influence: A Theory of Poetry* (New York: Oxford University Press, 1997).

61. Rorty, *Contingency*, 164.

62. Ibid., 13.

63. Ibid.

64. Ibid., 45.

65. Ibid., 80

66. Ibid., 187.

67. Ibid., 80–81.

68. Ibid., 79–80.

69. Rorty, *Achieving Our Country*, 85.

70. Rorty, *Contingency*, 89.

71. Stephen Macedo, *Liberal Virtue: Citizenship, Virtue, and Community in Liberal Constitutionalism* (Oxford: Clarendon Press, 1991), 68.

CHAPTER 4   TERRY EAGLETON

1. Flannery O'Connor, *Wise Blood* (New York: Noonday Press, 1949), 224.

2. Terry Eagleton, *Literary Theory: An Introduction*, 2nd ed. (Minneapolis: University of Minnesota Press, 1996), 169.

3. Ibid., 170

4. Terry Eagleton, *The Ideology of the Aesthetic* (Oxford: Basil Blackwell, 1990), 1.

5. Valentine Cunningham, *Reading After Theory* (Malden, MA: Blackwell, 2002), 53.

6. Richard Rorty, in *Against Bosses, Against Oligarchies: A Conversation with Richard Rorty*, ed. Derek Nystrom and Kent Puckett (Charlottesville, VA: Prickly Pear Pamphlets, 1998), 53.

7. Jean-Michel Rabaté, *The Future of Theory* (Malden, MA: Blackwell, 2002), 1.

8. Terry Eagleton, "Base and Superstructure Revisited," *New Literary History* 31 (2000): 231–240.

9. *The Eagleton Reader*, ed. Stephen Regan (Oxford: Blackwell, 1998), 289–290.

10. Ibid., 247.

11. Eagleton, *Literary Theory*, x. In addition, Eagleton wrote a screenplay that served as the basis for Derek Jarman's film *Wittgenstein*, and the philosopher appears as a character in his novel *Saints and Scholars*.

12. Eagleton, *Literary Theory*, 8.

13. Ibid., 19–20, emphasis in original.

14. Ibid., 13.

15. Ibid., 15.

16. Ibid., 21.

17. Karl Marx, "The German Ideology," in *The Marx-Engels Reader*, 2nd ed., ed. Robert C. Tucker (New York: Norton, 1978), 173.

18. Eagleton, *Literary Theory*, 23.

19. Ibid., 25.

20. Ibid., 59.

21. Ibid., 174.

22. Ibid., 170.

23. Terry Eagleton, *Ideology: An Introduction* (London: Verso, 1991), 23.

24. See Richard Rorty, "The Pragmatist's Progress," in *Interpretation and Overinterpretation*, ed. Stefan Collini (Cambridge: Cambridge University Press, 1992), 106.

25. Eagleton, *Literary Theory*, 68–70.

26. *The Eagleton Reader*, 63.

27. Ibid., 37.

28. Terry Eagleton, *Saints and Scholars* (London: Verso, 1987).

29. Eagleton, *Literary Theory*, 57.

30. Eagleton, *The Ideology of the Aesthetic*, 33.

31. *The Eagleton Reader*, 291.

32. Ibid.

33. See Simon Stow, "'An Unbecoming Virulence': The Politics of the Ethical Criticism Debate," *Philosophy and Literature* 24 (2000): 185–196; Richard Posner, *Public Intellectuals: A Study of Decline* (Cambridge, MA: Harvard University Press, 2001), 239.

34. Norman Geras, *Solidarity in the Conversation of Mankind: The Ungroundable Liberalism of Richard Rorty* (London: Verso, 1995).

35. *The Eagleton Reader*, 285.

36. Terry Eagleton, *The Illusions of Postmodernism* (Oxford: Blackwell, 1996), viii.

37. Eagleton, *The Ideology of the Aesthetic*, 11.

38. Eagleton, *Literary Theory*, 178.

39. Ibid., 184.

40. Raymond Williams, *Marxism and Literature* (Oxford: Oxford University Press, 1977), 2.

41. Ibid., 80.

42. Karl Marx, *Early Writings* (London: Penguin, 1992), 426.

43. "Art, then, is for Marxism part of the 'superstructure' of society." See Terry Eagleton, *Marxism and Literary Criticism* (Berkeley: University of California Press, 1976), 5.

44. Engels, for example, offered an account of a zigzag dialectic. "The economic situation is the basis, but the various elements of the superstructure—political forms of the class struggle and its results, such as the constitutions established by the victorious class after a successful battle, etc., juridical forms, and especially the reflections of all these real struggles in the brains of the particular participants, political, legal, philosophical theories, religious views and their further development into systems of dogma also exercise their influence upon the course of the historical struggles and in many cases determine their form in particular." See Engels, "Letter to J. Bloch," quoted in *Marx and Engels on Law*, ed. M. Cain and A. Hunt (New York: Academic Press, 1979), 56.

45. Eagleton, *Marxism and Literary Criticism*, 75.

46. John Berger, *Ways of Seeing* (New York: Penguin, 1991).

47. Karl Marx, *Surveys from Exile* (London: Penguin Books, 1973), 226.

48. Eagleton, *The Ideology of the Aesthetic*, 4–5.

49. Eagleton, *Literary Theory*, 40.

50. Ibid.

51. G. A. Cohen, *Karl Marx's Theory of History: A Defence* (Princeton, NJ: Princeton University Press, 1978), 216–296.

52. Eagleton, *Literary Theory*, 24.

53. Williams, *Marxism and Literature*, 206.

54. Eagleton, *Literary Theory*, 59.

55. Eagleton, *Ideology: An Introduction*, 23.

56. Paul Goodman, quoted in Philip Roth, *Reading Myself and Others* (New York: Vintage, 2001), xiii.

57. See, Simon Stow, "Worlds Apart: Ursula K. Le Guin and the Possibility of Method," in *The New Utopian Politics of Ursula K. Le Guin's The Dispossessed*, ed. Laurence A. Davis and Peter G. Stillman (Lanham, MD: Lexington Books, 2005), 37–51.

58. This is, of course, in a sense, a *spoken* world, but it comes to us in *written* form.

59. Terry Eagleton and Derek Jarman, *Wittgenstein: The Terry Eagleton Script: The Derek Jarman Film* (London: British Film Institute, 1993), 13.

60. A novel that Eagleton sees as "deeply reactionary." See Eagleton, *The Illusions of Postmodernism*, 54. For a more interesting account of this problem, see Christopher Ricks, "Literature and the Matter of Fact," in *Essays in Appreciation*, ed. Christopher Ricks (Oxford: Oxford University Press, 1998), 306–307.

61. Stanley Fish, *There's No Such Thing as Free Speech . . . And It's a Good Thing Too* (New York: Oxford University Press, 1994), 51.

62. Eagleton, *Ideology: An Introduction*, 197.

63. Ibid., 211.

64. Ibid., 58.

65. Eagleton, *The Ideology of the Aesthetic*, 7.

66. Eagleton, *The Illusions of Postmodernism*, 56–60.

67. See, for example, Terry Eagleton, *Heathcliff and the Great Hunger: Studies in Irish Culture* (New York: Verso, 1996); Eagleton, *The Truth about the Irish* (New York: St. Martin's Press, 2000).

68. Such as, for example, his reading of *Hard Times*, where he cuts through some of the more strained readings of the text. See Terry Eagleton, "Critical Commentary," in *Hard Times*, ed. Terry Eagleton (New York: Methuen & Co., 1987), 1–8.

69. This is not to say, of course, that such questions cannot be interesting. See John Sutherland, *Is Heathcliff a Murder?: Great Puzzles in Nineteenth-Century Literature* (Oxford: Oxford University Press, 2002).

70. Eagleton, *Literary Theory: An Introduction*, 71.

CHAPTER 5   JUDITH BUTLER

1. Jeanette Winterson, *Art Objects* (New York: Vintage Books, 1995), 165.

2. Judith Butler, *Gender Trouble: Feminism and the Subversion of Identity*, 10th anniversary ed. (New York: Routledge, 1999), xxxii.

3. Butler's doctoral dissertation, *Recovery and Invention: The Projects of Desire in Hegel, Kojève, Hyppolite, and Sartre*, Yale University, 1984—later published as Judith Butler, *Subjects of Desire: Hegelian Reflections in Twentieth-Century France* (New York: Columbia University Press, 1999)—dealt with the concept of desire in Hegel's *Phenomenology* and the reception of, and reaction to, that work by Jean Hyppolite, Alexander Kojève, and Jean-Paul Sartre.

4. Richard Rorty, *Contingency, Irony, and Solidarity* (Cambridge: Cambridge University Press, 1989), 133.

5. Though, as Butler notes, many outside the Academy have found her work to be a platform for activism and artistic expression. See Butler, *Gender Trouble*, xvii.

6. Judith Butler, *The Psychic Life of Power: Theories in Subjection* (Palo Alto, CA: Stanford University Press, 1997), 145, emphasis added.

7. Butler, *Gender Trouble*, xix.

8. At times, Butler's tone can even be a little arch: "The fact that my friends Slavoj and Ernesto claim that the term 'Phallus' can be definitionally separated from phallogocentrism," writes Butler of the work of Žižek and Laclau, "constitutes a neologistic accomplishment before which I am in awe. I fear that their statement rhetorically refutes its own prepositional content, but I shall say no more." See Judith Butler, Ernesto Laclau, and Slavoj Žižek, *Contingency, Hegemony, Universality: Contemporary Dialogues on the Left* (New York: Verso, 2000), 153.

9. See, for example, Martha C. Nussbau, "The Professor of Parody: The Hip Defeatism of Judith Butler," *The New Republic* (February 22, 1999).

10. "It is no doubt strange and maddening to some, to find a book that is not easily consumed to be 'popular' according to academic standards. The surprise over this is perhaps attributable to the way we underestimate the reading public, its capacity and desire for reading complicated and challenging texts, when the complication is not gratuitous, when the challenge is in the service of calling taken-for-granted truths into question, when the taken for grantedness of those truths is, indeed, oppressive." See Butler, *Gender Trouble*, xviii. In addition to Nussbaum's famously intemperate piece on Butler, the journal *Philosophy and Literature* awarded Butler first place in its 1998 "Bad Writing Contest."

11. See "Can the 'Other' of Philosophy Speak?," in *Undoing Gender*, ed. Judith Butler (New York: Routledge, 2004), 232–250.

12. This may, in part, explain some of the shrillness in the debate between the in-group and the out-group: so strongly identified is Butler with this subsection of the public that criticism of her work is seen to be a criticism of the group itself. Ironically, this phenomenon seems to be the by-product of a certain type of identity politics that Butler's work seeks to undermine.

13. Butler is well aware of this problem: her own version of "methodological reading." "Whatever you say," she writes, "will be read back as an overt or subtle manifestation of your essential homosexuality. (One should not underestimate how exhausting it is to be expected to be an 'out' homosexual all the time, whether the expectation comes from gay and lesbian allies or their foes)." See Butler, *The Psychic Life of Power*, 94.

14. See Butler, *Undoing Gender*.

15. Quoted in James Miller, *The Passion of Michel Foucault* (Cambridge, MA: Harvard University Press, 1993), 211.

16. Butler, *Subjects of Desire*, 23.

17. Ibid., 18.

18. Ibid., 19.

19. Ibid.

20. Ibid.

21. Butler, Laclau, and Žižek, *Contingency, Hegemony, Universality*, 25.

22. See, for example, Judith Butler, *Antigone's Claim: Kinship between Life and Death* (New York: Columbia University Press, 2000), 5, 22. Her concern with reading and philosophical writing is also manifest in Judith Butler, *Bodies That Matter: On the Discursive Limits of "Sex"* (New York: Routledge, 1993), where she discusses "rude and provocative readings" (36), as well as what it means to read for absence (37).

23. See, for example, Butler, *Bodies That Matter*, ix, xii, 123; Butler, *Subjects of Desire*, xiv. Butler's self-defensiveness is also pertinent here. In addition to the example cited earlier, see also Butler, Laclau, and Žižek, *Contingency, Hegemony, Universality*, 136, 36; Judith Butler, *Excitable Speech: A Politics of the Performative* (New York: Routledge, 1997), 142, 62.

24. Butler acknowledges the problem of texts being used as "evidence" for preexisting claims. In her discussion of Žižek's use of the Spielberg movie *Jaws*, Butler asks whether "the instance of popular culture [can] be used to illustrate this formal point which is, as it were, already true, prior to its exemplification?" See Butler, Laclau, and Žižek, *Contingency, Hegemony, Universality*, 26.

25. Butler, *Antigone's Claim*, 22.

26. Butler, *Bodies That Matter*, 151.

27. Ibid., 172.

28. Butler, *Subjects of Desire*, xix.

29. Or it *can* rock the reader back in this way, depending, of course, on the reader.

30. Arthur C. Danto, *The Transfiguration of the Commonplace: A Philosophy of Art* (Cambridge, MA: Harvard University Press, 1981).

31. Winterson, *Art Objects*, 60.

32. Michel Foucault, *The Order of Things: An Archaeology of the Human Sciences* (New York: Vintage, 1990), 3–16.

33. Butler, *Excitable Speech*, 77, emphasis in original.

34. Ibid.

35. Butler, *Bodies That Matter*, 36–37.

36. Butler, *Excitable Speech*, 77.

37. Butler, *Bodies That Matter*, 57.

38. Butler, Laclau, and Žižek, *Contingency, Hegemony, Universality*, 3.

39. Butler, *Antigone's Claim*, 1.

40. Butler, *Subjects of Desire*, 4.

41. Butler, *Gender Trouble*, 181.

42. Ibid., emphasis in original.

43. Ibid., 175.

44. Butler, *Bodies That Matter*, xi.

45. See, for example, Butler, *Excitable Speech*.

46. Butler, *The Psychic Life of Power*, 44, emphasis in original.

47. Butler, *Bodies That Matter*, 195.

48. Butler, *Excitable Speech*, 126.

49. Butler, *Bodies That Matter*, 7. It is hard not to wonder, however, what a non-temporal or nonspatial sense of "before" is in actuality. Claims such as these perhaps are partly responsible for some of the hostility in Nussbaum's critique of Butler's work. See also, Butler, *The Psychic Life of Power*, 2; Butler, *Excitable Speech*, 2, 161.

50. See, for example, Butler, *The Psychic Life of Power*, 44, 145, 49.

51. See, for example, Butler, Laclau, and Žižek, *Contingency, Hegemony, Universality*, 14; and Butler, *Excitable Speech*, 13.

52. Butler, *Bodies That Matter*, 3–4.

53. Ibid., xii. Butler, it might be noted, qualifies even this move with the phrase "in part."

54. Judith Butler, "The Question of Social Transformation" in *Undoing Gender*, 204–231.

55. Butler, *Bodies That Matter*, 18–19.

56. Butler, *Gender Trouble*, 188.

57. Butler, *The Psychic Life of Power*, 82.

58. A "parting shot" is, however, the quintessential last word.

59. Sara Silah, *Judith Butler* (New York: Routledge, 2002), 13, emphasis in original.

60. Alexander Nehamas, *Nietzsche: Life as Literature* (Cambridge, MA: Harvard University Press, 1985), 3.

61. Miller, *The Passion of Michel Foucault*, 65.

62. Butler, *Subjects of Desire*, 20.

63. Butler, *Excitable Speech*, 161.

64. Ibid., 98–99.

65. Ibid., 2.

66. Ibid., 22, emphasis in original.

67. Ibid., 102.

68. Butler, Laclau, and Žižek, *Contingency, Hegemony, Universality*, 160.

69. Butler, *Antigone's Claim*, 74.

70. Butler, *Gender Trouble*, xx.

71. Butler, Laclau, and Žižek, *Contingency, Hegemony, Universality*, 266.

72. Cited in Miller, *The Passion of Michel Foucault*, 233.

73. For a summary of such criticism of Foucault's work, see J. G. Merquior, *Foucault* (London: Fontana, 1985).

74. Butler, *Excitable Speech*, 2.

75. Butler, *Bodies That Matter*, 191.

76. Butler, *Gender Trouble*, viii.

77. Butler, *Excitable Speech*, 38.

78. Butler, Laclau, and Žižek, *Contingency, Hegemony, Universality*, 277.

79. Ibid., 14. See also Butler's assertion that "we should devise and justify political plans on a collective basis," 158.

80. Butler, Laclau, and Žižek, *Contingency, Hegemony, Universality*, 15.

81. Ibid.

82. Ibid., 17.

83. Ibid., 19.

84. Michael Sandel, *Liberalism and the Limits of Justice* (Cambridge, MA: Harvard University Press, 1982). For the subsequent debate, see Charles Taylor, *Sources of the Self: The Making of the Modern Identity* (Cambridge, MA: Harvard University Press, 1989); John Rawls, *Political Liberalism* (New York: Columbia University Press, 1993).

85. Butler, Laclau, and Žižek, *Contingency, Hegemony, Universality*, 167.

86. Butler, *Bodies That Matter*, 53.

87. Butler, Laclau, and Žižek, *Contingency, Hegemony, Universality*, 13.

88. *The Portable Greek Historians*, ed. M. I. Finley (New York: Penguin Books, 1959), 492.

89. See John Seery, *Political Returns: Irony in Politics and Theory from Plato to the Antinuclear Movement* (Boulder, CO: Westview Press, 1990).

90. Butler, *Bodies That Matter*, 29.

91. Ibid., 221.

92. Ibid.

93. Butler, "Can the 'Other' of Philosophy Speak?," 242.

94. Judith Butler, *Precarious Life: The Powers of Mourning and Violence* (New York: Verso, 2004).

CHAPTER 6
HOW TO READ A NOVEL IN A DEMOCRACY

1. Azar Nafisi, *Reading Lolita in Tehran: A Memoir in Books* (New York: Random House, 2002), 38.

2. Jonathan Rose, *The Intellectual Life of the British Working Classes* (New Haven, CT: Yale University Press, 2001), 4.

3. Valentine Cunningham, *Reading After Theory* (Malden, MA: Blackwell, 2002), 52.

4. Jürgen Habermas, *The Structural Transformation of the Public Sphere: An Inquiry into a Category of Bourgeois Society*, trans. Thomas Burger (Cambridge: MIT Press, 1991), 29.

5. Nafisi, *Reading Lolita*, 39.

6. John Seery, *America Goes to College: Political Theory for the Liberal Arts* (Albany: State University of New York Press, 2002), 43.

7. Elizabeth Long, "Textual Interpretation as Collective Action," *Social Discourse* 14:3 (1992): 112.

8. Alfred P. Kazin, quoted in Stephen Braun, "The Oprah Seal of Approval," *Los Angeles Times*, March 9, 1997, 8.

9. For a discussion drawing on empirical examples, see Simon Stow, "The Way We Read Now: Oprah Winfrey, Intellectuals, and Democracy," in *The Oprah Affect: Critical Essays on Oprah's Book Club*, ed. Cecilia Konchar Farr and Jaime Harker (Albany: State University of New York Press, forthcoming).

10. Cecilia Konchar Farr, *Reading Oprah: How Oprah's Book Club Changed the Way America Reads* (Albany: State University of New York Press, 2005).

11. David Miller, "Deliberative Democracy and Social Choice," in *Democracy*, ed. David Estlund (Oxford: Blackwell, 2001), 299.

12. Martha Nussbaum, *Poetic Justice: The Literary Imagination and Public Life* (Boston: Beacon Press, 1995), 6.

13. Quoted in Jean Bethke Elshtain, *Augustine and the Limits of Politics* (Notre Dame, IN: University of Notre Dame Press, 1998), 57.

14. Jean-Michel Rabaté, *The Future of Theory* (Malden, MA: Blackwell, 2002), 100.

15. Julian Barnes, *Flaubert's Parrot* (New York: Vintage Books, 1984), 75.

16. Stow, "The Way We Read Now."

17. Richard Rorty, "The Inspirational Value of Great Works of Literature," *Raritan* 1 (1996): 13.

18. Cunningham, *Reading After Theory*, 3.

19. Quoted in Garry Wills, *Augustine* (New York: Penguin Books, 1999), xiv.

20. Cunningham, *Reading After Theory*, 86.

21. Stacy Schiff, *Vera (Mrs. Vladimir Nabokov)* (New York: Random House, 1999).

22. Vladimir Nabokov, *Lectures on Literature* (New York: Harcourt-Brace & Company, 1980), 1.

23. Quoted in Martha Nussbaum, *Cultivating Humanity: A Defense of Reform in Liberal Education* (Cambridge, MA: Harvard University Press, 1977), 35.

24. Jeanette Winterson, *Art Objects* (New York: Vintage Books, 1995), 60.

25. Sheldon Wolin, *Tocqueville between Two Worlds: The Making of a Political and Theoretical Life* (Princeton, NJ: Princeton University Press, 2001).

26. See, for example, Patrick J. Deenen, *Odyssey of Political Theory: The Politics of Departure and Return* (Lanham, MD: Rowman & Littlefield, 2000).

27. Simon Stow, "Written and Unwritten America: Roth on Reading, Politics, and Theory," *Studies in American Jewish Literature* 23 (2004): 77–87.

28. Italo Calvino, *The Uses of Literature* (New York: Harcourt-Brace & Company, 1986), 128–129.

CHAPTER 7   BEYOND THE DOLOROUS HAZE

1. Plato, *Phaedrus and Letters VII and VIII*, trans. Walter Hamilton (London: Penguin Books, 1973), 97.

2. Richard Rorty, *Contingency, Irony, and Solidarity* (Cambridge: Cambridge University Press, 1989), 133.

3. Joseph H. Lane Jr., "The Stark Regime and American Democracy: A Political Interpretation of Robert Penn Warren's *All the King's Men*," *American Political Science Review* 95 (2001): 812. An earlier version of Lane's paper was awarded the prize for the best paper presented in the "Politics and Literature" organized section at the 1999 American Political Science Association Meeting, suggesting that it is regarded as some of the best work currently being done in the discipline.

4. Paul A. Cantor, "Literature and Politics: Understanding the Regime," *PS: Political Science and Politics* 28:2 (1995): 193.

5. Lane, "The Stark Regime and American Democracy," 826.

6. Ibid., 818.

7. Ibid., 826.

8. Richard Posner, *Public Intellectuals: A Study of Decline* (Cambridge, MA: Harvard University Press, 2001), 239.

9. Lane, "The Stark Regime and American Democracy," 826.

10. Cantor, "Literature and Politics," 194.

11. Marx, it might be noted, accounted for both agency *and* structure. "Men make their own history, but they do not make it just as they please; they do not make it under circumstances chosen by themselves, but circumstances directly found, given, and transmitted from the past." See *The Marx-Engels Reader*, ed. Robert C. Tucker (New York: Norton, 1978), 595.

12. Lane, "The Stark Regime and American Democracy," 827.

13. Philip Roth, *Reading Myself and Others* (New York: Vintage Books, 2001), 30.

14. Plato, *The Republic of Plato*, trans. Allan Bloom (New York: Basic Books, 1991), 38, 360c.

15. Ibid., 39.

16. Ibid.

17. Ibid., 196.

18. Jonathan Rose, *The Intellectual Life of the British Working Classes* (New Haven, CT: Yale University Press, 2001).

19. See Brian Stock, "Ethics and the Humanities: Some Lessons of Historical Experience," *New Literary History* 36 (2005): 1–17.

CHAPTER 8   CONCLUSION

1. Philip Roth, *The Human Stain* (New York: Vintage Books, 2000), 84.

2. "Washington Official Resigns over Comment," *New York Times*, January 27, 1999, A17. The official was later reinstated.

3. John Seery, *America Goes to College: Political Theory for the Liberal Arts* (Albany: State Univeristy of New York Press, 2002).

4. Hanna Pitkin, *Wittgenstein and Justice*, 2nd ed. (Berkeley: University of California Press, 1993), 299.

5. See, for example, Simon Stow, "'An Unbecoming Virulence': The Politics of the Ethical Criticism Debate," *Philosophy and Literature* 24 (2000): 184–196.

Index

179